-7

F

Date Due

F

WITHDRAWN

Labor Unions
in Action

LABOR UNIONS
IN ACTION

A STUDY OF THE MAINSPRINGS OF UNIONISM

---

by Jack Barbash

Lecturer, The American University, Washington, D. C.
University of Wisconsin, School for Workers

HARPER & BROTHERS
NEW YORK AND LONDON

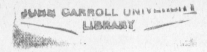

CONTENTS

v

CONTENTS

My purpose in writing this book is to erect a framework from which contemporary union functioning can be appraised constructively. Such facts as I have used to fill in the framework are illustrative rather than exhaustive.

In defining "contemporary" I have limited myself to the period from 1933 on, which I believe constitutes a whole new era in the development of the American labor movement. As I write this introduction I have the feeling that 1945 and 1946, in which I did most of my work, mark the end of that era, a contingency I did not foresee when I began to think about this book.

The perspective throughout, with the exceptions clearly indicated, is that of the union spokesman who is candidly describing and interpreting his own behavior. It is no part of my intention, therefore, to appraise unionism from the standpoint of the employer, the public interest, the unorganized worker or, for that matter, from the standpoint of my own sentiments about these matters. The justification I advance for this approach is that no appraisal of unionism, from whatever angle, can be useful unless we first gain some insight into how the unionists themselves realistically view their policies and actions.

Another observation is perhaps in order about my approach. For two reasons I have deliberately underemphasized the *formal* aspects of unionism: that is, provisions of union constitutions, verbatim terms of collective agreements, etc. The first is the fact that these phases have already been given adequate treatment. (If the reader is not yet familiar with these materials, he will find them noted among the lists of references in the back of the book.) The second is my conviction that an intelligent understanding of American unionism requires comprehension of kinds of behavior which cannot normally be encompassed in formalized documents.

I have tried to deal with my materials in a detached and dispassionate way. Considering my own sympathies, it is likely that this is hardly possible in a subject full of explosive overtones as anything associated with the labor movement must inevitably be these days.

Since this is my first book I want to acknowledge my debt to Fannia M. Cohn, J. B. S. Hardman, David J. Saposs, William M. Leiserson, and Selig Perlman, all of whom have taught me much about the labor movement. For the opportunity to teach at the University of Wisconsin School for Workers over a period of years I am grateful to Ernest Schwarztrauber and Vidkuun Ulriksson. My worker-students at the School for Workers made it possible for me to learn a great deal about the union as a day-to-day process, an opportunity I would otherwise have been deprived of. My friend Morris Weisz read the manuscript at various stages and his advice was uncommonly helpful. Of course, none of the persons named here can properly be held responsible for the defects in this book, nor should any agency by which I happen to have been employed be associated with the views expressed.

Chapters VIII and X have previously appeared in the Industrial and Labor Relations Review and the Antioch Review, respectively.

This enterprise would have been completely impossible for me if I had not had the help and encouragement of my wife.

JACK BARBASH

Silver Spring, Maryland
November 23, 1947

Labor Unions
in Action

THE UNIONS AND
THE AMERICAN ENVIRONMENT

No POLITICAL DEMOCRACY HAS OFFERED A MORE HOSTILE ENVIRONMENT
to unionism than has the United States. And this hostility has imparted
to American unionism a character and temper unlike those of any other
labor movement.

Industrialism in American life moved out of its period of fitfulness after
the Civil War. And as industrialism moved "with a stride that astounded
statisticians,"[1] the businessmen who were its advance agents took over
economics, politics, church, and culture, and shaped them to their own
ends. Individualism was the philosophical rationalization by which this
process was given respectability. Nobody has comprehended the sweep
of individualism in this period more epically than the late Vernon
Parrington when he wrote:

. . . individualism had become the inalienable right to preempt, to exploit,
to squander. Gone were the old ideals along with the old restraints. The
idealism of the forties, the romanticism of the fifties—all the heritage of
Jeffersonianism and the French Enlightenment—were put thoughtlessly away,
and with no social conscience, no concern for civilization, no heed for the
future of democracy it talked so much about, the Gilded Age threw itself
into the business of money-getting. From the sober restraints of aristocracy,
the old inhibitions of Puritanism, the niggardliness of an exacting domestic
economy, it swung far back in reaction, and with the discovery of limitless
opportunities for exploitation it allowed itself to get drunk. Figures of earth,
they followed after their own dreams. Some were builders with grandiose
plans in their pockets; others were wreckers with no plans at all. It was an

anarchistic world of strong, capable men, selfish, unenlightened, amoral—an excellent example of what human nature will do with undisciplined freedom. In the Gilded Age freedom was the freedom of buccaneers preying on the argosies of Spain.[2]

Labor's first wholesale challenge to the "conquering hosts of business enterprise" was an attack both on the fundamental rightness of business enterprise and on the expression it took in particular kinds of business behavior. The Knights of Labor, from secret beginnings in 1869, reached a point where it was identified with murderous red revolution in seeking to undermine big business individualism by agitation and by strikes. Some notion of how the Knights were regarded by workers may be sensed from the following verse sung to the revival hymn tune "Hold the Fort" and sounded off by Chicago workers after the Knights' foray against Jay Gould's Wabash Railroad in 1886.

> Toiling millions now are waking—
> See them marching on;
> All the tyrants now are shaking,
> Ere their power's gone.

> Chorus:

> Storm the fort, ye Knights of Labor,
>   Battle for your cause;
> Equal rights for every neighbor—
>   Down with tyrant laws! [3]

The New York *Sun*, then as now, a newspaper of the respectable groups in the community, reflected the concern of these substantial elements over what seemed to them the dangerous and growing power of the Knights.

Five men in this country control the chief interests of five hundred thousand workingmen, and can at any moment take the means of livelihood from two and a half millions of souls. These men compose the executive board of the noble order of the Knights of Labor of America. The ability of the President and Cabinet to turn out all the men in the civil service, and to shift from one post to another duties of the men in the army and navy, is a petty authority compared with that of these five Knights. The authority of the late Cardinal was, and that of the bishops of the Methodist Church is, narrow and prescribed, so far as material affairs are concerned, in comparison with that of these five rulers.

They can stay the nimble touch of almost every telegraph operator; can shut up most of the mills and factories, and can disable the railroads. They can issue an edict against any manufactured goods so as to make their subjects cease buying them, and the tradesmen stop selling them.

They can array labor against capital, putting labor on the offensive or the defensive, for quiet and stubborn self-protection, or for angry, organised assault, as they will.[4]

Not alone through strikes, but through the boycott in which they were eminently successful, did the Knights build a reputation as a formidable foe of the status quo. The threat which the Knights were supposed to constitute to capitalism was underscored by its leaders' denunciation of the wage system and their urgings "to abolish the wage system" and to substitute a system of co-operation. "There is no good reason why labor cannot through co-operation own and operate mines, factories, and railroads." [5]

There are many explanations as to why the Knights of Labor failed, ranging from organizational ineptness to the orthodox historical judgment that wage earners were not ready for its philosophy of "an injury to one is an injury to all." Whatever the explanation, this much is a fact—the Knights did go out of business and they were not successful in weakening the sway of big business over conditions of work.

Samuel Gompers's conception of a labor movement, given form and shape in the American Federation of Labor and its constituent unions, was the next stage in the evolution of labor's adaptation to the realities of industrial life. For Gompers, the Knights were "purely sentimental and bereft of all practical thought and action." [6]

And then the trade unions went about tailoring a labor movement that would come into less harsh conflict with the accepted attitudes of the business community. The process of adaptation was characterized by an articulate renunciation of revolution and revolutionary ideas by labor spokesmen in the AFL. Against a background of disastrous strikes carried on by the Knights, the eschewing of revolutionary ideology was followed through in some unions by what seemed to be a great reliance on the methods of industrial peace—arbitration and the trade agreement. Yet for all this, the unions could not, before the New Deal, assail successfully the mainstays of American industry—the mass production industries. Whatever major sorties into mass production union organization were engaged in were repulsed with primitive violence and passion by industry and, in behalf of industry, by government.

It is an ironic turn that a labor movement whose dominant elements went to such lengths to divorce themselves from revolutionary ideologies should have been met by systematic and calculated oppression when it ventured forth from its strongholds of organization in the building, service, and small employer unit metal trades into the fastness of steel, coal, and textiles. Where in the history of the radical-minded labor organizations of Europe is it possible to find chapters comparable to Homestead, where in 1892 an armed battle took place between three hundred Pinkertons hired by the Carnegie Steel Company and the striking workers; to the anthracite strike of 1902, during which the leading coal operator wrote to a minister pleading for some concession to the striking miners, "the rights and interests of the laboring man will be protected and cared for, not by the labor agitators, but by the Christian men to whom God in His infinite wisdom has given control of the property interests of the country"; to "Bloody Ludlow" in 1913, where during the coal strike in the Colorado Fuel and Iron Corporation a Congressional investigating committee reported "that government existed in Southern Colorado only as an instrument of tyranny and oppression in the hands of the operators"; [7] to the 1919 Steel Strike, in which one labor strikebreaking detective agency employed by the steel industry instructed its operatives to "call up every question you can in reference to racial hatred between these two nationalities [Serbians and Italians]." [8]

To know that these are not exceptional illustrations selected for their shocking qualities one must go through the seventy-odd volumes of the hearings of the Senate Civil Liberties Committee headed by Senator La Follette, and to draw the inevitable conclusion that the corporations which used professional spies, strikebreakers, and terrorists represented the aristocracy of American industry.

More than economic calculation was involved in the large employers' bitter antipathy to union organization. The economic cost of opposing unionism came high and the managers of industry, we know now, could have come to terms with the unions, as many did and have, without endangering their profit position. George Baer's enunciation of the "divine right of property" was probably not far from one of the basic motivations of most of the large employers in their opposition to unionism. Their opposition was not only an economic response, it was a moral crusade. Listen to this interchange between Congressman Foster, who directed the investigation of the House Committee on Mines and Mining into the Ludlow "massacre," and John D. Rockefeller, Jr., who controlled the Colorado Fuel and Iron Corporation at the time.

Q.—But the killing of people and shooting of children has not been of enough importance to you to communicate with the other Directors and see if something might be done to end that sort of thing?

A.—We believe the issue is not a local one in Colorado. It is a national issue whether workers shall be allowed to work under such conditions as they may choose. As part owners of the property our interest in the laboring men in this country is so immense, so deep, so profound that we stand ready to lose every cent we put in that company rather than see the men we have employed thrown out of work and have imposed upon them conditions which are not of their seeking and which neither they nor we can see are in our interest.

Q.—You are willing to let these killings take place rather than to go there and do something to settle conditions?

A.—There is just one thing that can be done to settle this strike, and that is to unionize the camps, and our interest in labor is so profound and we believe so sincerely that that interest demands that the camps shall be open camps, that we expect to stand by the officers at any cost. It is not an accident that this is our position—

Q.—And you will do that if that costs all your property and kills all your employes?

A.—It is a great principle.

Q.—And you would do that rather than recognize the right of men to collective bargaining?

A.—No, Sir—rather than allow outside people to come in and interfere with employes who are thoroughly satisfied with their labor conditions. It was upon a similar principle that the War of the Revolution was carried on. It is a great national issue of the most vital kind.[9]

The ingenuity expended by management in devising alternatives to free unionism evoked a high order of creative talent in industrial relations. These efforts have generally been summed up under the name "company unionism." One scheme known as the "industrial democracy" plan provided for a House composed of employee representatives, a "Senate manned by management representatives and a Cabinet" made up of representatives of top management. Employee representation plans, works councils, shop committees were other kinds of formal designations through which management sought to frustrate, in a resourceful way, free union organization. A prominent personnel man who favored these devices put it bluntly: "After all, what difference does it make whether one plant has a 'shop committee,' a 'works council,' a Leitch Plan . . . or whatever else it may be called. . . . They can all be called 'company union' and they all mean the one fundamental point: The Open Shop." [10]

Only during World War I, in the period before the New Deal, did unions encounter a measure of toleration, but this required the active intervention of the federal government in behalf of collective bargaining—a development with mixed consequences since it served as a spur to company unionism. After the war the lid was on unionism again. Hostility of employers understudied by government continued unabated. Even the prosperity of the middle twenties failed to encourage anything like a corresponding upswing in the growth of unionism.

Except for sporadic upsurges, the characteristic adjustment of the unions to the hostility of large employers and the government was the infusion of an inferiority complex with respect to their ability to organize large-scale industry. By way of compensation, perhaps, the unions instead made the most of their relatively favorable position in the trades and industries in which small-scale business predominated.

Here and there, immediately before and after World War I, the radical unions sought to breach the wall that shut off big industry to union organization. The IWW showed great zeal in prosecuting their organizing efforts in the mass production industries. But this was more than offset by its lack of financial resources and by the intensified fury with which the radical union was destroyed precisely because it was radical—to say nothing of the organizing weakness that came from confusing a union organization job with agitation for political causes. The unions on the railroads were the only exceptions to the barrenness of labor organization in large-scale business. But the railroads were unique among large enterprises in that they were dependent on groups of skilled craftsmen who could not easily be replaced by strikebreakers.

One inescapable fact emerges from the whole course of union history in the United States: labor organization could not successfully persevere in industries where large aggregates of business power were in belligerent opposition to unionism and where the relationship between business and government was such that the latter was made part of the general onslaught against unionism in general and in particular.

The growth of unionism that followed the election of the Roosevelt administration to power, and which is the major concern of this book, is inextricably intertwined with the favorable climate created for union organization in a positive and energetic fashion by government. It was only through the wholesale intervention of government in its behalf that unionism could overcome the overpowering disabilities that an antagonistic environment had contrived.

CHAPTER II

HOW AND WHY
UNIONS ARE ORGANIZED

THE PROCESS OF SUCCESSFUL ORGANIZATION OF WORKERS INTO UNIONS is one of accommodation to a wide variety of situations. Essentially involved are tactics and improvisations rather than predetermined techniques and methods. There is no certified body of principles which can take the place of the common-sense intuitions and vigor required to make an effective adjustment to the complex of social forces characteristic of every union organizing situation.

WHY WORKERS JOIN UNIONS

Higher wages and shorter hours are obvious reasons for workers' joining a union. Even so, the wages and hours inducement is put in terms of status. The organizer's appeal is more "Look what the fellows in the union doing the same work are getting" rather than "Conditions are very bad in your shop." During the steel industry organizing campaign in 1937, the Steel Workers union research department deliberately set out to collect material on wage inequalities and this was promptly fed to the organizers. "Who said a craneman is worth twenty cents more in Pittsburgh than in Chicago?" proclaimed loudspeakers outside of plant gates in the Chicago area.[1]

The appeal of "more" rarely functions alone in motivating a worker to sign a union application card. For one, the improvement over existing conditions which the union organizer promises or can deliver is hardly ever so markedly higher that it can serve as a basis for a stirring "before-

and-after" type of appeal. An organizer's manual prepared by the Long-shoremen's union asserts in this connection, "Don't make rash promises of immediate gains and fabulous wages."[2] For another, employers who want to spike the union's guns will frequently match or even better union conditions in order to keep the union out of the plant during an organization drive. In another manual, prepared by the Women's Trade Union League, a situation is described in which "the organizer concluded that next time she would get the workers ready and call a strike . . . before the manufacturers had time to raise wages and thus prevent a strike."[3] The southern textile organizing drive of 1946 by the AFL and CIO unions in the field evoked substantial wage increases by nonunion mills.

Another potent motive for joining a union is the worker's interest in eliminating favoritism by management. The insistence with which the union representative normally puts forth the claim for a seniority system in a newly organized plant reflects the high value workers place on seniority as a method of ensuring understandable objectivity in lay-offs and rehiring. Golden and Ruttenberg, with much experience in organizing steel workers, observe that the appeal against favoritism is "perhaps the organizer's strongest appeal." The appeal is couched in terms of

Join the union so you can get a square deal. When you get a contract with seniority protection you don't have to worry every morning when you get to work whether you'll have a job when you come home at night; you won't have to worry about the boss firing you because he don't like the color of your hair, or of promoting a younger man to a job you should have because he's a member of the same fraternal order as the boss; and you won't have to shine the foreman's shoes [or some other colloquialism] to get a nickel raise or a better job—it'll be yours if you have the years of service to get it and can do the job.[4]

The antifavoritism motivation is set in another context by the Marine Firemen:

For prior to the unionization of the industry, you hunted your jobs on the docks and the ships. You stood around in the rain and the snow when a ship came in, and waited for an opportunity to ship. When your chance finally did come, some contemptuous shipping master crooked his finger with a "Hey, You!"

You got pushed around plenty, brother. You stood around, and saw the guys with pull and drag get the jobs. Guys from college making a trip for fun and getting on a ship because they knew the port captain or the chief engineer or a big stockholder in the company. You wore out plenty of shoe leather prowling from ship to ship and dock to dock.

The cards were stacked against you! Favoritism was rife! The guy that was the lackey got first preference. You got shoved around in an atmosphere of uplifted noses and superiority complexes, for you were "the crew." Focsle hands. Trash! Tripe! Scum of the universe, and devoid of all humane consideration! [5]

Favoritism on the part of small employers can be just as effective in impelling unorganized workers to join a union. In the needle trades, where the operations are relatively small scale, the unions have utilized the equal division of work as a strong selling appeal, since a sore point among workers in "slack" seasons has been favoritism in dividing the work load which under a piecework system determines the take-home pay.

Without the union, the hugeness and impersonality of modern industry leaves the average worker feeling overwhelmed in a forest of procedures and levels of authority. The union provides an outlet for the worker to channel and give constructive and emotional expression to his "gripes" and problems without fear of retaliation.

In general, nonpecuniary motivations loom larger in workers' calculations than many employers have realized. The UAW-CIO organizers in the Ford campaign were frank to assert that the oppressiveness of Ford supervision surveillance was much more fruitful in getting workers to join the union than was the anticipation of wage increases. Brendan Sexton, who was active in the Bethlehem Steel organization campaign, says that the union got little for the workers at first in the way of increased wages. But what was important to them was the promise of protection from arbitrary discipline that the union offered.

Where unions exercise effective control over employment opportunities—through the closed shop or its variants—joining the union is a matter of course. In the building trades, for example, where this situation prevails, the prospective member seeks out the union representative rather than the other way around. It is relevant to note in this connection that the closed shop is a capitalization of intensive organizing activity in the past—sometimes in the remote past. During the war much of the increase in union membership was of either the closed-shop or "maintenance of membership" variety. Vigorous union campaigns in the war period were the exception rather than the rule. In the case of maintenance of membership there was, however, relatively little defection from union ranks during the allowable "escape" period, which may be an indication that once the workers were in the union they wanted to stay in.

Even though there may be no *formal* closed shop prevailing in a plant where union membership predominates, the new worker, even if he is so disposed, cannot long persist in a refusal to join the union, against the social and other kinds of pressures exerted on him by his fellow workers. A steel shop steward says, "When a new man comes into our shop he has twenty days to qualify. . . . If that man . . . gets close to qualifying it is the duty of the office and the shop steward to inform that man that there is a union in the shop and that he is expected to join. We are not asking him to join, we expect him to join." [6] On the railroads the closed shop is forbidden by law. As a matter of practice, however, it is difficult for a worker to remain in the good graces of fellow employees on organized roads if he holds out against joining the union. The nonunion worker in these situations finds it extremely hard to get adequate handling of his grievances. This fact the union members on the job are at great pains to point out to him. In extreme cases the organized workers will refuse to work with "free riders."

In large-scale organization drives, joining the union involves for many workers nothing else than "climbing on the band wagon" once the leaders among the workers in the plant have been brought into the union and the fear of employer retaliation is broken down. Then joining the union is a matter of being in the swing of things and remaining out of the union is risking the hostility of the group. It was this bandwagon urge that was undoubtedly responsible for much of the gain in union organization during the NRA period.

The responsiveness of the intellectual climate to social reform that characterized the 1930's has stimulated something which can be called "sentimental unionism." This kind of unionism grows out of the disposition, of intellectuals particularly, to be in the vogue. Thus liberal ministers of the gospel organized a ministers' union. Many college professors and free-lance intellectuals in the United States, for whom the benefits of collective bargaining could not be great, have joined and have even organized unions.

Many workers join a union because it provides them with an outlet of expression for their aspirations to leadership. The company unions in the steel and telephone industries, for example, provided a training ground for many of the local union leaders, and in the case of telephones for the national leadership as well. When many of these people began to feel restricted by the limitations of company unionism they were ripe for the appeal of the organizers of the free unions. As it turned out, the leadership qualities developed in the company unions were easily transferable to the free union environment.

The open interest of workers in free unions can be minimized by oppressive employer tactics. Yet no organization situation can be so bleak that the union organizer cannot find a few hardy souls who will consent to act as a union nucleus. To these people unionism is a cause. Not even in such places, during the early and middle thirties, as the Harlan County coal fields or throughout the automobile industry, where organized antiunion terrorism was the order of the day, could the desire of at least a small nucleus of workers for a free union be obliterated.

The ultrabelligerent type of American employer who responds to a union organizing drive only in terms of suppression suffers from a blind spot, which makes him unable to comprehend the tenacity with which, under violent suppression, some workers will keep alive their desire for unionism of their own choosing. The discovery through an NLRB election that a large majority of his workers wanted an outside union as against his own despotic-benevolent paternalism so shocked Henry Ford that, with little pressure on the part of the union negotiators, he conceded in quick succession to what were token demands for the closed shop and the checkoff.

WHY UNIONS ORGANIZE

From this brief exploration into why workers join unions it is appropriate to see what lies behind the *union's* interest in organizing workers. Unions will organize workers because they are sometimes attracted by the potential income from dues and initiation fees. Union leaders moved by this interest will on occasion appraise a proposed organizing drive on the basis of whether it will bring in more than it will cost, which is what occurred when the leader of an important union was being urged to carry on a campaign to organize farm workers. More typically, however, financial strength of unions is derived not from organizing workers but from holding on to the workers once they are brought into the union, which is a task of a different order. In short-run terms at least, most organization campaigns cost substantially more money than is realized by dues and initiation fees. In fact, a common inducement during an organization drive is the elimination of initiation fees. Both AFL and CIO unions in the southern drive are following the practice of either eliminating the initiation fees altogether or of charging some nominal amount. The cost of District 50's organizing campaign of the United Mine Workers came to about $2,500,000. It is not likely that the 50,000 members in District 50 will ever justify this expenditure in dues income.

The motives of many pioneer organizers of unions in particular industries can be traced more to idealistic and perhaps ideological impulses than to any other factor—idealistic, because they did not stand to gain in any material way from their efforts; ideological, because the motive power for union organization was a conception of the union as a vehicle for social change if not social revolution. Terence Powderly, one of the outstanding labor leaders of his day, in telling of his own conversion to unionism recalled that John Siney, a monumental figure in coal unionism, "was the first man I ever heard make a speech on the labor question. . . . I caught inspiration from his words and realized there was something more to win through labor than dollars and cents for self." [7]

Uriah Stephens, one of the founders of the Knights of Labor, brought to that founding strong religious and idealistic strains. What estranged Stephens from the Knights was no issue of high policy but a modification of the initiation ritual to make it acceptable to the Catholic Church. The origins of unions in the needle trades are indissolubly bound up with the revolutionary ideologies of their Jewish founders. Henry Miller, the first president of the International Brotherhood of Electrical Workers, used his own resources for the most part to organize the early locals of the IBEW. When he died in 1896 from an electric shock there wasn't enough money left to pay his funeral expenses.

Even in more current times, new unionism is accompanied by outlook of men and women whose main drive is to spread the gospel of unionism rather than more businesslike objectives. Without Heywood Broun, it is possible that there might have been no American Newspaper Guild and it is not likely that Broun needed the protection of a union to safeguard his own livelihood. For the Reuther brothers, helping to organize a union in the automobile industry was part of a way of life. The involvement of the International Ladies' Garment Workers in the organization of the mass production industries through the Committee for Industrial Organization was essentially an idealistic enterprise, since the sizable outlay of funds and effort could not have been justified in terms of a commensurate benefit to the organization of clothing workers.

New unionism, under the best of circumstances, is the kind of undertaking that in large part can be carried on only by individuals who will be satisfied with other than pecuniary compensations. Who else would voluntarily submit themselves to the arduous and backbreaking effort involved in establishing union organization in new fields and territories, but people to whom union organization is part of a larger goal? The initiative in the new age of unionism of the 1930's was largely that of the CIO. It is not a coincidence that the men and the few women who played important roles in bringing unions to steel, automobile, rubber, aluminum, and the other mass production industries were of an idealistic bent. Men like Powers Hapgood, Franz Daniel, Adolph Germer, E. J. Lever, and Clinton Golden, to name those who come to mind at once, were in the front line of the organization drives of the thirties, not because this was the easiest way to earn a living but because unionism to them fulfilled certain ethical and social objectives.

In their own way and according to their own capacities, the non-professional union organizers working on a full-time job in the plant whose union activity consisted in nagging their bench mates to join the union, or in working on a stubborn nonunionist over a glass of beer after hours or during lunchtime, are also giving expression to a belief in unionism as a philosophy. The more sensational union organization drives have obscured the important extent to which this kind of volunteer yet effective union organization work has been responsible for sizable gains in union membership. The so-called craft unions in the metal trades, for example, have gained much of their accessions to membership in this mouth-to-mouth fashion. Frank Fenton, AFL director of organization, says, "The pioneers of the labor movement have ever been its volunteer organizers." [8]

When a union passes the evangelical stages and settles down, one of the most compelling motives in its organization work is to minimize wage competition in its industry. Unions naturally have a stake in keeping their organized establishments in business profitably. To the extent that this is endangered by the fact that nonunion firms paying lower wages can undersell the union firms, there is a crucial obligation on the part of the union to organize these firms. Sidney Hillman put the matter very succinctly when he said, "We have always fought in the non-union markets to protect ourselves in the union markets." [9] A Textile Workers (CIO) publication discussing its agreement in the American Viscose Corporation notes in this connection: "The ability of the Union to win gains for Viscose workers has not alone been due to its activities in the plants of the Company. No one corporation could afford to raise wages far above its competitors. The strength of the TWUA lies in its national organization." [10] The factors important in this connection are (1) the relative importance of labor costs in the total cost of production; (2) in geographical terms, the dimensions of the market area—i.e., local, regional, national, or international; (3) the importance of price competition in the marketing of the product.

Under pressure of New York union restaurant owners, the Hotel and Restaurant Workers were forced into an expensive organization campaign against the Horn and Hardart restaurant chain in New York City. For the same kinds of reasons, the laundry workers' unions are on the constant alert to organize laundries within a 30- or 40-mile radius in a given area. Since laundering is essentially a local industry, there is no vital interest in organization for purposes of stabilizing wage costs over the country or over a state.

Women's dresses are sold in what amounts to a national market, which means that the manufacturers in New York City are in direct competition with every other manufacturer producing dresses in a given price range. The tendency of clothing manufacturers to move from high-wage areas results in what the clothing unions refer to as the out-of-town problem.

The International Ladies' Garment Workers' Union maintains a highly efficient organization to run down manufacturers who seek to escape from the union's wage and hour standards. By dint of great resourcefulness and even detectivelike ingenuity, the ILGWU has been able to catch up with these "runaway" shops and bring union conditions to their employees wherever they may be. This persistence is not alone a matter of a sentimental desire to extend union organization, but it is a matter of life and death for the union. The economics of the clothing industry lends itself admirably to fly-by-night employers, and unless the union demonstrates proper vigilance it may find itself with a large unemployed membership. Indeed, this out-of-town and runaway shop problem is one that is common to all the so-called needle trades industries, and all the unions, therefore, share the interest in organizing to prevent undesirable wage competition which, when it is successful, succeeds in undermining the organized segments of the industry. The Com-

petitive Shops Department of the UAW-CIO has a task of the same
order in preventing undesirable wage competition by unorganized plants.

Even when the economic reason for organizing competitive firms is
not very apparent, union negotiators find themselves in a difficult psychological bargaining position with unionized employers who tax the
union with its inability to impose union conditions over the whole
industry.

Union organizing is undertaken frequently to reinforce the claims of
the sponsors for position, power, and influence in the labor movement.
The organizing activities of the United Mine Workers District 50 in
chemicals, railroads, dairy farming, utilities, and a host of other industries was undoubtedly related to John L. Lewis's bid for power in the
labor movement. The substantial assistance which Sidney Hillman and
the Amalgamated Clothing Workers gave to the organizing of textile
workers is cited as another case in point where desire for high position
in the labor movement motivated union organizing activity. The development of the CIO is in part an outgrowth of the aspirations of its
proponents to positions of influence in American labor and in the community at large. In turn, the heightened organizational activity of many
AFL unions like the Electrical Workers, the Carpenters, and the Machinists was in definite response to the challenge the CIO threw down
to them.

Workers are organized to extend the influence of political ideological
groups in the union movement. At various stages of Communist party
strategy, its policies of dual unionism or rival unionism have stimulated
organizing campaigns, not because the unions already in the field were
inadequate but because they were not controlled by the Communists.
During the early thirties, when the American Communists directed the
Trade Union Unity League, organizing campaigns were undertaken in
the clothing and coal industries where long-established unions already
existed.

Racketeers who have established themselves in labor unions organize
workers and even employers as a quid pro quo for protection against
violence. Leaders of the Detroit teamsters were indicted by the state
court for extorting money from independent retailers for the privilege
of picking up their stocks at the wholesale markets. The indictment
alleged that the extortion took the form of the sale of permits. In the
same indictment it was charged that grocery merchants were compelled
to join the union by force.

Then, the job of running a *vital* union generates a certain dynamic of its own in the same way that a businessman seeks constantly to expand irrespective of whether he needs to expand in order to exist. Many unions, too, engage in organizing activity simply because that is their reason for existence. Thus, unions will go after an unorganized firm simply because of their conviction that every worker in the industry should be in the union and every employer should be in a collective bargaining relationship with the union.

FACTORS AFFECTING ORGANIZING ACTIVITY

The reason why "tactics" is a more fitting word to describe the manner in which the organizer adapts himself to a situation than, say, "techniques" or "methods" is that no two situations are alike. It is the purpose of this section to outline the range of factors affecting union organizing.

In the past decade or so, the most decisive influence on the tactics of union organizing has been the passage and the Supreme Court validation of the National Labor Relations Act. Without the active intervention of government in this way, establishing unions would have been extremely more difficult than it is, and in many instances the task would have been impossible. By and large, the National Labor Relations Act transformed the organizing process from an underground movement to a more or less open and aboveboard enterprise. This does not mean that in substantial numbers of cases organizing is not met by systematic opposition, but such cases are fewer than they were before 1937. The fact also that the act provides for a method whereby the majority of a group of workers can choose its collective bargaining representative has served to funnel the course of a union's organizing activity toward the clearly defined objective of persuading a majority of the workers to vote for it in an NLRB election. Before the act, the objectives of organizing activity were never so explicitly defined.*

Another decisive influence is the strike sanction. Without the right and the ability to strike union organizing cannot be successful. In wartime the inability of the union to strike is offset by establishing machinery which will, at least in part, effect the kinds of union gains possible in peacetime, only by a test of strength.

* See concluding section of Chap. VIII for discussion of effect of Taft-Hartley law on organizing activity.

The will and energy and other personal qualities that union leadership brings to a situation are also of importance in shaping the character of organizing activity. The events after 1933 stimulated a new hopefulness in union leadership and this reflected itself in the zeal and resourcefulness with which unions embarked on organizing drives in contrast to the fitfulness of union organizing in the twenties.

An important variable factor involved in union organization is the character of the working force. A clinical analysis of union organizing by the Women's Trade Union League illuminates the influence of this factor (reflected in this case in a predominance of women workers) on the tactics of union organizing.

In the white goods trade . . . the girls are younger and of different nationalities. The Jewish girl is likely to marry early, and the young girls in the white goods trade do not feel themselves a permanent part of the industry. Many of the foreign-speaking workers, Russians, Italians, Spaniards and others, do not understand or speak English. The strength of the organization came through a big strike in 1913. Many of the workers who have come into the industry since the strike do not know how much the union has accomplished. The girls change frequently from shop to shop. You may convert ten girls in a shop one week, and only five of them will be employed there the next week. In a recent campaign three months were spent, and the workers had changed their position before the results could be seen. New workers had taken their places, and these were not members of the union.[11]

Skilled workers are easier to organize into unions than are unskilled, for a number of reasons. Unionism in the United States started among the higher skilled and, therefore, among the better paid workers. Skill generally brings with it a higher measure of literacy and a more dynamic standard of living. Certain strategic considerations also account for the greater susceptibility of the skilled worker to union organization. His skill gives him a stock in trade and consequently a greater measure of bargaining power with his employer. From the point of view of the organizer, the highly skilled worker is invariably the person whom those with lesser skill look up to and follow. Moreover, the strike sanction is more formidable when it is the skilled workers who are likely to be involved in the strike.

In organizing Negro Pullman porters into the Brotherhood of Sleeping Car Porters, A. Philip Randolph, who came to the union movement as a Socialist, associated the labor movement with the highest aspirations of religion. Talking to the Pullman porters, Randolph said once, "The Negro Church representing the working class population can serve the race nobly in championing the cause of labor and yet remain true to its traditions, since Jesus Christ was a carpenter and all his disciples workmen."

"Fight on, brave souls," said Randolph another time. "Long live the Brotherhood! Stand upon thy feet and the God of Truth and Justice and Victory will speak unto thee."

The idea of the self-sufficient strength of the Negro was another appeal Randolph used. "Thus by all gods of sanity and sense Brotherhood men are a crucial challenge to the Nordic creed of the white race's superiority. For only white men are supposed to organize for power, for justice and freedom." [12]

Employer attitudes to unions influence the kinds of tactics that will be brought to bear in a given organizing situation. In directing the Textile Workers Organizing Committee, Sidney Hillman was able to persuade many textile employers that unions might be a good thing for them without resorting to more vigorous action. When Henry Kaiser began his wartime shipbuilding operations he was convinced of the desirability of friendly union relationships, and the metal trades unions in the AFL on the West Coast were able to get into the shipbuilding industry on the ground floor. Here again vigorous organizing tactics were not needed to bring workers into unions.

On the other hand, the spirited opposition to unions by Sewell Avery of Montgomery Ward forced the Department Store Workers (CIO) to engage in a forceful organizing drive which extended not only to the Montgomery Ward workers but to the communities in which the Ward stores were operating, and even to consumers all over the nation. The opposition mustered by Mr. Avery and his associates against the union proved to be beyond the resources and capacity of the single international union originally involved, and the CIO itself had to set up a Montgomery Ward Organizing Committee. In a city as favorable to union organization as New York, the Hotel and Restaurant Workers could not crack the determined opposition which Horn and Hardart (Automat) massed against the union.

Similarly the social attitudes, cultural backgrounds, and economic alignments in a community will affect the kind of organizing campaign a union conducts. The CIO organizers in the southern campaign are emphasizing the fact that in bringing Negro workers into unions the CIO is concerned with economic objectives and not objectives of social equality. In combating the CIO drive, the AFL leaders are characterizing the CIO as Communist. The CIO, with reason, feels that its organizing task in the South would be impossible if it were associated with a philosophy so repugnant to the prevailing culture as racial equality. Communism evokes the same kind of taboo and so, as the spokesman for the rival union, President William Green, in a radio address aimed at southern industry on the occasion of the launching of the AFL drive, declared, "Grow and co-operate with us or fight for your life against Communist forces." [13] To deflate the charge of communism against the CIO, Van Bittner, director of the Southern Organizing Committee, called a special press conference to repudiate support from a "Help Organize the South Committee" in New York headed by Representative A. Clayton Powell and tinged with Communist connections. Bittner and his advisers were impressed with the clear need for ridding the drive of even the slightest suspicion of Communist support.

Ideally, the union organizer does nothing that will engender unnecessary bad feelings toward him in the community, particularly if it is a small community. Whatever his personal views on politics, religion, sex, and temperance, he will not air them if they run counter to prevailing attitudes of the community or of the workers whom he is seeking to induce to join the union.

The extent to which one organizer sought to integrate himself into the life of the community is illustrated by the experience of Gregory Bardacke in persuading clothing workers in an upstate New York community to join the union. Bardacke learned Italian so that he could talk to the parents of the workers as well as to the workers themselves. He steeped himself in Italian history and, in talking with the older folks, he associated the objectives of the union with the ideals of Garibaldi and Mazzini. He cultivated the friendship of the local ministry, the leaders of the farm groups, and the fraternal organizations and even of the businessmen. To the farmers he explained how their prosperity depended on decent wages for city workers. Among the businessmen he distributed statements of other manufacturers who had found collective bargaining helpful to their business. With the churchmen, he contended that unionism was but a practical application of the basic precepts of Christianity. In short, Bardacke viewed his organizing task not only in terms of persuading workers to join the union, but also in terms of developing a community environment sympathetic to the idea of unionism.

The presence of an already established labor movement in a community will influence the task of new union organizing. The organizing of garment workers by the Amalgamated Clothing Workers in coal towns was substantially assisted by the unionized miners. In so-called union towns the central labor bodies frequently initiate organizing campaigns on their own or provide encouragement and advice to individual unions. The central labor body knows much about the community and the workers that is of value to the organizer. Moreover, the established local unions in a community have jurisdictional and other interests which must be taken into account and resolved. Frank Fenton says, in citing a co-ordinated drive to organize the P. Lorillard Company tobacco workers, "With the campaign co-ordinated by the central labor union and the international representatives the joint committee is responsible for fostering the spirit of co-operation and guarding against efforts to obtain special advantage. [Divisive] efforts can wreck any co-operative undertaking." [14]

The general attitude to labor of the government of a city can make a great deal of difference in the task of the union organizer. An extreme case of violent antiunion opposition was to be found in Harlan County, Kentucky. Here the coal operators maintained a reign of terror for United Mine Workers organizers, largely through the utilization of organized government. Harlan County is, of course, an extreme case and the reaction of the general run of communities is somewhat more tolerant of union organizers. A more common obstacle is the enforcement of city ordinances prohibiting "littering and cluttering" against the distribution of union handbills.

The temper of the times is an influential factor in the job of union organizing. For obvious reasons workers are more easily induced to join unions in relatively prosperous times—and, of course, the bargaining power of the union is greater when labor is relatively scarce. It is not an accident, for example, that the peaks of union membership coincide with wartime prosperity and relative shortage of workers. Union organizing is also accelerated by the favorable disposition of the country toward social reform, and unions as agencies of social reform. There is no question but that the effect of the proclaimed sympathy to unions by the Roosevelt administration, and the deflation of big business omniscience, was one of the most important if not the most important factor in the recovery of union strength in the 1930's. The American Plan, i.e., the open shop and the glorification of rugged individualistic virtues in the

1920's, although a period of economic expansion, created an atmosphere in which union organizing and its implicit challenge to normalcy was beset with hopeless difficulties and frustrations.

How Workers Are Organized into Unions

The way in which workers join unions generally follows one of two broad patterns. In the one way, the workers in a plant are able to organize themselves into a more or less cohesive group without substantial assistance from professional union organizers. In the other, an established union will assign one or more professional organizers on the union payroll to initiate a campaign.

A period of extensive self-organization of workers into unions was ushered in by the NRA and its Section 7a when the unions were spreading the idea with considerable spirit that "President Roosevelt wants you to join a union." Organization in the automobile industry was for the most part a spontaneous affair, particularly in the concentrated production centers. On-the-spot observers describe Flint and Detroit as cities in which union organization was running like a fever. With the fear of joining a union broken down, the automobile industry, with the exception of Ford, cracked wide open and workers applied for union membership faster than they could be handled. Catching the infection of unionism from the auto workers, milk wagon drivers, railway guards, and soda dispensers formed long queues before the UAW local offices, clamoring for union membership.

There are many cases like that of the employees of a public utility in an Ohio city which was experiencing a steel organization drive in 1936. One day the workers, without outside urging, decided they wanted to organize into a union. Since the leaders of the group knew little about union organization, they appealed for assistance to the only labor leader they knew about, and he happened to be an official in the teamsters' union. The assistance was immediately forthcoming with little concern that public utilities were about as far from the teamsters' jurisdiction as any enterprise could conceivably be.

When a full-time organizer is utilized, his tactics are adapted to the peculiar requirements of the situation. The teamsters may organize by the simple expedient of stopping a truck and inquiring of the driver if he is a union member. If he isn't, the proposal to join is put to him then and there. Or, because of their strategic position in the distribution process, organized teamsters may refuse to deliver to plants employing non-union teamsters. Getting merchant seamen to sign up with the union calls for the organizer to board the ship on which the men are employed. In plants employing large numbers of workers, the organizer distributes leaflets at the gate. If he can't get them to take leaflets, he may have to visit them individually.

A device used where a plant may not be ready for an open organizing drive is what is known as the "inside organizer." The task of the inside organizer is difficult and tedious because he has to persuade workers to join the union without seeming to function like a professional organizer, which is what he is in many cases. The use of this kind of organization device is resorted to in situations where for any number of reasons an outside organizer finds it difficult to get access to the workers in the plant.

Says Joseph Buckley, who carried on "inside" organizing activity aboard merchant ships:

When you go aboard an unorganized ship it is not with purpose of telling the world in general your business. Keep to yourself at first. Study your shipmates. Every fo'c'sle has a leader to whom most of the men are drawn. When you are sure of your ground, bring the subject of unions into the ordinary conversation; don't try to force it upon men. If your subject is interesting their normal curiosity will make them listen. Bring your subject to the point and don't drag it along. Let the men understand you. Above all, get them to respect you.

A worker on the job trusts a worker who approaches him in the same capacity. He feels the other fellow has an understanding of his economic life better than an outsider.

It is important that you do your job and stay sober. Then you can prove your ability to protect your shipmates when the brass hats attempt the usual exploitation found on these unorganized ships.

Brute strength in organization shows stupidity and lack of understanding. So do prejudices when displayed in an argument, whether the men around you hold the same prejudices or not.

Your job is to gain the confidence of the crew; understand their weaknesses and fears; know their hopes and ambitions. Only then can you organize them.[15]

Like any other persuading job, union organizing has its tricks and stratagems. In an organizing situation in the women's garment industry "where the employers' known opposition to unionism made it necessary to avoid openly identifying any of the workers with the union, a resourceful organizer planned a raffle; the names and addresses entered on the stubs of the raffle tickets comprised a good working list for house to house canvass. In other places, offers of free cosmetics and of cooking recipes have produced names and addresses without laying the workers open to the employers' suspicion." [16]

If the plant or establishment that is being organized is susceptible of mass consumer opinion, this too will have a bearing on tactics. The American Communications Association, organizing telephone workers on the West Coast, urged that if union people having "occasion to call central or long distance [will] just make some mention of the CIO it will be encouraging to them because the company is using every means possible to discourage and intimidate these people from coming into the CIO." [17]

The tactics of organizing are also a matter of who happens to be doing the organizing. There are organizers who temperamentally are "hell raisers" and are sent into situations in which high-powered pressure on management and on the workers appears to be required. This kind of person is not suited to recruiting unorganized workers who need to be worked on slowly and patiently.

The effective organizer is a "good mixer" whatever other qualities he may have. He must also be a good beer drinker. Beer, the experienced organizer has found, is an indispensable catalytic agent in every organizing situation. The most telling arguments for unionism are frequently made in the congenial atmosphere generated by a couple of glasses of beer.

Whatever the personality of the organizer, it is clear that the job requires a combination of salesmanship and idealism: salesmanship, because the job requires cultivation of the art of getting along with different kinds of people; idealism, because the job is extremely difficult, the pay is small, and the commodity being dispensed is essentially an idea.

In the following detailed account of an organizing campaign by Alan Strachan for the UAW-CIO, we get some insight into the kinds of tactics required in a systematic campaign by a full-time professional organizer.[18] In the fall of 1939, Strachan, then an organizer for the United Automobile Workers, was assigned to organize the workers at the Stark Equipment Company, a small manufacturer of automobile parts in Hanan, Michigan, which was in competition with the unionized gear and axle plants in Detroit. The Hanan environment was not conducive to union organization at the time of Strachan's arrival. Hanan is a small town of some 4,000 population in which the company was the major enterprise in the midst of a farming area. The year before, the UAW had lost an NLRB election to an independent union.

Although the UAW had received 300 votes in that election, only seven workers from the plant showed up for the first meeting called by Strachan. The temper of the workers who came to the meeting was one of quiet despair about the possibility of reviving union strength in Hanan, but they agreed to meet weekly.

Strachan then began to compile a list of the more likely prospects for union membership. The men regarded as leaders were singled out for special treatment. Strachan made his first contact at a farm and the conversation took place while his prospect, whom we shall call Keith, was milking a cow. In describing the ensuing conversation, Strachan points out that at no time did he use high-pressure methods in getting Keith to sign a union card. Instead, the conversation proceeded leisurely and concerned itself with general union matters. Keith was cordial but reserved. He remembered the last fiasco—he had his farm and he wasn't doing too badly at the company. Strachan argued that comparable plants under UAW contracts were working under better conditions—better pay, seniority, and the protection of a powerful national organization like the UAW. Keith said he'd think it over and agreed to come to the next meeting.

Eight people showed up at the next meeting. After asking a few questions about the organization, Keith asked for an application card and signed it. Strachan felt that, as a result of Keith's joining, the struggling local gained stature in the community and a few other workers were more inclined to join. Strachan also made a desultory attempt to bring the leaders of the independent union into the UAW, but apparently without success. Their chief complaint was that the CIO allowed aliens to hold office.

Meanwhile Strachan initiated a weekly mimeographed bulletin which he labeled *Sparks from Starks*. The early issues of *Sparks from Starks* tried to appeal to the workers' common sense—showing them the advantage of unionism—pointing out other notable examples in other plants. This did not seem to have too much effect. A gossip column was started. Everybody in town read the bulletin and there were demands from all quarters for copies. The publisher of the local weekly newspaper told Strachan it was competing with his circulation. The independent union at the plant was the target of most of the mockery in the gossip column. For instance, the independent gave a dinner to celebrate its second year of existence and the gossip column, written in the style of Walter Winchell, insinuated that before anybody touched the soup it was tested to make sure that the CIO hadn't poisoned it. The door prize, said the gossip column, was an autographed picture of John L. Lewis. Another reason Strachan thinks *Sparks from Starks* caught on was the inclusion of a recipe column for the women. He was told that the women opened their husbands' mail and read it directly it arrived.

The bulletins had to be mailed because they couldn't feasibly be distributed at the gate. The company had built the plant in piecemeal fashion and it sprawled all over a sizable area. There were no fences or gates. Workers entered the plant across fields, through back yards, in any way most convenient for them.

Strachan says he went to special lengths to make himself a respected member of the community during his stay. He made his personal life blameless. He made a special point of buying his supplies in Hanan and patronizing local professional people. Unostentatiously, he let them know that he was a CIO organizer. In choosing a doctor he chose one who was on the local school board, keeping in mind that the school auditorium would be useful for large union meetings. Although Strachan saw no positive gains from this approach, he feels that it minimized local opposition to union organization.

Every evening Strachan made individual house calls. He had considerable difficulty in finding the houses of some of the workers. Three visits were the most he could do in any evening for his hours were limited to the period between after-dinner and an early bedtime. He soon learned that it was pointless making a call after 9:30 P.M. In one house he had the embarrassing experience of getting the family out of bed when he arrived at 9:40.

After Strachan had been in Hanan about two months, the membership increased to eighty. During the next two months it rose to ninety. Union membership was not growing fast enough despite the intensive effort and Strachan almost decided to report to the regional director that it was not possible to organize the Stark Equipment Company. On second consideration, he decided to give the campaign another month's trial. He obtained from the International an agreement to waive the payment of dues for ninety days and to reduce the initiation fee to $1. This helped some, for those few who were continuing to pay dues were very critical of the others who had allowed their dues to lapse. The dues concession placed everyone on an equal basis.

It was about this time that the campaign really started to catch on and workers began to sign application blanks in accelerated numbers. A $25 prize was offered to the person signing up the most members and a $15 prize to the runner-up. The night before the deadline the three beer gardens in the town were the scene of an unprecedented union drive by those who were out to win the coveted prizes. Strachan had decided in the beginning that he would not ask the NLRB for an election until there were 500 signed applications. At the NLRB election of the previous year, the UAW had claimed 600 members and the company union 600, with the result that the UAW polled about 300 in the actual election. When Strachan had 496 applications for union membership, the NLRB was petitioned for an election. The UAW-CIO received 525 votes, about 65 per cent of the votes cast.

The over-all picture in any given organizing situation is set by the motives that impel the workers to join the union, the motives of the union in organizing the unorganized, the cultural and economic climate in which the organizing process occurs, and the personality of the organizer. Differences in organizing tactics are accounted for by interplay of these factors and not by differences in fundamental philosophies of organizing, or of anything else.

CHAPTER III

UNION STRUCTURE AND JURISDICTION

THE SIGNIFICANCE OF STRUCTURE IN AMERICAN UNIONS IS THE resourcefulness men have shown in shaping it to meet the practical requirements of maintaining and extending union organization. By and large, however, academic tradition in studying unions in the United States has decreed a different outlook on the significance of structure, and consequently public discussion has become excessively concerned with the merits in the abstract of craft vs. industrial unionism.

FORMAL UNION STRUCTURE

The formal stratification of union structure in the United States is well known, and for our purposes needs to be treated only briefly. At the top are the two great federations, the American Federation of Labor and the Congress of Industrial Organizations.[1] In a technical sense both are federations (although only one uses the word in its official name) because they are both made up of autonomous international unions. [2]

The AFL is the larger of the federations, encompassing unions with a membership on the order of seven millions. The CIO claims a membership in its affiliated unions of six millions. The AFL is composed of 102 international unions, 196 federal unions, and 4 departments. The CIO is made up of 38 international unions and 103 local industrial unions.[3]

The meaningful story of the American labor movement is essentially the story of the international unions. The international union on the whole is a self-contained unit. Without the international unions, the federations have no meaning and not much substance. The reverse is not true. The international unions can and have functioned without affiliation to the federations. Within recent years, the United Mine Workers, the International Ladies' Garment Workers' Union, the International Association of Machinists, and the Amalgamated Clothing Workers have at one time or another been unaffiliated. The Railroad Brotherhoods, i.e., the Engineers, Conductors, Firemen, Trainmen, Signalmen and Dispatchers, although working together with many AFL unions in the Railway Labor Executives Association are not affiliated to either of the federations. In turn, the international unions are made up of constituent local unions. The local unions, in varying degrees, derive their sustenance, guidance, and direction from their respective internationals.

We have run over briefly the main line of union structure—the federation, the international, and the local. There are, however, tangential lines of structure which fill out the total picture. On the federation line of authority there are, in the case of the AFL only, the departments, about which more will be said later. Here it is enough to list them: Metal Trades, Railway Employees, Building Trades, Maritime, and the Union Label. The departments charter local councils on city-wide and county-wide bases. The CIO has no form of organization comparable to the department. Also on the federation level is the local union affiliated directly to the federation, not through an international. The AFL calls these federal unions. The CIO uses the term "local industrial union."

For purposes of sponsoring legislation and mutual aid, the AFL locals in every state form state federations of labor and, in the larger cities, central trades and labor councils. The opposite numbers in the CIO are the state and city industrial union councils respectively.

THE IDEA OF STRUCTURE IN ACTION

At the outset it is important to recognize that the type of structure (i.e., broadly speaking, craft or industrial) has no point when applied to either of the large federations since they are made up of international unions of widely varying structural characteristics.

One system of classification of union structure runs: craft, multiple craft, trade union, semi-industrial, industrial, and miscellaneous.[4] An analysis of the structure of 85 out of the 102 international unions in good standing in the AFL in 1938 revealed the following distribution as among the types enumerated above.

Type	Number of Unions	Membership
Craft	12	25,800
Multiple Craft	19	458,300
Trade Union	13	814,800
Semi-industrial	27	611,000
Industrial	10	815,600
Miscellaneous	4	294,600

Although no comparable analysis has been made of the international unions affiliated to the CIO, there is considerable, though not so much, variety in the types of jurisdiction, as even a crude examination indicates. For example, the Amalgamated Clothing Workers might be termed a semi-industrial union since it normally excludes maintenance and clerical workers in the men's clothing industry. The Federation of Architects, Engineers, Chemists, and Technicians (subsequently merged with the Office Workers) may be classified as a multiple-craft union claiming only the professional and technical personnel in industry. Then there are such internationals in the CIO as in the maritime industry: the Inland Boatmen's Union of the Pacific, Marine Cooks and Stewards Association of the Pacific Coast, and Marine Engineers Beneficial Association;[5] and the Newspaper Guild and the United Office and Professional Workers, which, whatever they are, are clearly not industrial unions in any accurate use of the term.

The practical significance of the idea of craft and industrial unionism in concrete situations is illuminated by the way in which individual unions seek to have the National Labor Relations Board determine the size of the appropriate bargaining unit in representation cases. Both AFL and CIO unions, in the majority of instances in which they petition the NLRB, want industrial bargaining units although CIO unions request industrial units more frequently. The NLRB experience is singularly impressive because it provides an opportunity to appraise the force of an idea in a context of action, not of debate or discussion.

The organization of the Pacific Coast district by the Sailors' Union of the Pacific provides a practical illustration of how exigencies rather than philosophical speculation is the motive power behind union structure. As Harry Lundeberg tells it:

In the latter part of 1940, the NMU (CIO) signified their intention of moving in on the Pacific Coast to organize the tankers. The Sailors' Union of the Pacific then officially requested the Marine Cooks and Stewards' Assn. and the Marine Firemen, Oilers and Watertenders Assn. to state their position in regard to organizing the Stewards and the Firemen in the tankers on the coast, in order to offset the NMU's attempt to move in. The Marine Cooks and Stewards went on record to the effect that they were not interested in the tankers, and gave the NMU (CIO) a blanket authority to move in on the tankers. In fact, they also paid for one of the organizers to help the NMU organize the tankers. The Marine Firemen, Oilers and Watertenders Assn. also refused to organize the tankers, stating it was not worth while. Thus, the two other unlicensed organizations definitely chose to ignore the tankers and left the field open for the NMU.

The membership of the Sailors' Union of the Pacific immediately went on record, on a coastwise scale, instructing the Secretary to take immediate steps to organize all departments in the oil tankers on the Pacific Coast, and to use any and all means to do the job. It was very clear to the membership of the Sailors' Union that this step was necessary in order to block the NMU from getting a foothold on this coast. Should they have been successful in organizing the firemen and the cooks in the tankers, then the next step would have been to move in on freighters and coastwise vessels.

Inasmuch as we were a deck organization, and the NMU was requesting an election for all three departments in one, and as on the Pacific Coast the three departments have their separate setups, in order to circumvent the possibility of lumping sailors, firemen and cooks together, we then established the Pacific District of the Seafarers' International Union of North America, Engine Department, and the Pacific District, S.I.U. of N.A., Steward's Department. We were, at that time, not too sure of what the feeling of the Stewards and black gang would be towards us in an election. That was the reason for establishing the Pacific District. If the National Labor Relations Board had granted an election lumping all three departments together, we might have been in a position to lose the election and lose the Deck Department.[6]

What emerges from this analysis is: (1) The international unions affiliated to the AFL are characterized by great variety in respect to policies they follow with regard to type of structure—certainly by no means exclusively craft as is fashionably assumed. (2) Industrial-type unions are more predominant in the CIO though not so completely that the CIO can appropriately be considered a federation of exclusively industrial unions.*

The local unions show an even greater variety of structural types. The fact that an international union is essentially industrial does not, in many instances, preclude constituent local unions covering a narrower jurisdiction. The reverse is true as well; that is, an international union which is nominally craft in structure contains within it locals which are in effect industrial unions.

The Amalgamated Clothing Workers (CIO) and the Ladies' Garment Workers (AFL) contain locals whose jurisdiction is limited to one craft, the cutter. (The cutters are the highest skilled workers in the garment industries.) The latter union introduces another variant— locals whose jurisdiction is based on industry lines and then on language groups. Thus, Local 89 covers only Italian workers in the dress industry in New York except cutters. Local 22 covers all other workers in the dress industry except cutters and pressers.

An industrial union like the United Auto Workers-CIO, as a matter of effective organization, gives recognition to the significance of craft lines through the organization of a Tool and Die Council and a Maintenance Council. These councils are not locals nor do they bargain directly with employers, but they are designed to take into particular account the special interests of the men in the higher skill brackets.

The position of the skilled worker in the industrial union is aptly put in a UAW-CIO publication: [7]

Because the shop problem of the skilled man is different from that of the production worker, and every person will have to admit they are, a frank discussion of them is not "Craft Unionism" but is, on the contrary, "Sound Unionism." There can be no question as to the loyalty of the skilled workers to the industrial form of organization in the mass production industries. All they ask is that their problems be given adequate recognition. As a minority group within a great industry they are frequently overlooked and they resent being called "Craft Unionist" when they raise their difficulties on the floor of the Local.

Many of the teamsters' locals (AFL) will, to all intents and purposes, cover all the workers in the motor transportation industry in a given

---

* Hereafter, to simplify the discussion, we shall use the terms "craft" and "industrial" to signify the types of union structure.

area. In this situation these locals may be said to be industrial. At the same time, in laundries, wholesale and retail trade, a teamsters' local will include the drivers only. In these situations the locals are functioning as craft unions.

Craft unions will frequently join to bargain as one unit with employers. The railroad unions in and out of the AFL have on many occasions been able to present a single front to the railroads in collective bargaining negotiations. Although the printing trades have a long historical tradition of craft independence, co-operation, deliberate and otherwise, among the various crafts on the national and local level is not uncommon. Emily Clark Brown notes:

> In practice, the negotiations of the strongest craft frequently set the stage for the others, which then get approximately the same settlement. The typographical union is often the leader, partly because its locals include newspaper members, and so are in a strong position to wage a strike if necessary.[8] . . . In recent years local unions (in different crafts) frequently cooperated in organizing new plants through the Allied Printing Trades Council and sometimes in the name of the council brought cases to the National Labor Relations Board.[9]

Philip Taft, a discerning student of labor affairs, has observed in connection with the building trades:

> The departments [i.e., the Building Trades Department, Metal Trades Departments, etc. in the AFL] have enabled the craft unions to achieve greater unity in their dealings with the employer through the authorizing of a common committee to conduct negotiations for all the crafts, and by provisions for the simultaneous expiration of contracts, or contractual clauses permitting withdrawal of membership from a job in the event of a controversy with another craft employed in the same industry.[10]

In an important NLRB representation case in the telegraph industry between several AFL unions, commercial telegraphers, federal unions, and the Electrical Workers, on the one hand, and the American Communications Association-CIO, in opposition, it was the AFL so-called nonindustrial unions that petitioned for the company-wide unit and the ACA that sought the less inclusive city-wide bargaining units. The reason for this alignment was quite understandable—the AFL unions had an over-all majority company-wide but fell short of a majority in one of the constituent units which the CIO controlled.

The wartime industrial relations situation with its resulting improvement in the bargaining position of the unions has spurred many of them to unusual efforts to enroll workers in their organizations. Many of the craft unions have really become "industrialized" in respect to many of the industries in which they have been organizing. The outstanding example is the International Association of Machinists and its inclusion of virtually the whole range of skills in the aircraft industry. The Boilermakers, though not quite so inclusive in its coverage, has nevertheless included in its jurisdiction many workers who are not boilermakers. Similarly, such large industrial unions in the CIO as the UAW, the United Steel Workers, and the United Electrical Workers have not permitted themselves to be limited by industry-classification demarcation lines and have organized workers in fields more or less remote from their basic industry ties.

As to the efficiency of the various types of structure, no worth-while wholesale generalizations will hold up in the face of the facts. Craft unions failed to build lasting unions in automobiles and rubber but industrial unions succeeded. Industrial unions, although some attempts were and are being made, failed in the building trades and on the railroads—here craft unions have been pre-eminently successful. In the machinery, aircraft, and shipbuilding industries both industrial and craft unions have been able to develop effective organizations. In the white-collar employments there are only a few unions of any consequence, either craft or industrial.*

THE JURISDICTIONAL DISPUTE—WHY?

Interunion disputes over jurisdictional claims are more common among craft unions than among industrial unions though the industrial unions are by no means free from controversies of this sort.

Primarily, jurisdictional disputes occur because each union is concerned with maximizing its own job opportunities, particularly but not exclusively when there is not enough work to go around. Holding up their union's side in a jurisdictional dispute is what the rank and file of the membership demand from their leaders. When election time comes around, no fact in a candidate's record for re-election is more potent in many unions than his ability to win for his union in jurisdictional controversies with other unions. At the 1946 convention of the Car-

---

* See concluding section of Chap. VIII for effect of Taft-Hartley law on structure.

penters Union the major portion of Secretary Frank Duffy's nomination speech for President Hutcheson is on the theme, in Duffy's words, "that General President Hutcheson has been successful in settling jurisdictional disputes of the Carpenter [sic] with other trades." [11]

One of the reasons that the consciousness of jurisdictional rights has a stronger hold among AFL unions than among CIO unions is that the AFL unions are older and have, therefore, had more time to give their vested jurisdictional interests deeper roots. That jurisdictional consciousness is a function of age is suggested by the practical nonexistence of jurisdictional disputes in the earlier period of the CIO and the cropping up of these disputes as the CIO unions have become older.

A dispute now traditional in the annals of labor is the controversy between several AFL internationals and the Brewery Workers. The Brewery Workers claimed every worker in the industry—the Carpenters and Teamsters each put in separate counterclaims. In fact the Carpenters, because of their consistent strength in the AFL, have played a prominent role in some of the most important jurisdictional disputes. Over a period of years the Carpenters have been involved in what a prominent Carpenters' official referred to as "numerous annoying jurisdictional disputes" [12] with the Sheet Metal Workers over the installation of sheet metal products in building construction and with the Concrete Workers over the building of wooden forms incidental to concrete work in construction.

A share of every AFL convention session is taken up by jurisdictional disputes. Brought before the 1938 AFL convention were disputes between the Building Service Employees and the Hotel and Restaurant Employees over maintenance employees in hotels and between the Upholsterers and Carpenters over the furniture industry; at the 1939 convention, between the Wall Paper Craftsmen and the Pulp and Sulphite Workers over wallpaper mills; at the 1941 convention, an important dispute between the Carpenters and Machinists over the installation and erection of machinery; at the 1943 convention, between the Lithographers and several printing trades unions over offset work; at the 1944 convention, between the Railway Clerks and the Railroad Telegraphers over clerical work being carried on by the telegraphers.

In 1945 the CIO Executive Board found it necessary to establish a Jurisdiction Committee, which took as its first assignment the dispute between the Department Store Workers and the Longshoremen. The Amalgamated Clothing Workers and the International Ladies' Garment Workers have had their conflicts over "mannish-type" women's clothes. The Farm Equipment Workers (CIO) have charged the United Automobile Workers (CIO) with raiding agricultural equipment plants. The United Electrical Workers have had jurisdictional difficulties with the Steel Workers and the Auto Workers. The Transport Workers have competed with the UAW. On occasion locals within the same international union will get into jurisdictional conflict as in the case of Local 91 of the Ladies' Garment Workers which had been charged with luring away plants engaged in the production of "snow suits" from the higher wage cloak and suit locals in the same international. The New York locals of the Bakery and Confectionery Workers came into open conflict with each other over the fancy cake bakers.

The organization of the departments in the AFL has been one of the ways through which attempts have been made with varying success to minimize the consequences of jurisdictional disputes. Least effective has been the Building Trades Department. Although it has gone to extraordinary lengths in establishing impartial tribunals, this department has not been able to prevent aggrieved unions, usually the losing side, from refusing to abide by decisions. The Metal Trades Department has not sought to enter into jurisdictional conflicts as directly as has the Building Trades Department. On the whole, these disputes have been much less troublesome among the metal crafts. The Railway Employees Department has been moderately successful in maintaining interunion harmony in the industry and such disputes as do occur rarely break out into open warfare.*

Jurisdictional disputes as a disrupting influence are not an inevitable outcome of the existence of craft union structure, as the British experience should suggest. The structural fabric of British unions is a scramble of craft, industrial, and so-called general unions, the last a kind of catchall type of organization. Yet the British unions have been remarkably free from interunion conflict, possibly because, as the U.S. Commission on Industrial Relations in Great Britain reported: "The Trades Union Congress . . . has consistently taken the stand that no union has an exclusive right to organize any class of worker." [13] In the United States, the Bricklayers (AFL) and the Steel Workers (CIO) have worked together in the same plants without engaging in disputes

---

* See concluding section of Chap. VIII for effect of Taft-Hartley law on jurisdictional disputes.

of consequence. This holds true as well for the UAW-CIO and various craft unions such as the Patternmakers (AFL) and the Die Sinkers (independent). That many unions can live together peaceably without engaging in jurisdictional disputes or in finding more or less satisfactory resolutions of their differences suggest that the will and intent to settle conflicting jurisdictional claims or the lack of them is a powerful factor in the persistence of rivalries of this kind.

The much-stressed idea of craft union consciousness of American unions is much too facile to serve as the wholesale explanation of the virulence of jurisdictional disputes in union behavior. To be sure, craft union consciousness exists and causes jurisdictional disputes. The psychological basis of craft union consciousness is really craft pride— the pride of a man who has mastered an intricate job through long and arduous application. Veblen called it "the instinct of workmanship." Craft consciousness has become institutionalized into a restrictive vested interest largely as the result of the impact of scarcity of job opportunities. Jurisdictional disputes are minimized (not eliminated completely, however) when there are enough jobs to go around, as the war experience suggests.

Conversion from *peacetime* civilian to war production in particular plants did not generate much jurisdictional conflict. The fact that plants which, in peacetime, produced automobiles turned to the production of such unrelated items as rocket bombs, ammunition, and tanks furnished the ingredients of jurisdictional strife; yet none of consequence occurred. Full employment left little time or inclination for jurisdictional disputes.

The context in which jurisdictional disputes are set has other complicating features. The labor movement in the United States lacks the binding tie of a positive economic philosophy like socialism, which, whatever its other meanings in practical union affairs, commands a kind of allegiance to larger goals which tends to override immediate jurisdictional interests. If the professing of an ideology by union leaders does not completely eliminate jurisdictional conflict it at least exercises a restraining influence. It is this influence which accounts in part for the relative absence of jurisdictional conflict in Great Britain.

The introduction of new materials is an obvious factor in jurisdictional disputes particularly where the union jurisdiction is based on material, as in the case of the Carpenters. The shift from wood to metals has been responsible for much of the Carpenters' involvement in jurisdictional disputes. Changes in industrial technology are equally obvious as a cause of jurisdictional disputes. The introduction of the offset press has been responsible for a long-standing dispute between the lithographers and the printing pressmen. Changes in style in the garment trades have had a comparable effect on jurisdictional claims in the apparel industries.

Jurisdictional disputes arise out of the catch-as-catch-can character of union organizing. When the UAW signed its agreement with Ford it found that it had unwittingly acquired maritime workers on the Lake transport properties of the Ford Empire. This became the basis for a minor disagreement with the NMU, which ended when the maritime workers were turned over to that union.

The economic organization of particular industries has some bearing on the incidence of jurisdictional disputes in those industries. The contracting system in the construction industry, whereby a total construction project is subdivided among several employers, undoubtedly constitutes a breeding ground for jurisdictional disputes. Too much, however, should not be made of this causal relationship. In the case of the motion picture industry, for example, where there is substantial integrated control of employment policies, jurisdictional disputes are frequent. In general, jurisdictional disputes find smaller scale enterprises a more favorable climate in which to exist than in larger scale operations, possibly because the occurrence of these disputes tends to vary in part with the economic strength of the employers and their capacity to impose some kinds of restraints on interunion warfare.

One must also take into account the normal propensity of people who stake out claims either to resist encroachments or to seek to extend their sway over related areas of activity. This holds true whether the claims are of an intellectual kind, as in the case of professional societies and societies for the promotion of something or other, or as in the case of unions, government agencies, and private corporations, where the claims are to more material things such as jobs. These commonplace observations are made here to suggest that the jurisdictional dispute is not a union monopoly but run-of-the-mill aspect of most intergroup relationships.

Then there is what has sometimes been called "union imperialism." William Hutcheson, whose Carpenters Union has been involved in more jurisdictional disputes than any other union, has been pointed to as one of the most effective of the union imperialists. "Once wood," Mr.

Hutcheson has said, "it is always the right of the carpenter to install it, no matter what the new material is." [14]

An official of the Masters, Mates and Pilots charges Joseph Ryan of the Longshoremen with "piracy of our legal jurisdiction within the American Federation of Labor . . . by the issuance of four charters dual to ours," Ryan "not content with local piracy in New York . . . has invaded our locals in Baltimore, Norfolk, Philadelphia, and in New Orleans." Ryan's tactics are "circulation of libel about groups he wishes to smother, coercion of men and interference with their duties by refusing to handle freight which they bring to SS piers." [15]

On other occasions charges of union imperialism have been made against James Petrillo of the AFL Musicians for his claims to the several categories of employees other than musicians in radio broadcasting; against Harry Bridges of the CIO Longshoremen for his attempts to organize in the service trades; and against John Lewis for the efforts of District 50 of the Miners to organize among others, construction workers, paper and pulp workers, and dairy farmers.

Political differences sometimes underlie rival union claims. The long-standing dispute in the CIO between the Longshoremen and the UWRDSEA is at least in part stimulated by the fact that the Longshoremen usually follow the Communist party line, whereas the leaders of the latter union are militantly anti-Communist. The conflict between the Conference of Studio Unions and the Moving Picture Machine Operators (both AFL), which has tied up movie production on the West Coast for lengthy periods, is alleged to stem from the strong Communist influence in the Conference leadership.

AFL leaders are not insensitive to the consequences of jurisdictional warfare. Edward Weyler, as an officer of a state federation and, therefore, frequently caught in the middle of these disputes, has warned:

I see three things happening, that if continued, will spell disaster, maybe destruction, to our A. F. of L. labor movement. First, the growing dislike and contempt of trade unionists for commonly called unfair picket lines. Second, the regretful shaking of heads of union sympathizers and the constant loss of their support because of the unnecessary inconvenience imposed upon them. Third, the greatest weapon the C.I.O. is swinging at us is our jurisdictional disputes and our lack of ability to correct them. I can name numerous cases where we have lost to the C.I.O. in organizing campaigns, because of our lack of unity.[16]

AFL and CIO and the Issue of Structure

The division between the AFL and the CIO has been widely attributed to unresolvable differences over ideas of structure, the AFL being the exponent of craft unionism and the CIO being the exponent of industrial unionism, according to this view. The preceding material in this chapter lends itself to the interpretation that American unions have not characteristically, in their *day-to-day* activities, attached themselves unalterably to either craft or industrial structure. Indeed, it would be strange to comprehend why practical men (and the contemporary union leader is practical if he is nothing else) would be disposed to go to such trouble over structure. Candor compels the admission that craft vs. industrial unionism as such involves no issue of high principle. In short, divorced from the personalities, pressures, and group loyalties, there is no question of real substance in a conflict between craft and industrial unionism.

This is not to say that the CIO-AFL conflict is not based on issues. There are issues involved—weighty and momentous issues—and personalities too. On the surface, the differences between the AFL and the CIO (when it was the Committee for Industrial Organization rather than, as it became later, the Congress of Industrial Organizations) was over the granting of unrestricted charters to organize the mass production industries like rubber, steel, and automobile. The AFL contended that the jurisdictional rights of its existing affiliates would have to be safeguarded. The CIO maintained that such safeguarding of jurisdictional claims would defeat permanent organization in mass production industries. Probing beneath the surface of this conflict one finds, in addition, many more real differences dividing the respective protagonists. The setting in which the difference arose offers some illumination on this score.

The New Deal provided an environment for the organization of unions unprecedented in the history of the nation. For the first time there was at least a presumptive case that with the aid of a sympathetic government the seemingly impregnable fortress of belligerent anti-unionism which large-scale industry had successfully constructed could be breached.

The dominant leadership of the AFL had found the problem of organizing workers in these industries a backbreaking and frustrating job.

Such unions as were organized evaporated with the first sign of adversity. Professor Selig Perlman, a profound and penetrating student of the American labor movement and not unsympathetic to the AFL, writing in 1928 observed in this connection:

The psychology of a big majority of leaders today [is] a curious blending of "defeatism" with complacency. Every union leader admits that the organization of labor must be expanded into the basic industries . . . But at the first encounter with the difficulties of the task—difficulties which are admittedly enormous, made up as they are of the employers' active opposition and of the inertia on the workers' part begotten by the Coolidge prosperity and by "welfare capitalism,"—or in many cases even before such an active encounter, union officers and organizers lose their hearts for the task, and rarely proceed beyond expressions of good intentions. Thereupon having gone through the motions of organizing in new fields, and thus eased their organizer's conscience,—the same leaders settle down to a smug survey of the well oiled machinery of their little organizations which suggests at least a suspicion that these leaders might not entirely welcome too many members, whose alignment in the politics of the union would at best be uncertain.[17]

The judgment was perhaps on the harsh side, underemphasizing the appalling magnitude of organizing, say, steel workers into unions and the systematic terrorism that was invoked against union outsiders who sought to challenge the reign of industrial feudalism. In essence, however, Perlman's appraisal conveys accurately something of the attitude of dominant union leadership later opposing the CIO—the lack of spirit to tackle what seemed a prodigious undertaking and the threat that the CIO offered to the control and traditions of the movement. On balance the conclusion is inescapable that one of the real differences between them, then, was that the CIO wanted to organize and the AFL didn't.

But that is not the whole story. Looming as large is the fact that the leading personalities of the CIO were increasingly feeling out of place in the strategic councils of the AFL—a restlessness excited in part by the new hopes which the Roosevelt New Deal was raising.

John L. Lewis, the chief architect of the CIO, in a speech which became his swan song to the convention of the organization he had built, recited with great feeling:

For many years I was a delegate representing a great organization to the annual conventions of the American Federation of Labor, and during most of those years I was the President of the largest affiliate organization in the American Federation of Labor and yet, during all of those years of participation—and I was something of an active, vigorous young man in my own way—*during all of those years I never even achieved the chairmanship of a standing committee in the American Federation of Labor.*[18] [Emphasis added.]

Lewis was clearly not at peace with his lot in the AFL.

The second-rung personalities in the formation of the CIO were all men who had really never "arrived" in the higher councils of the AFL. David Dubinsky of the International Ladies' Garment Workers' Union, with his Jewish Socialist background, found his own union at odds ideologically with the top-side AFL leaders on many issues. Sidney Hillman of the Amalgamated Clothing Workers had only recently seen his organization admitted into the AFL and it meant little to him. It was hardly likely that a Johnny-come-lately like Hillman could hope to reach the heights of AFL dominance. Along with Charles Howard of the International Typographical Union, the significant characteristic of the men under Lewis was that their own unions stood little to gain in a bolt from the AFL and from a campaign to organize in the mass production industries. Hillman and Dubinsky were already engaged in vigorous organization drives, and Howard's printers needed the other printing crafts in the AFL and couldn't function effectively without them. The motivation for these men was the achievement of authority and reputability in a labor movement more congenial to their aspirations. Lewis's interest in the CIO was also conditioned—it is difficult to say how much—by the need to organize the steel industry workers as a prerequisite for organizing the miners in the "captive" coal operations of the steel industry.

The meaning of the CIO-AFL controversy is less as a conflict over opposing conceptions of structure and more as a conflict between the ins and the outs, in which ideas of structure served as the medium through which the debate could be respectably carried on in public. It is a good illustration of the way in which the requirements of the debater's technique to rationalize his interests in terms of higher philosophy beclouds the real substantive issues at stake. This is not to say that many spokesmen in both AFL and CIO were not sincere when they sought to put the conflict on a more cosmic plane. But, sincerity conceded, it is nevertheless possible to see that there were more compelling considerations at work.

The fact that both AFL and CIO have been able concurrently to build powerful movements is hindsight proof that, given sympathetic environment, energy, and resourcefulness, an effective union organization job can be done irrespective of theoretical disagreements over structure.

This chapter has sought to establish both a positive and a negative approach to the problem of structure in American unions. On the positive side we have stressed the notion that a working understanding of structure can be acquired only by some appraisal of the surrounding circumstances in particular cases. On the negative side we have tried to discourage the idea that a specific structure is an open-sesame to effective labor organization or that, conversely, the prospects of effective organization can be written off in advance because of structure.

UNION GOVERNMENT
AND ADMINISTRATION

THE ORGANIC DOCUMENTS OF THE GOVERNMENT OF ANY ORGAN-
ization never adequately encompass or reflect the intangibles and the
unwritten government. The theory underlying the provisions for checks
and balances in the United States Constitution are, in large degree,
negated by the realities of party politics. Similarly, in union government, the constitutions and by-laws of unions give way to more timely
and real considerations of a kind which this chapter seeks to explore.

FORMAL UNION GOVERNMENT

The outlines of the formal government of unions are embodied in
their constitutions and conform to American democratic tradition and
practices. The highest authority in both AFL and CIO is the annual
convention composed of elected delegates from the affiliated international unions, state and local central bodies, and the federal unions in
the AFL and the local industrial unions in the CIO. Between conventions, the supreme authority is a convention-elected executive board
or council headed by a president. The administration of policy is carried on by a full-time president and secretary-treasurer directing a number of staff departments dealing with organization, legislation, law, information, research, and education.[1]

The point commonly made with respect to the authority of the federations over the constituent international unions is that it is limited
in much the same way that the authority of the federal government

over the states is limited; with the exception of expressly delegated powers, the internationals are completely autonomous. The crucial authority of the federations is the allocation of jurisdiction to the constituent unions. Under the AFL, five departments function to coordinate the interests of the international unions in particular fields. These departments are Metal Trades, Construction, Railway Employees, Maritime, and Union Label. The departments function through conventions, an executive council, and a permanent president and secretary-treasurer.

The government of international unions follows generally the pattern set by the federations. A minor deviation is that in a number of instances a referendum may supersede the convention as the highest authority. The conventions of the international unions are not, as in the case of the federations, typically held annually, but at longer intervals ranging from every two years to indefinite. An executive board elected by the convention, or in a few instances by referendum vote, directs the international between conventions, and the members of the executive board are made up of a president, secretary-treasurer, and executive board members who are, as a matter of practice if not law, also officers of subordinate units. While the precise degree of authority of the international over the locals varies considerably as among internationals, it is in any event substantially greater than the authority of the federations over the internationals. The locals are completely creatures of the international. Policy is positively laid down for the locals by the international and the locals are subject to the direction of their respective internationals with respect to a wide range of functions ranging from collective bargaining negotiations to the administration of union finances. The local union is the primary unit in union government. The local union membership meeting lays down policy and its decisions are carried out by an executive board usually composed of members who are working at their trade. Whether or not there are full-time officers depends on the size of the group and the state of the treasury.

Reference has already been made to the state bodies of organized labor, the AFL State Federations and the CIO State Industrial Union Councils. These units operate under a charter issued by their respective federations. The general practice is for these regional bodies to hold an annual convention composed of delegates from the local unions in the appropriate area, which elects an executive board and full-time officers, usually a president, secretary, or a legislative representative. The city central labor bodies also are made up of delegates from appropriate local unions, an executive council and perhaps one or two full-time officers.

A per capita payment by affiliated units is the method uniformly followed to defray the expenses of all the federated organizations, as well as the international unions; i.e., the national federations, the AFL departments, and the state and local bodies. In the last analysis, the per capita payments come out of the dues paid by individual members to their local unions.

In the discussion that follows it will not be possible to do more than explore the underlying realities in a few strategic areas of union government.

Force of Tradition

The currents of mutual aid, equalitarianism, and fraternalism are the tradition of the American labor movement and have influenced the ways in which unions have set themselves up to do their work. The pull of mutual aid is traceable to the origin of many unions as beneficial institutions concerned deeply with providing financial assistance in illness, death, and unemployment. Expressive of this tendency is an early declaration of the Cigarmakers that one of the primary objectives of unionism is to provide a system of benefit payments which saves the workers "the humiliation and degrading influence that surround charity and the poorhouse." [2]

The pioneers of unionism also articulated strong convictions about the rights of man and a conception of democracy as universal equality and brotherhood. In an environment hostile to unionism, union pioneers like Sylvis, Debs, Gompers, and Stephens talked in terms of unionism as an inevitable and logical extension of the idea of democracy. Organized labor's early pronouncements for free and universal education are manifestoes for democracy in the grand manner of Paine and Jefferson, and indeed, the quest for social status was a significant force in molding the shape of early American unionism.

Fraternalism stems from the "joiner" sentiment in the social life of the nation. Unions have not been immune from the same influence of secret handshakes, elegant titles, and solemn rituals. Contributing also to the secrecy of much of early unionism was the violent hostility of the reputable citizens of the community.

The influence of tradition is reflected at least superficially in the frequency with which such words as "brotherhood" and, to a lesser extent "order," "protective," and "beneficial" appear in the full names of some of the older unions. There is the United Brotherhood of Carpenters and Joiners, the International Brotherhood of Electrical Workers, and the Grand International Brotherhood of Locomotive Engineers.

The fraternalistic roots of the labor movement are manifested too in the designations of officers in some of the older unions. In the Locomotive Engineers, the highest officer is called the "Grand Chief Engineer." The Machinists have "Grand Lodge Representatives." The constituent units are known as "Lodges." The CIO Steel Workers also call their locals "lodges." In the Brotherhood of Railway Signalmen the chief executive is the Grand President.

The impact of history is reflected in the word "amalgamated" that appears occasionally in the names of organizations and epitomizes precisely that fact—namely, an amalgamation of hitherto separate international unions. The Amalgamated Meat Cutters and Butcher Workmen and the Amalgamated Association of Streetcar and Electrical Railway Employees may be cited in point. The desire to incorporate the history of the union in its official name has been responsible for some rather breath-taking names; to wit, the International Association of Marble, Slate and Stone Polishers, Rubbers and Sawyers, Tile and Marble Setters Helpers and Terrazzo Helpers; the Hotel and Restaurant Employees International Alliance and Bartenders International Alliance and Bartenders International League of America; the International Alliance of Theatrical Stage Employees and Moving Picture Machine Operators of the United States and Canada.

AUTONOMY OF THE INTERNATIONALS

On paper, the relationship between the AFL and the CIO and their respective internationals appears to be basically the same—federations of autonomous internationals. Actually, however, there are historical and personal considerations which give greater authority to the CIO in dealing with its internationals.

In origin, the CIO was an organizing mechanism perhaps more than it was anything else. With the exception of the internationals, which had a previous existence of some consequence in the AFL, the unions affiliated to the CIO owe much to it in the way of financial and organizational assistance. The AFL, by contrast, has not directly organized workers in any large magnitudes. The brunt of organization work has been borne by the internationals without significant assistance from the AFL. The difference between the AFL and the CIO in this respect is seen in the current southern organizing drive. The CIO activities here are under the definite control of the CIO as such. The main responsibility in the AFL drive is vested in the affiliated internationals.

Again, with a few important exceptions—the Amalgamated Clothing Workers and the Steel Workers—no CIO unions have been able to build substantial treasuries. In the postwar strike wave of 1945-1946, the striking CIO unions in automobiles, electrical products, meatpacking were in serious financial straits. The AFL unions in the metalworking, construction, and railroad trades, which constitute the core of AFL strength, are all in excellent fiscal shape.

There are personal elements which account for the greater authority of the CIO in dealing with its internationals. The initial drive of the CIO unions was associated with one individual—John L. Lewis. Lewis exercised enormous influence on the conduct of the internationals—an influence which meant far beyond the constitutional proscriptions. Much of that influence was a matter of Lewis's personal temperament. In large part it was also a matter of being head of a powerful international union—the Miners—which had made substantial contributions to CIO organizing activities. When Lewis stepped down, he was succeeded by Philip Murray who, by this time, had become head of the Steel Workers. Murray became president of the CIO because he was the only CIO leader of any stature who was acceptable to the divergent groups within the CIO: the Communists, the anti-Communists, and Sidney Hillman. Murray was fully aware of the fact that he was beholden to no particular group for his position. Murray's personal qualifications are also considerable. His standing as CIO president is somewhat heightened by the fact that there are few leaders of constituent internationals even now who are of Murray's experience and stature in the labor movement.

In the AFL, William Green is a leader among many who are at least on an equal footing. Also, international union executives like Tobin of the Teamsters, Hutcheson of the Carpenters, Tracy of the Electricians have power roots in important international unions. From 1934 on, Green, who had succeeded Samuel Gompers because he was supported by the Miners, lost the support of the Miners and, therefore, lost the support that was singularly responsible for his accession to office.

For all these reasons the CIO, as such, and Philip Murray exercise more extensive authority over the internationals—largely extraconstitutional—than is the case in the AFL. Murray has been known to reprimand international presidents when he felt that their activities ran counter to CIO policy. One such occasion occurred during the war when followers of the Communist party line in the CIO supported national service legislation in direct conflict with CIO policy, which was sharply opposed to this legislation. Murray has also been firmer in dealing with jurisdictional rivalries within the CIO. The importance of Philip Murray in the internal affairs of the internationals is suggested by the fact that at the 1946 convention of the UAW the question as to whom Murray was supporting for the UAW presidency became a highly charged issue. At the 1946 CIO convention, Murray was powerful enough to persuade international union leaders of Communist persuasion to agree to a resolution disavowing Communist interference in CIO affairs. Later Murray was able to induce CIO top leaders of both Communist and anti-Communist leanings to withdraw from the Progressive Citizens of America and the Americans for Democratic Action, strongholds respectively of Communist and anti-Communist movements. Any such relationship between the AFL or William Green and the affairs of the internationals would be unthinkable. Jurisdictional disputes among the AFL unions as one aspect of this federation-international relationship are handled with anything but firmness and decisiveness.

THE UNION CONVENTION

The convention is uniformly the highest union lawmaking body. The union convention is much like conventions of other types of organizations—political, fraternal, business, and veteran; therefore, in important measure the convention is as much a ceremonial occasion as it is a vehicle for the formulation of policy.

In most instances the union convention is an expertly managed affair designed to give the delegates and, through them, the membership a sense of the union's importance. The communication from the President of the United States or from the governor of the state in which the convention is held, the parade of speeches of senators, representatives, cabinet members, government administrators, and top-side leaders of labor are in the nature of testimonials to the reputable status the union holds in the community and in the labor movement. The conventions of the more important unions provide an important morale builder and a reward for many delegates isolated in small communities for whom the international union may be hardly more than an address to which the monthly local per capita payment is sent. The convention provides an opportunity for a few men from each local to have what approximates a good time at the union's expense. In terms of the arduous day-to-day job of being an active union member in his local, the delegate thinks this is not excessive compensation.

As in all large deliberative bodies, the real decisions at a convention are made in committee rooms and places other than in formal debate on the convention floor. This is true of Democratic and Republican conventions, the Congress, and of United Nations Conferences, and is just as true of a union convention. There are usually several hundred, even several thousand, delegates at a union convention and deliberation on matters of policy on a wide variety of issues on the floor of the convention does not flourish under such circumstances.

Most resolutions coming out of the committees are adopted in perfunctory fashion. On certain issues, however, there occasionally develops heated discussion, and the action of the convention as such is not altogether a cut-and-dried routine. Such an issue was the whole question of the industrial organization of the mass production industries at the AFL conventions in the middle thirties. At the 1940 CIO convention there was a rustle of disagreement over the issue of unity between the AFL and the CIO with the delegates of the Amalgamated Clothing Workers standing almost alone in their criticism of the CIO's progress on unity. Differences over jurisdictional claims or increases in per capita payments are invariably responsible for some conflict at AFL conventions. The issue of Negro rights in certain AFL unions is certain to raise controversial discussion sharpened by A. Philip Randolph, president of the Brotherhood of Sleeping Car Porters.

An unusual convention in terms of the extent of controversy is that of the UAW-CIO. In part an outcome of the intense group factionalism and in part the general cussedness of the rank-and-file delegates, controversy is the rule rather than the exception. Elections are hotly contested. Issues such as incentive wage policy evoke heated disagreement—and even when the officers do agree among themselves, the delegates vote down dues increases and raises for the officers. During the 1936 convention of the Amalgamated Clothing Workers, so unusual was the sight of open controversy that a pained hush spread over the Cleveland Auditorium when Joseph Schlossberg, then secretary-treasurer, stood up to oppose the union's endorsement of President Roosevelt for a second term.

At conventions in which there is a Communist minority controversy arises on general political issues and over candidates for office. At the 1946 Shipyard Workers-CIO convention an open break developed between the administration group headed by President John Green and the Communist-dominated group led by Philip Van Gelder. Several of the conventions of the Teachers (AFL) were characterized by much open disagreement between Communist and anti-Communist forces over the election of officers and the expulsion of Communist-controlled locals from the federation. Conventions of the American Newspaper Guild, the Lumber Workers (CIO), the United Electrical Workers have seen a conflict of forces based essentially on a Communist and anti-Communist alignment.

These illustrations do not, of course, exhaust the instances of controversy on the union convention floor, but the record is clear that such controversy is usually the exception rather than the rule. This is true of the convention down the line from the federations to the internationals to the state meetings.

THE EXECUTIVE BOARD

The main force in most international unions is that of the executive board. In the larger internationals the executive board is composed of full-time officers of the union. This situation is typically not a matter of constitutional provision but the reflection of a normal tendency—when a union leader manages to achieve enough influence to be elected to the national executive board he also has enough standing to qualify for a full-time job with the union. The fact that they are full-time officers puts them in a favorable position to keep informed of union and industry problems. It also puts them in a more favorable position to line up support in their own behalf. The executive board, when it is united, will generally be able to persuade the convention to accede to its recommendations.

In some executive boards one strong man pretty much dominates the body. In others the executive board represents a coalition of trade divisions—geographical, national, racial, and factional interests—with influence in the union. In fact, the domination of an executive board by one man may be more apparent than real because the leader has minimized open opposition by having previously taken into account the diverse interests in the union.

Even where an executive board is politically unified it may run into difficulties if it does not give adequate representation to important non-political groups within the union. The International Executive Board of the Transport Workers Union (CIO), which is generally regarded as part of the Communist group in the CIO, discovered that the 1946 union convention balked at accepting the selections from the airline group chosen by the nominations committee, and was successful in electing the man who appeared to be the choice of the airline workers themselves rather than the nominations committee. As one delegate opposing the nominations committee designation put it, "I must go against any procedure that says that the International Executive Board will dictate who are going to be members of the International Executive Board." [3]

Men like Lewis of the Miners, Bridges of the Longshoremen, Petrillo of the Musicians, Hutcheson of the Carpenters, and Murray of the Steel Workers, it is fair to say, occupy positions of dominance on their executive boards and there is no record of any recent serious challenge to this dominance. On the other hand, the UAW-CIO executive board is a synthesis of factional interests headed on the one side by Walter Reuther and by George Addes and R. J. Thomas in a loose coalition on the other side. The Typographical Union is a good illustration of an executive board which lacks a central dominating figure, but in which decisions depend upon the tugs and strains of diverse interests.

The semiautonomous trade department in several internationals is self-sufficient except for certain general administrative functions. This autonomous status is, in most instances, a concession on the part of the international to bring a previously independent union within its own organizational structure. The Journeymen Tailors in the Amalgamated Clothing Workers, the Dyers and the Hosiery Workers in the Textile Workers (CIO), the Sawmill and Lumber Workers in the Carpenters are cases in point of "little internationals" within internationals in that the larger group exerts no significant policy-making influence over a nominally subordinate unit.

CENTRALIZATION AND DECENTRALIZATION

One of the most crucial features of union government and administration is the degree of control exercised by the international over its locals. Constitutional provisions will define the tolerances within which local unions can negotiate agreements, call strikes, and conduct the administrative aspects of their operations. In general, this will range from the comparative freedom that characterizes the Hosiery Workers in the Textile Workers Union, the Sawmill Workers in the Carpenters, and the locals of the building trades unions to the close direction and supervision characteristic of the Machinists Grand Lodge, the Steel Workers, and the International Ladies' Garment Workers' Union.

Whether or not there is in fact close supervision of the locals by the international depends on many factors. The scope of the market within which the union operates is of ranking importance although not always controlling. The Carpenters, Bricklayers, Operating Engineers, Barbers (CIO and AFL), Newspaper Guild, Office Workers (CIO), operating within what is essentially a local market, have considerable leeway in negotiating agreements and calling strikes. The Boilermakers, the United Garment Workers, the Machinists, the Auto Workers (CIO), and the Steel Workers, operating in a national market, exercise by constitutional provision veto power over important aspects of local union functioning.

The extent to which organization in the first instance arose out of local initiative will influence the degree of control in fact over the locals. In the Rubber Workers, the strongholds of union power were built in many instances by the workers on the spot without much aid or assistance from the international. And some local officers and local unions are prone to resist dictation from the international headquarters. Many federal locals in the AFL and the local industrial unions in the CIO, organized as they were in many instances without significant assistance from the federations, function without substantial controls from above.

Factionalism is another influence which tends to break down the discipline of an international over a subordinate unit. The Trotskyist-minded Dunne brothers controlling the AFL teamsters in Minneapolis fought Dan Tobin bitterly, and in turn were subjected to sharp attack by the international. In the Rubber Workers, Sherman Dalrymple, the president, found himself powerless to stem the tide of unauthorized strikes in Akron by the Goodyear local led by George Bass, who had opposed Dalrymple for the presidency. President Harvey Brown of the Machinists removed the alleged Communist-dominated lodge leadership in Oakland, California, and put the local in the hands of a grand lodge receivership.

In the middle thirties, when the CIO was still a committee in the AFL, factionalism as an influence undermining discipline was quite common. Local adherents of the CIO in internationals dominated by a leadership of a different mind were at constant odds with one another. In this connection, one of the bitterest battles raged between Joseph P. Ryan, president of the International Longshoremen's Association (AFL), and Harry Bridges, then president of the West Coast District. The councils of federal locals formed directly under the AFL in rubber and autos were in a state of constant rebellion against the parent organization.

International unions operating in industries with a recent history of company unionism seek to exercise substantial control over their subordinate units as a way of guarding against the possibility of the local leadership reverting to a state of employer-domination. The president of the Pullman Car Porters virtually has the authority to control the local grievance committee operations and can, therefore, remove a local grievance committee chairman if he is so disposed. This provision stems from the long and bitter battle the union has had to fight against company unionism in the Pullman system. The National Federation of Telephone Workers, an unaffiliated group, is currently conducting a campaign urging its constituent groups to authorize stronger controls by the national union by way of destroying the ties that some local federations may still have to their managements. The condition of "perpetual autonomy" that characterizes the present relationship between the local units and the national organization stands as a bar to positive action on the part of the NFTW in ridding some of its local groups of company influence.

"Strong men" in the local unions can entrench themselves in position where the international finds it inexpedient to challenge their hegemony. Dave Beck, head of the Teamsters' Union in the Northwest, is one such strong man. In the same region, court action was required to oust Tommy Ray from his sway in the war-inflated Boilermakers' Union. Luigi Antonini, head of the Italian Dressmakers local of the Ladies' Garment Workers, is the unchallenged head of that local.

A "strong man" as head of the international will encourage the development of extraconstitutional control of local units by the international. John Lewis has put the case for "provisionalism," as his suspension of district autonomy is called, in broad terms of efficiency and democracy.

It is not a fundamental principle [provisionalism] that the convention is discussing. It is a question of business expediency and administrative policy as affecting certain geographical areas of the organization. It is a question of whether you desire your organization to be the most effective instrumentality within the realm of possibility for a labor organization or whether you prefer to sacrifice the efficiency of your organization in some respect for a little more academic freedom in the selection of some local representatives in a number of districts.

. . . What do you want? Do you want an efficient organization or do you want merely a political instrumentality? [4]

Dan Tobin of the Teamsters also has made out the general case for strong international discipline.

. . . Where there is no discipline in a trade union and no head authority, it is bound to get into trouble. Where there are no international leaders to advise and direct, and sometimes compel, local unions to respect the rights of employers and to carry out their agreements, there is apt to be irresponsible action.[5]

The matter of international discipline over local units was seen in another ramification in the Amalgamated Clothing Workers when it was found necessary to revise the constitution in order to empower the international to remove local officers who were charged with racketeering.

The function of the international as a service agency to its locals has been used as a selling point by the international office of the Teamsters in urging the independent newspaper drivers to become part of the international.

The International Union protects unions in legal affairs that involve the International Union. The International Union has established and maintains one of the best statistical departments, with high class, trained technicians, graduates of the best colleges in the country, and investigators equal to any in the labor movement. And we charge our local unions nothing for this service.

This service has been responsible for the prevention of strikes and for enormous increases in wages since it was established three or four years ago. One of our statisticians, Dave Kaplan, a graduate of the University of Wisconsin, spends almost his entire time in New York to help our local unions there. What a great help it would be to the newpaper drivers in their negotiations to have the benefit of this service.

In addition to this, we have national legal advisers and helpers, and we advise and help local unions through this legal department whenever the question becomes a matter that would deal with the International.

In addition to this, we have a legislative department that protects us as much as possible in dealing with legislative matters in Washington and our International Union is as well known on Capitol Hill and has as much influence as any labor organization in America.[6]

The international representative tends to be more seasoned and carry greater prestige in dealing with employers. In general, the international representative brings to bear on a given situation a broader industry outlook, a diversity of experience in union affairs, and independence from possible employer influence which local units cannot normally command. This is realized by many local unions, and their chief complaint is that they do not get *sufficient* guidance from the international. In a document remarkable for candor in appraising their own shortcomings, the International Brotherhood of Paper Makers finds:

One cause for dissatisfaction in the past [among locals] has been the slowness with which an international representative has arrived in town in response to a request. An outstanding example is in the case of one mill which was shut down last year by a spontaneous strike of several days duration. It was some three days later before an international representative arrived in town.[7]

Much in the same vein is the report of the Textile Workers Union (CIO) that

We wish it were possible to report that the majority of our field workers are engaged in the primary task of organizing new workers. Unfortunately this is not the case. Although a part of our staff is able to devote full time to this work, the largest number by far is engaged in servicing local unions by negotiating and administering contracts, handling grievances and otherwise assisting the locals to carry on their business.[8]

The rapid growth of unionism in the past decade has far outstripped the capacity of local people to handle their own affairs in competent fashion; therefore, the valid need for assistance from the international office on a wide variety of matters. The importance of the international union as a service agency has increased perceptibly with the active intervention of government in labor affairs. Appearance before government tribunals demands a measure of technical expertness which many local units on their own cannot provide. The widening of the scope of collective bargaining to include such matters as wage incentives and job evaluation, to cite but one instance, also has put a premium on the specialist. The tendency for collective bargaining to be corporation-wide and industry-wide has further emphasized the importance of the international as against its subordinate units. To leave local units on their own in the face of inexperienced leadership and complex problems would be dangerous to the survival of many unions.

Some mortality of local unions is caused by the absence of guidance and direction from the international. In a few cases this is due to the isolation of the local units from the main roads of union activity. In areas where a large union predominates, there is a tendency for it to acquire plants in apparently unrelated jurisdictions simply because it *is* in a position to service these groups.

The rapid growth of unionism has also outstripped the administrative resources of the internationals to provide the kind and frequency of direction that local units require in a period of fast-moving events. In one important union, whose name it would be inexpedient to divulge, the subordinate units deal with subsidiaries of a giant corporation on a more or less unco-ordinated basis without any significant guidance and direction from the international. This is not a deliberate policy on the part of the international, but results from a sheer lack of competent manpower to provide the kind of guidance that is called for. The investigation of the Paper Makers referred to above notes in this connection: "There is a feeling in some [local] quarters that the International Union has no clear cut policies in connection with the many matters which they have to deal." [9]

The question as to whether control of union policy is becoming more or less centralized cannot be answered in any pat fashion. The facts are that there are tendencies in both directions and the absence of a secular trend in any particular direction. Pulling in the direction of centralization are such factors as increasing movement toward industry-wide bargaining, the increasing element of technical expertness in collective bargaining, the widening of the scope of collective bargaining, the expanding role of government in economic affairs, and the broadening of union interests. Offsetting this trend toward pyramiding of responsibility is one large consideration: the way in which on-the-job grievances are handled has never ceased to be the central day-to-day concern of the rank and file of the membership. In the nature of these matters, the international office cannot adequately do a wholesale job in this area of union administration. To the extent that local grievances continue to be as important as they are now, the centralization process in matters of consequence to the average union member will not undermine the vital position that the local organization holds in the scheme of union matters.*

The extent to which the international directs the affairs of its subordinate units has no necessary relationship to the degree of democracy in the government of particular unions. John Lewis's permanent receiverships in some of his districts does mean a denial of democratic participation by the local membership in the conduct of its business. But the injection of the international office of the UAW in the Packard local because it was discriminating against Negroes means an extension of democracy. In short, whether centralized discipline is good or bad depends on whether the objective of the discipline is good or bad.

The problem of *enforcing* union discipline among the membership as an aspect of union government is beset with the same conflicts that we observe in the other aspects of union functioning. On the one hand, the union must be able to protect itself from attack from within its own ranks; on the other, as a democratic institution it must provide mechanism for a fair hearing for those accused of offenses against union rules and morality.

The major kinds of offenses can be summarized under two headings: (1) violation of union rules relative to strikes and standards of wages, hours, and working conditions; (2) alleged breaches of union discipline arising out of a factional struggle within the union. The judicial process typically follows a pattern something like this: The union member committing the alleged offense is brought up on charges before his local union. If the charges are upheld, the accused member has the right to appeal successively to a district body, the international executive

---

* See concluding section of Chap. VIII for effect of Taft-Hartley law on centralization.

board or the international president, and the tribunal of last resort is the international convention. As a practical matter, the convention rarely overrules the decision of the executive board or of the international president.

With a few striking exceptions, the actual operation of the judicial process in unions comes as close to dispensing justice as the peculiar character of the situation allows, and perhaps a little more. Philip Taft remarks, on this point, "The judicial procedure of the union is not an instrument for dispensing abstract justice, but is a means for keeping the union intact and effective. . . ." [10] And in another place he says, "From our knowledge of union history, we may conclude that machinists, printers, railway unions, hatters, some of the garment trades, and a number of other unions are not in danger of abuse of power by the top officials. It would be unsafe to say as much for the unions in the building trades and in the coal mining industry." [11]

Several cases may reveal something of the character of union judicial proceedings. Several members of a Boston local of the Teamsters were charged with and (after trial by their local) convicted of having participated in "an unlawful or rump strike." The local ordered expulsion. The defendant members appealed to the district joint council, which modified the sentence to a fine and temporary suspension. The local then appealed to the executive board, which sustained the judgment of the joint council. [12]

The 1943 convention of the UAW-CIO heard, on appeal, the case of three members of a local union—shop committeemen—charged with conduct "unbecoming union officers" because they failed "to represent a union member properly before management" and because they took "workers off their jobs during working hours in order to frame the fictitious charges against union members." They were accused also of "conducting an inquisition by cross-examining members in an incriminating manner before supervision" and "of attempting to incite race difficulties by asking Negro workers to strike against the white race." A local trial committee found the defendants guilty as charged and the sentence was the suspension of the privilege of running for office. The General Council, which heard the case on appeal, lacking a two-thirds majority vote, did not sustain the verdict of the trial board. Instead, suspension for thirty days was ordered. The defendants, dissatisfied with this decision, appealed to the General Executive Board for a reversal and for reimbursement of pay lost because of the pro-

ceeding. The Executive Board upheld the decision of the General
Council and the defendants appealed to the convention, which adopted
the recommendation of the convention's Grievance Committee set up
to hear these cases, and which had recommended a denial of the appeal.[13]

The judicial process in the unions has its seamier sides. The American Civil Liberties Union describes a case which involved

the editor of an opposition paper "We Pay Dues Too" in a State, County
and Municipal Workers (CIO) local of New York. He vigorously attacked
the union leaders for following the Communist Party Line. The administration tried him on charges of saying in his paper that union officials had
opposed the Selective Service Act before and after its enactment. At the
executive board hearing he was charged with wilful, deliberate misrepresen-
tation of the union's position. Defense counsel replied that the local had
sent delegates to the American Peace Mobilization conference in April 1941,
showing the union officers had followed the Communist Party line and opposed the Selective Service Act. The defense also argued that the executive
board was biased and urged that the trial body be elected by the membership. The executive board—consisting of the officials accused of Communist
policy—sat in judgment against their political opponent and suspended him
from the union for a year. He sued in the courts, and the case is now
pending.[14]

In another case coming to the attention of the American Civil Liberties
Union, a New Jersey teamster in the face of antagonism of the local
union officers was elected shop chairman for his "barn." He was expelled, as the court found later, without the serving of a charge and
without a hearing for making "derogatory remarks about the local's
president and vice-president." [15] Members of the Moving Picture Machine Operators' Union in New York, when that organization was
under the leadership of Sam Kaplan, who sought accounting of union
funds through court action, were either expelled or fined up to $1,000.

QUALIFICATIONS FOR MEMBERSHIP

Qualifications for union membership with respect to race, citizenship,
sex, and political affiliation are not uncommon. The extent to which
union membership is restricted on these grounds is motivated by a fusion
of economics, expediency, ideology, and folklore. Special reference is

made to Negroes in this account because they are the population group most seriously affected.

The economic nexus functions in barring certain groups in the population from union membership because these groups are presumed to exercise an unwholesome competitive influence in the labor market. Thus, Negroes, women, and foreign-born workers, particularly those of Eastern European and Oriental origin are considered to be inherently low-wage workers whose presence in the labor market, at least in bad times, exercises a depressing influence. Negroes and foreign-born workers have, in the past, been used as organized strikebreakers on the railroads and in the automobile industry, for example.

The force of economics operates favorably in behalf of these groups when they have predominated in an industry before union organization in the industry was established. In these cases, discriminatory policies aimed against them would be clearly inexpedient, all other factors aside. This consideration has dictated the admittance of Negroes in the white-controlled hod carriers' and bricklayers' unions, and measurably influenced union admission policies with respect to the automobile industry (Ford particularly).

In general, a period in which employment opportunities are expanding rather than contracting facilitates the relaxation of membership restrictions. For example, the Boilermakers admitted Negroes to full union membership under the pressure of wartime manpower shortages and, it should be added, of government through the Fair Employment Practices Committee.

Perhaps the kind of prejudice divorced from pecuniary elements that the union member as part of the population at large manifests toward Negroes and the colored races in general is at least as potent a force in barring Negroes from union membership as is the economic factor. The average union member is also an average American and, as such, he shares the deep-rooted color prejudices of the average American. Consequently, in the South in the unions whose national leadership has the most enlightened attitudes the problem of assimilation of Negro workers is still serious and beset with much conflict. CIO Textiles and Steel in the South are cases in point. Even in the Midwest, the UAW-CIO (another union with an aggressive antidiscrimination policy) locals have had grave racial conflicts.

The CIO unions and the AFL unions, like the ILGWU, Actors

Equity, and the Millinery Workers have been motivated in their union admission policy by a positive philosophy in which equal treatment of all races has been an article of faith. These unions have, therefore, faced up to the race problem, not by reluctant and grudging compromise but by deliberate and conscious planning, as witness the presence of a fair employment practice department in both the CIO and the UAW, and the importance of interracial experiences in the educational activities of the ILGWU and the Textile Workers. Actors Equity is waging a broad campaign to alter the restrictive admission policy of the National Theatre, the only place of the legitimate theater, in Washington, D.C.

The Communist unions have always pursued vigorous antidiscrimination policies as a matter of political ideology and tactics. In most of the unions that sought to integrate Negroes into the life of the organization as a matter of affirmative belief, it is safe to say that the national leadership has been far ahead of its rank-and-file membership in this respect.

Herbert Northrup,[16] who has done the most exhaustive study of union policies and attitudes toward Negroes, has classified these according to unions which exclude Negroes: by ritual—to wit, the Machinists; by constitutional provision—notably the unaffiliated brotherhood and AFL railroad unions; by "tacit consent"—as in the case of the Electrical Workers and the Plumbers; by unions which "afford Negroes only segregated auxiliary status," like the Blacksmiths, Railway Clerks, and Sheet Metal Workers.

ASPECTS OF UNION FINANCES

"The modern labor union," Philip Murray and coauthor M. L. Cooke say, "has in many respects become a big business."[17] To this observation, a delegate to the convention of the Carpenters adds documentation: "I think we will all agree that this [the Carpenters' Union] is big business. The operation of this [Carpenters'] home is big business. The operation of the printing plant in Indianapolis is big business. The Statistical Department of this United Brotherhood compares with the largest statistical bureaus in any sort of a business or industrial organization."[18]

Administering the financial phases of union administration involves the collection of dues, initiation fees, and assessments, and the record keeping incidental to these activities. Union financial administration means also disbursing of unemployment, strike, sickness, and death benefits, auditing the account books of subordinate units, payment of "per capita" to affiliated organizations, investing the union's funds in securities and real estate, and operating as an employer would with perhaps thousands of workers in its own right. The nature of these enterprises has introduced a large measure of businesslike procedure into the internal affairs of unions which runs counter to the mood of equalitarian idealism of which unions are an expression.

Part of the impact of this businesslike systematization of union affairs has been to create in the minds of the ordinary members in some aspects of their dealings with the union apparatus a conception of the union as an impersonal mechanism. Most of the members' points of contact with their union—paying dues, receiving "sick" benefits—are conducted more in the atmosphere of a bank than they are of a fraternal organization. The tendency toward financial massiveness is one of the factors in creating a perceptible gulf between the union administration and the union members. From the rank-and-file member's point of view, the union is "the office." It is this which must have been in the mind of the secretary-treasurer of the CIO Shipyard Workers when he observed that "there should be very little 'lost time' drawing out of union funds" and expressed as his "earnest hope that we will return to the days of militant rank and file unionism when it was deemed a mark of honor for a Union brother to give his services to our cause without reimbursement for 'lost time' if it did not interfere with his livelihood." [19] And from a much older union we observe the same kind of reaction when the Grand Lodge auditor of the Machinists complains that there has been a deterioration in trade union morality in expending union funds for wasteful and frivolous purposes because "the newer members have not been grounded in sound union principles." [20]

The conflict between equalitarianism and efficiency has reflected itself nowhere so sharply as in the financial structure of unions. High salaries for union officials are regarded as contrary to good trade union principles. The conflict of ideas about union salaries is between those who say that no union officer should receive more than the best paid worker in a plant and those who assert that the requirements of efficiency and effective representation of union interests warrant the payment of salaries more nearly like executives than of workers.

The equalitarian feeling among the workers is still strong, as the Typographical Union discovered when a referendum to increase the salaries of the vice-presidents was defeated by the membership. Vice-President Elmer Brown lamented the

failure of the membership to compensate them for added cost which resulted in their elevation to office and the high cost of living and added tax burden will in no way affect the service these officers will render to the membership of the ITU. Any person who runs for office in the ITU with any expectation that he is going to be materially compensated for his effort is in for sad disappointment. Like ministers, ITU officials must be satisfied with the compensation that comes with the knowledge that they are doing something for the benefit of those they are privileged to serve.[21]

In the convention discussion over raising the salaries of the general officers of the Carpenters' Union, a delegate voiced the modern business approach to salaries. "Organized labor has taken a position in the world where it is a part of business. It has now reached the point where we must pay and take care of our officers in proportion to the amount of business we do." [22]

Philip Taft's researches with respect to salaries of union officers reveal that the remuneration of local officers bears some relationship to the going scale of wages in their particular craft or industry. Thus, the average weekly salary of a local union officer is on the order of $75. The salary of the international officers in general is not characterized by any such relationship. On average, the salaries of international officers, other than the chief union executive, is on the order of $5,500 per year, $6,500 for officers in AFL unions and something under $4,000 for CIO unions. The salaries of the chief union executive averages about $6,500; $7,000 for AFL executives and $6,000 for CIO.

The president of the UAW-CIO, a union with a million members, gets $9,000. It required a heated convention debate to get it raised from $5,000. The president of the Rubber Workers gets $4,000 and the United Electrical Workers president gets about $3,500. The Newspaper Guild president gets no salary and is a working newspaperman. The Pulp and Sulphite Workers president receives $6,500. The Ladies' Garment Workers head receives $12,000. In the higher brackets, the largest salary appears to be that of the Teamsters president at $30,000; the presidents of the Miners and the Railway Clerks receive $25,000; Steel Workers, Musicians, and the AFL get $20,000. In terms of other employment of comparable responsibility in private industry, these salaries are low.

The equalitarian influence is discernible in the typical goldfish bowl environment in which the routine financial transactions of unions generally take place. The convention reports of the executive boards, or the union periodical, usually include what are, on the whole, fairly elaborate financial statements showing in detail the disbursements and the income of the unions. Indeed, one of the features that make many union periodicals such deadly reading is the inclusion of financial minutiae page after page. The Hod Carriers Union is an exception. In its most recent financial statement it covered the period 1911 to 1941 in one report.

One of the most revealing of the financial reports is prepared by the Typographical Union. In a recent issue of the Journal there appeared a graphic presentation of how the union spends the $5.80 per month which a member earning $250 per month pays:

$4.15—old age pension
.85—mortuary benefit
.50—maintenance of union printers' home
.30—economic activities (.05 of which goes for the Journal)

The financial statement of the Newspaper Guild provides the raw data for a really effective appraisal by the membership, or anyone else for that matter, of how the union's money is spent. For example, it is possible to learn that for a quarter year the editor of the union periodical received $845 and the research director received $885; $13,523 was spent for organizational activities and administrative costs came to $10,-770 during this period.[23]

It is safe to say that, on an average, the financial reports of unions have been revealed publicly in greater detail and with greater frequency than that of the typical corporation. This is particularly significant because, until the Taft-Hartley law was passed, no comparable legal compulsion on the unions existed with respect to the publication of financial details.

As a general tendency, the drift is away from incorporating elaborate benefit schemes in the dues systems, a common characteristic of the older unions. The newer unions tend to collect dues only for what the Typographical Union calls "economic" activities. Again, this movement away from the union financing of fraternal activities is accounted for in large part by the wider prevalence of government-sponsored social security, by the inclusion in the unions of workers in the lower skilled categories who look toward collective bargaining for the benefits traditionally provided by the union alone, and by the inefficiency of many of these systems. "Benefit systems," said Matthew Woll, "where they are still in operation are a constant source of trouble. . . . Their assessments must be raised constantly to meet rising ages, and increases of assessments are always resented. All manner of complications result. . . . Few union operations are today productive of as much woe and uncertainty as the benefit systems that remain in operation." [24]

The financial structure of a union may have other purposes than those of raising funds to defray the expenses of running the union. High initiation fees are, in some instances, used to restrict union membership, particularly in closed-shop industries. At one time or another locals of the Moving Picture Machine Operators charged initiation fees of from $300 to $1,000 for precisely that purpose. Other unions whose initiation fees have come within that range include the Cement Masons, the Bill Posters, and the Carpet and Linoleum Layers. The dues system is sometimes viewed as a way of attracting a type of membership which will stick to the union in bad times as well as good. This is the sense of the attitude of an official of the Boilermakers who says, "They [the CIO] sell a cheap class of organization. This organization is wanted by those who have no desire to pay dues and no desire to continue in business when the cut-backs come." [25] The international office of the Teamsters take only 30 cents out of the minimum monthly dues of $2, leaving the local with a sizable proportion of the members' dues. This, it is felt, serves as an incentive for the locals to engage in vigorous organizing activity and to hold their members once they are organized.

The financial phases of union administration have felt a trend toward greater authority in the international. Millis and Montgomery note:

> Historically, policy with respect to initiation fees and local dues was the concern of the locals, not of the internationals but this has undergone very considerable change as the internationals have performed new functions and gained more power. The change is explained in part as incidental to the financing of the international but more so by efforts to protect against weakness in this direction or that.[26]

THE LOCAL MEETING

In theory, the union meeting of the locals should constitute the core of union government. The local union meeting in practice, however, is not a creative institution except when issues in great controversy arise, such as an increase in local dues, or the calling of a strike, or when a factional dispute develops so that the leaders of the factions work hard to get the vote out. As Will Herberg says, as long as things go along evenly the union meeting is "merely a plebiscitary body and in the more democratic unions, also a medium through which the directives of the leadership are transmitted to the masses of members and the members aroused and inspired." [27]

The Paper Makers investigation presents an account of a union meeting which the experienced observer can recognize as being generally applicable.

Business drags on and on until late hours. A few members argue every question repeatedly while others sit silent. The chairman allows a speaker too much time or too many opportunities to be heard. Discussion is not limited within reason. No committees are appointed or make reports. Correspondence is left at home or passed over because it is "too long and just a lot of hooey anyway." Outsiders are seldom invited and when one is present it is so late by the time the program reaches him, the members wish he would make it short so they may go home.

Some of our meeting halls are dreary, cheerless, uninviting places.[28]

Undoubtedly the rapid rate at which workers have been brought into unions and the failure of most unions to do an adequate job of assimilating the newer membership have had something to do with the indifference of rank-and-file members to the run-of-the-mill local meeting. The problems that are closest to the individual worker's concerns are normally taken up on the job or through the grievance machinery, leaving little of vital moment for discussion at the local meeting. Finally, routine meetings of all types of organizations are not commonly attended by any large segment of the membership and labor organizations are no exception.

The sparse attendance at local meetings makes it easier for a few insiders to control the local. Where there is a concern to get members to attend, some locals have resorted to the expediency of fining members for failure to attend or have tried to dress up the meeting through the use of guest speakers, movies, and other kinds of inducements—without much success, it must be said.

The problem of the unions has been to shape a traditionalism, developed in a less complicated environment which still exerts a powerful contemporary pull, to the requirements of functioning in a mass production business society. The tendency has been for the unions, in conducting their affairs, to become more businesslike in a literal sense of the term. Large memberships, government intervention in economic affairs, the tendency toward expansion in and increasing complexity of the scope of collective bargaining are all factors causing a certain bureaucratization (if that is a word) of the unions' operations in contrast to the earlier informal equalitarianism of beneficial societies.

CHAPTER V

COLLECTIVE BARGAINING

THE COLLECTIVE AGREEMENT IS THE MEDIUM THROUGH WHICH THE major stresses and strains of the employer-union relationship are stabilized for at least a brief period. Although normally a written document embodying the terms of wages, hours, and working conditions which the union and management agree to, it is frequently more than that, being understandings, oral commitments, and tacit acceptance of common practice.

Irrespective of the social attitudes of union leadership, no union of consequence opposes the making of a collective agreement as a matter of principle, although here and there it may be opposed as a matter of expediency. For an earlier generation of left-wing union leadership, the collective agreement was class collaboration and a transgression of the class struggle. Such inhibitions are no longer of importance in practical union affairs.

WAGES AND HOURS

Wages, and hours as a function of wages, are in the first rank of importance for the union in the collective agreement. The basic principles which underlie the union's position on wages can be stated briefly:

1. More pay and shorter hours.
2. Maintaining equilibrium in the formal and informal status arrangements among the workers in the plant.

3. Protecting the competitive position of the plant, industry or whatever unit of operation is involved in a particular collective bargaining
situation.

The force of the principles will become more apparent as this discussion
develops.

The precise way in which these principles are achieved is, however,
a matter of expediency and not of basic principle. This was clearly
demonstrated in the laboratory provided by the wage stabilization program administered by the National War Labor Board. When the traditional avenues of wage increases—explicit increases in wage rates and
explicit reduction in hours—were closed, the battleground shifted to
more esoteric outlets, the so-called "fringe issues"—vacations, lunch
periods, and travel time, merit progression systems, bonuses, incentive
schemes, and job classification programs. In fact, a whole new strategy
of wage payment was evolved to provide opportunities for getting wage
increases which would not run afoul of stabilization policy.

These principles are the keystones of functioning union attitudes with
respect to methods of wage payment. The International Ladies' Garment Workers over a period of years shifted back and forth between
piecework and timework. In 1916 the ILG cloakmakers, after having
accepted piecework, opposed it because it gave an undue competitive
advantage to the sweated contract shops. In 1933 the New York cloakmakers agreed to restore piecework because they were on their way
toward developing more efficient mechanisms to control the contract
shops. In the New York dress industry sections of the ILG a complicated
technique has been evolved of setting uniform piecework rates on the
basis of time studies and price ranges in which the product is to be sold.
The union participates fully in this rate-making process and would be
opposed to a return to simple time methods of payment.

The International Typographical Union opposed piecework but found
it frequently impossible to impose its will on the constituent local unions
who chose to cling to piecework systems. The ITU has voiced the
traditional attitude of labor in general to piecework and incentive systems by pointing to the "disruptive individualism inimical to the co-
operation necessary for the establishment and maintenance of adequate
union rates," [1] which piece rates caused. Given the extensive local
autonomy that prevailed in the ITU, it was many years before the International was disposed to get tough about piecework. Piecework per-

sisted because, for a small part of the composing room at least, it was more profitable. In building construction, piece-rate systems are clearly inapplicable when one recognizes the virtual impossibility of setting production standards. Consequently, time payment stands unchallenged.

The automobile worker appraises piecework incentive schemes against a background of speed-up. The opposition to speed-up was one of the potent arguments that got auto workers to join the UAW in the first place. During the war, in this union, the attitude toward incentive schemes became an issue in political conflict between the group headed by Reuther, who opposed it, and that of George Addes, who favored it. Addes's support was alleged to have stemmed from the fact that incentive schemes were part of the Communist party wartime line. As Victor Reuther put it:

Piecework systems would have the result of further intensifying the problem of wage inequalities, and differentials will block the union's efforts to establish an industry-wide wage agreement based upon equal pay for equal work, and will further demoralize workers who are, at present, getting less money for doing the same work.[2]

On the other hand, the United Electrical Workers, with what it regarded as a win-the-war program, favored incentive schemes:

Our experiences in these plants provide the living proof that incentive piecework plans, bonus systems, etc., can be controlled by the union, and be prevented from becoming devices to speed up the employees and cut rates.[3]

In another place the UE says:

It is not enough for us to demand "equal pay for equal work regardless of sex, race or creed." The problem is too complex to be so easily disposed of.[4]

As a tenet of faith, unions are opposed to incentive payments, but the practical union rank-and-file leader tries to make the best of a wage incentive scheme if he has to. And whether he has to or not depends on whether the union is in a strong enough bargaining position to support its opposition. This is essentially the attitude of an executive board member of the Mine, Mill and Smelter Workers:

In the Casting Division where we have numerous piecework or incentive systems I have been asked by workers on numerous occasions what I think of piecework. Trying to answer is like advising your best friend whether to continue living with his cantankerous wife. The obvious answer is, you married her—if she is bad, reform her and if you can't, then you had better see the chaplain.

Piecework is something like that . . . if you have it and it's bad, then reform it and if you're still dissatisfied, then you'd better see your negotiating committee and ask them to divorce it from the next contract.

I personally wouldn't want to work under piecework. If I want to burn myself out fast, I can find more pleasant ways to do it. The tendency under piecework is to work at a pace which one can hardly keep up year after year. However, it is a matter of choice and taste for each shop. It's like spinach—while I don't like it, some do . . . so, I'll continue disliking it and others will continue eating it.[5]

The AFL Electrical Workers assert in the same spirit: "It should be significant that all job evaluation, piece work, bonus and such schemes are conceived in the minds of employers and their agents. We have yet to learn of any such plan being devised by or on behalf of labor." [6] Yet the same pamphlet concludes with, "Nothing in this pamphlet should be construed as to bar local unions from using any and all legitimate means in efforts to secure equitable wage rates." [7]

The Steel Workers (CIO) joined with management representatives in a painstaking job survey of the steel industry leading to an evaluation system, not because the union was especially in favor of the conception but because this was the only way in which the union felt that it could adequately protect the job-by-job allocation of a War Labor Board wage inequity award.

The belligerent union attitude that holds for wage incentive systems holds for other aspects of what used to be called "scientific management" —time study, job evaluation, and merit rating. In general, the union's position is that management's objective in installing these work rationalization systems, when it is not clearly a speed-up, is to exclude from the bargaining relationship as wide an area as it can get away with, on the ground that the work arrangements arrived at by these systems are "facts" or are matters of "management prerogatives," and therefore not subject to bargaining and *joint* determination.

In recent years the unions have employed their own engineers and technical experts, who have challenged the factual character of the findings of work rationalization. Outstanding among these is William Gomberg, the engineer for the International Ladies' Garment Workers' Union. Both in time study, which is basic to rate setting under incentive payment plans, and in job evaluation schemes, Gomberg has pointed out that the element of human judgment is considerable. "The evidence shows further," Gomberg says,

that the residual error of human judgment in the administration of these techniques is usually far greater than the percentage changes made in a wage scale as the result of collective bargaining negotiations. It can easily be seen therefore why no experienced union is prepared to leave these techniques to the unilateral judgment of management itself. Of course, this entails a corresponding obligation on the part of the union to equip itself with trained personnel that can cope with management engineers on their own terms.[8]

If and when the traditional union opposition to work rationalization schemes is surmounted, the union's strategy is to subject the details of these schemes to the give-and-take of collective bargaining. This does not necessarily mean that all unions or even most unions are interested in joint participation from the initial point of installation. While some unions do, others will accept management's right to install the system but vigorously reserve their right to subject certain specific application to the processes of the joint grievance machinery.

The point of the union's reluctance to participate fully with management in the installation and administration of work rationalization schemes is its fear of being "sucked in" to promote a technical program about which it is uncertain. The CIO Electrical Workers advise their local unions

to refuse to become a party to or be bound by any point rating systems which management may use to establish job evaluation. It should not appear in the contract. As with time studies the UE let the company use whatever method it pleases but under close union surveillance. If the result is satisfactory, well and good. If it is not the company will hear from us. The union should always reserve the right to challenge any job values which it finds unsatisfactory and to utilize any and all factors bearing on the case.[9]

When the union goes along with the installation of a time study system it does so "as a means of conserving the particular financial position of the particular union employer so that he could continue to furnish employment" according to the appraisal of a group of union engineering technicians.[10] The objects of union questioning in time study are likely to be such aspects as fatigue allowances, the representative character of the "average" worker whose operations are being timed, and the value judgments involved in setting the standard time an operation requires.

One auto worker says he "caught them [the management] . . . rating the most efficient and the youngest individual and not allowing 15 per cent for fatigue." Another auto worker relates that in a welding operation which he and a company engineer timed, the latter arrived at a rate of eight pieces an hour whereas "the actual time that I took on the man . . . was six pieces." In the technical jargon, the difference was between the observed time and the "average time" arrived at by the method of leveling.[11]

The AFL Office Workers offer advice to their unions in the same vein. "If complete participation is granted it may be accepted without however underwriting the plan as a union product. *Right of grievance should be reserved at all times.* Preferably the plan should not be made a part of the contract."[12]

Job evaluation sets up a relative standing of jobs in a plant according to such job factors as skill, responsibility, working conditions, and technical knowledge. The group of union engineering technicians referred to previously

were in agreement that under no circumstances could the job evaluation plan be used as the sole determinant of the relative wage structure. Aside from the relative job content measured by the job evaluation scheme would be such factors as

1. Irregularity of employment. . . .
2. The career prospects of the job. . . .
3. Market supply of and demand for the job. . . .
4. The traditional wage relationships which grew up historically.

As applied to particular jobs the union will frequently challenge the values assigned by management toward the end that the resulting wage rate will be raised from previous levels, or at least not reduced. The union will also seek to prevent the systematic application of job evaluation system from disturbing excessively the pattern traditional job relationships.

President Harvey Brown of the Machinists tells of a situation in a midwestern metal-working plant "organized by the Machinists and other crafts. Management installed a job evaluation system which in one department had the effect of substituting 12 different job analyses and what was more important 12 different rates, where only 1 rate for all the jobs had existed before. Immediately," Brown says, "production declined and employee discontent increased. Upon further investigation it was found that the employees had always functioned as a team: the employees were capable of operating each other's machines: and the employees, therefore, expected the same rate of pay." [13] Management, however, even when it had these facts, still supported the job evaluation plan. The union in the plant and the department foremen, it may be added, opposed its continuance.

In bargaining on wage incentive systems, unions recognize as crucial:

1. The minimum guaranteed rate, that is, the rate which will be paid irrespective of output.
2. The level of output at which incentive rates start operating.
3. The relationship between output and rate in the incentive curve itself, that is: will additional production of 1% compensate for at least 1% additional earnings, and finally,
4. Protection against changes in the relationship among (1), (2), (3) above to get more output at lower rates; in short, the speed-up.

It can be seen, then, that to the extent that wages are related by management to standards of output and job content the unions will be increasingly precipitated into an "invasion of management's prerogatives" (as the union's involvement in these matters is sometimes called), not because it is motivated by some philosophical tenet but because if the union is to hold the support of its membership it *must* protect wage rates no matter where that commitment leads to.

Union policy toward the relationship of wages to the cost of living reveals the same pragmatic rather than principled strains. As a matter of tradition, tying wages to the cost of living has been characterized by labor as "ridiculous and fantastic." [14] This attitude has carried over into more recent times. "As American trade unionists," says an official pronouncement of the Metal Trades Department of the AFL, "we have never accepted the unsound policy that wages must or should be geared to the cost of living. As a fundamental policy the idea is false." [15] Yet when the government's wartime wage stabilization program closed other opportunities for wage increases, both AFL and CIO did not hesitate to base a part of their argument for raising wartime wages on the fact that the BLS index was a gross underestimate of increases in wartime cost of living.

Equal pay for equal work is more than a slogan. No grievance can generate more friction among the workers themselves than the existence of disparate rates for the same kind of work, or derangements in the normal job hierarchy. The union looks upon the job of ironing out wage inequities as among the most important in maintaining the support of its membership, since one of the important reasons workers join unions in the first place is to achieve uniformity of treatment. Golden and Ruttenberg put it this way: "Wage equalization . . . is one of the most explosive jobs either unions or management together or separately can tackle." [16] Interplant or intercompany wage disparities, particularly as between organized and unorganized companies, put the union in a position where it must act to bring up the wages at the lower end of the range. This holds particularly true where labor costs constitute a relatively high proportion of total costs. In terms of the dynamics of union wage policy, the aim is generally to maintain a sensible relationship among various classes of wages as much as it is aimed at achieving some absolute goal of earnings for union members.

The problem of reconversion in the automobile industry was made more difficult by the problem of wage differentials between AFL maintenance workers employed by an outside contractor and the CIO maintenance workers employed by the plant. The possibly apocryphal story is told of an AFL maintenance worker on one side of a wall engaged in boring a hole when halfway through he meets a CIO inside worker boring the hole from the other side. Apparently the first question asked was "How much are you getting for this job?" The AFL man answered $1.75 an hour, the CIO man replied $1.10 an hour. There was no indication that the UAW-CIO maintenance men were dissatisfied per se with the $1.10 rate, but the fact that the AFL outside workers were getting more for the same work started a bitter controversy which was only sharpened when a War Labor Board decision granted the inside workers an increase of "only" 5 cents in the hourly rate.

The wage inequity problem applies not only to workers from different unions working in the same plant but more commonly to workers belonging to the same union. The union tactic is always, of course, to bring the lower rate up to the higher and not the other way around. In one steel mill employing about 5,500 workers, journeymen electricians found that they were earning 30 cents an hour less than production workers working alongside of them. The electricians pointed out that they had had to serve a four-year apprenticeship before they were deemed qualified, while the production workers had mastered their jobs in a few months. Management agreed to the justice of the electricians' stand, but maintained that it could not at one fell swoop eliminate the whole inequity. The issue was settled when those electricians earning less than the industry average for electricians were brought up to the average, those earning above the average were not to have their rates reduced.

Unions try to resist wage reductions, sometimes not too successfully, particularly on the downswing phase of the business cycle. Some unions accept the reduction only after a desperate struggle. Others accept the wage reduction on the basis of the employer's appraisal of the economics of the situation. Still other unions tacitly accept what amounts to a wage reduction but some transparent subterfuge is utilized to lighten the blow. Under any circumstances, the position of union leadership in accepting a wage reduction, no matter under what circumstances, is a hazardous one, involving as it does the danger of revolt in the rank and file.

The 1931-1932 agreement of the Hosiery Workers contained a reduction varying from 30 to 45 per cent when, as George Taylor put it, "they often had to choose between wage cuts and unemployment." [17] Although the union received a closed shop and checkoff in return, the reduction provoked a series of outlaw strikes culminating in a march of 5,000 hosiery workers on Reading, Pennsylvania, as the symbol of the hated wage reduction.

In 1932 the Railway Labor Executives Association, under the pressure of carriers' demands for a 15 per cent reduction, agreed to a wage "deduction" by which 10 per cent of each worker's wages was deducted, with basic rates nominally remaining unaltered. The deduction program was renewed annually until 1934 when wages were returned to the 1931 agreement. Although the building trades unions in many cities did not formally agree to reductions during the depression, there was a tendency to ignore the widespread practice among union members of working "below the scale." Even as John Lewis was proclaiming in the twenties "no backward step," the tide of wage reductions could not be stemmed in the face of the rapid disintegration of union standards in the coal fields.

The attitudes and policies of unions toward hours of work reflects the influences of equalitarianism, efficiency, and economics. The equalitarianism influence is articulate labor's long-standing advocacy of leisure for self-improvement and effective citizenship. The passion and zeal that organized labor has put forth, for example, in the 8-hour-day movement constitutes a vital chapter in American history. In the 1880's the hours movement assumed in the minds of many workers the proportions of a revolutionary upheaval. The consideration of efficiency is the outcome of the findings of scientific inquiry that increasing hours for individual workers reaches a point where it is accompanied by absolute diminishing output and heightened fatigue. These findings labor spokesmen have used to potent advantage in agitating for constantly reduced hours.

Finally, labor's attitude toward hours of work has been strongly conditioned by the fact that there are usually more union members and workers in general than there are jobs, and shorter hours are advocated as a method of spreading the available work more evenly. The force of this attitude is most critically demonstrated in the problem of overtime. The imposition of premium rates for overtime work, which is practically universal, is motivated by a desire to discourage overtime rather than to compensate for extra effort.

In the women's garment industry, during the slack periods in the middle thirties, working overtime (and overtime was given a highly restricted definition) was a union cardinal sin. Specially trained crews of loyal union members would roam the streets of the garment district of New York City after normal working hours in search of telltale slivers of light giving away the culprits who were working overtime in violation of union regulations. When the offenders were caught they were subjected to heavy fines. Harry Bridges has given expression to the traditional trade union sentiment against overtime when he writes: ". . . The conference of our longshore and waterfront local unions decided that the working of overtime by industrial workers, regardless of the wage received for such overtime work, was incompatible with labor's program of jobs for all." [18] The same penal notion of premium rates for overtime is voiced by Martin Gerber, a UAW-CIO regional director: "It seems to me downright silly to deny premium pay [for overtime] when thousands upon thousands of workers are walking the streets in search of employment." [19]

A full employment situation, it is clear, drastically modifies union hours policy. In the first place, limitation of the hours of work ceases to be an end in itself. With the need for spreading the work less compelling than in ordinary times, the unions put no obstacles in the way of increased hours. Indeed, given the increased pay envelope as a result of overtime, there was a marked tendency for workers to favor longer hours and one of the recruiting devices which many plants hard up for workers utilized was the appeal of longer hours. It is also worth noting that the unions—under some pressure, it is true—relaxed certain provisions of their overtime premium pay practices with respect to the conditions under which time and a half and double time were applicable. With the end of the war, unions are returning to their pressure for reduced hours of work. The Bridges statement referred to above was made in this context.

Over the long pull, unions have striven for reduced hours of work and aided by other forces have been largely successful. The 8-hour-day propaganda of the closing years of the nineteenth century has given way to the 6-hour day 30-hour week drive.

VACATIONS WITH PAY

The union's demand for vacations with pay, to be sure, is another form of increasing wages. And during the war vacation policy was one of the fringe issues by which the unions sought to get the fullest possible advantage of the wage stabilization program.

But it is more than an economic demand; it is a social objective. Like much of the underlying pressure for shorter hours, it is the way in which the union expresses the workers' interest in release, for a brief period at least, from the routine of the job. The idea of a vacation with pay is a warming one to the average workers and the union organizer will capitalize on it. In selling the advantages of union organization to the unorganized worker, the paid vacation is always high up on the list of inducements. When the paid vacation is illustrated in the union handout it will often be symbolized by a fishing trip or by a state of pleasant lassitude.

This approach to vacation with pay is reflected in the Textile Workers' Union (CIO) policy, which "has definitely discouraged all efforts to substitute a week's pay in lieu of the vacation, except in the interest of defense production [this was written in 1941], since the purpose of the entire provision is to provide adequate rest and relaxation to workers." [20]

Because of the casual nature of the employer-employee relationship in the highly seasonal apparel industries, the union has resorted to the device of the pooled vacation fund. As the president of the Ladies' Garment Workers has stated it, "Our union included vacation benefits under its health and welfare program because if it had not done so, the workers in our industries would have been deprived of paid vacations. Our industries are known for their irregularity of employment. Employers are small and business turnover is large. Circumstances force workers to change jobs frequently." [21]

For many years the printing trades unions frowned upon paid vacations, classing them as "gratuities." The monetary equivalents of the vacations should be incorporated in the wage rate, this policy held, and workers could provide vacations for themselves on their own terms by hiring and paying for substitutes. This policy has now been revised under the pressure of the Newspaper Guild's effectiveness in securing paid vacations for editorial and business employees and also the spread of paid vacations in industry generally.

This same conception of paid vacations as a "gratuity" and, therefore, a potential threat to the wage rate is voiced by the Boilermakers (AFL) with respect to the railroads:

. . . vacations are regarded by railroad management as being in the nature of an employer gratuity—a pure gift to their employes which, consequently, comes out of potential dividends to stockholders or increment to capital reserve; therefore, we may fairly anticipate that future wage movements will be compelled to recognize "paid vacations" as an element of wage compensation, and to be reckoned with accordingly. Our negotiating committees should be continually and well informed so the principle of vacation pay may not become an agency of compromise, to the detriment of actual standardization of hourly wages and overtime.[22]

SENIORITY

The typical worker's attitude toward seniority is reflected in the following from a recent member of the CIO Glass Workers in the South:

We union folks have come to appreciate that seniority clause in our contract just about more than anything else. . . . Seniority is valuable to us in more than one way. In cases of cut-backs it means our jobs which is more than money. The boss just can't up and fire us because he doesn't like us or because someone else tries to influence him to dislike us. He can't take us off our jobs to work somewhere else if we have the right seniority. He can't send us home first if there is a lack of work. . . . If we didn't have our union we wouldn't have our seniority nor our jobs. The boss would have us fired already because, well, maybe we're too large, too ugly, too old or maybe just anything.[23]

Seniority as a common provision in union agreements is of recent origin. The kind of protection that seniority provides is applicable only in a context where there are many groups of workers doing approximately the same work. In the smaller establishment the fact that there are few workers who have common skills minimizes the usefulness of a seniority protection. And it was only in the middle thirties that a union organization was able to make a sizable dent in the larger plants and by virtue of that fact to give meaning to the workers' demand for this kind of job protection. It was during the upsurge of labor in the mass production industries that seniority became a vital issue for the first time. The virtue of seniority as a standard for determining various aspects of employment status is that it is easily measurable and that, moreover, it has a certain ethical rightness—few will dispute the general principle that the older a worker is in point of service the greater priority he should be able to command.

When the unions spell out the kind of job security they demand from seniority, something like the following emerges: First, unions uniformly ask for a broader seniority unit than does management. Put another way, the union tries to minimize the area of management discretion and to substitute the automatic rule of seniority over as broad a field as possible.

Second, in formulating their policies on the size of the unit within which seniority should apply there are influences at work which may militate against the broadest possible application of seniority. These influences stem from the relationship of a particular union to other related unions and from contending forces *within* a given union. The Railroad Engineers seek to limit the seniority "district" to the worker's period of service as an engineer and not to include the period of service as a fireman, from which craft many engineers are promoted. The Firemen, on the other hand, organized in another union, want the seniority district to include the worker's service as both fireman and engineer—since if the promoted fireman is subsequently "bumped" from his engineer's job he would in turn "bump" a fireman junior in service to him.

Divergences in interest over the size of the seniority unit among members of the same union will frequently arise in some context like the following: During a period of expanding employment, production workers are upgraded into either maintenance or perhaps the tool and die shop. The men with long seniority in the tool and die shop are opposed to the upgraded worker having seniority dating from his first employment by the plant, but rather insist that his seniority, as far as layoff, say, in tool and die is concerned, date from his employment in the tool and die shop. In the latter case, the worker downgraded from tool and die retains his seniority in production and will in turn "bump" a worker with lesser seniority there upon his return.

Third, the unions aim to secure the utilization of the seniority principle, however delineated, to every applicable aspect of employment status: layoff, rehiring, promotion, opportunity for overtime work, and even opportunity to work on the newer equipment. The taxicab drivers in one city sought to incorporate in their agreement a provision that the older employees be given first preference to drive the newer model cabs.

Fourth, the unions want to participate in determining the weight attached to the factors that concededly qualify and modify the force of seniority. Most common is the ability to do the job, and many unions seek to prevent the weight given to competence from being an exclusively unilateral decision on the part of the employer. Manifestly, if competence as interpreted by management begins to override seniority it will negate the kind of protection against discrimination which is the first purpose of seniority. The Electrical Workers (CIO) note in connection with the 1946 Westinghouse agreement that "The 1945 contract provision 'upgrading of employees to fill available jobs will be based on seniority, if the employee can do the job' is continued and determination of ability to do the job does not rest solely with management," while the company demanded "the absolute right 'for the determination of ability to do the job' in upgrading." [24]

Finally, specified union officers such as stewards and committeemen are conceded to have a right to their jobs which transcends length of service and so it is common that these men are the last to be laid off and the first to be rehired. The unions feel that this is the only way in which the continuity of union plant leadership may weather the hazards of ups and downs in employment. It is also not uncommon that employees may take leaves of absence on union business and still keep their seniority rights.

In many industries, particularly those of a sharply seasonal character, seniority is not completely or even partially a practical way of enforcing layoffs. In some situations a combination of work sharing and seniority is resorted to. Hours of work must reach a specified minimum in the automobile industry before layoffs on the basis of seniority are put into effect. In the clothing industry equal division of the available work is the rule rather than seniority.

For industries like construction and maritime, share the work is based on the fact that the union as the exclusive source of manpower seeks to maintain some equitable distribution of work opportunities in the operation of its own hiring halls, through which workers are referred to jobs.

Unionism in industries in which smaller employee units predominate has not been seriously concerned with the ramifications of seniority, for a variety of reasons. In the smaller establishment workers can find job protection in less mechanical devices. Also, job interchangeability is limited and employment is more stabilized. For many years until comparatively recently the Pressmen and Bookbinders were not much concerned with seniority for these reasons. Changes in technology and the growth of large plants have altered this situation somewhat.

Union leadership is not insensitive to the criticisms leveled at seniority. The Paper Makers' investigation asks:

If employees are to be promoted when their time comes on the seniority roster and not before, is there danger of destroying initiative? Is there any incentive for an employee to learn the higher job, if he knows he will get it any way? In the post-war period, when we shall have to compete with tough foreign competition, will our companies be able to survive and will our jobs be secure if our production is low? Does strict seniority tend to lower level of skill and efficiency to that of the poorest man rather than raise standards of workmanship? [25]

In spite of these doubts and the vigorous criticism of management, there is no sign of any measurable diminution in the union's adherence to the seniority principle. The rank and file of the membership—it is they who are most tenacious in their attachment—have not been seriously convinced of a feasible substitute which will be free from personal favoritism.

More than wages and hours, which conceivably can be passed on by management in the form of higher prices, seniority represents a major inroad on the authority of the employer's exercise of one of his traditional prerogatives. From the worker's point of view seniority represents the most acute nonfinancial expression of the rank-and-file worker's desire for protection from arbitrary hiring and firing decisions of management.

Union Security

Under the category of union security we mean to include the various provisions of collective agreements by which unions seek to participate in the hiring of workers. Union security in terms of such provisions means substantially the closed shop, the union shop, or the wartime innovation of maintenance of membership. The closed shop is one in which the employer must get all his workers through union referral; the union shop is one in which the employer hires whomever he pleases but all employees must become union members within a specified time; under maintenance of membership workers who are members of the union at a given time must continue to be members as a condition of employment. In a way, the checkoff is a method of providing for union security because the union is assured a continuity of dues income by the very fact that the dues are deducted from the worker's pay envelope. All these variations on the union security idea have one important characteristic in common: the basic sanction in persuading the worker to join the union or to pay his dues is enforced by getting the employer to take punitive action against the worker.

The idea of union security stems from three facts about industrial relations in the United States: the historical opposition of employers to unions, union security makes easier the job of keeping the union together, and the absence of powerful motivating ideologies in the labor movement.

Self-protection has demanded pressure for union security provisions as a means of preventing the employer from hiring whomever he pleases in order to undermine the union organization in his plant. It was this kind of attitude that the Stamford local of the Machinists saw in W. Gibson Carey, president of the Yale and Towne Manufacturing Company, when in opposition to the union's demand for the continuance of union security he said, "We believe conscientiously that we have no right to invade the personal liberty of action of our employees. It is our position that no man or woman should be forced for any period or at any time either to belong or not belong to a union." [26] The union security issue was admittedly the chief factor in the union's calling a strike after an NLRB vote supported a walkout by a vote of 1,671 to 171. So deeply did the union feel about union security that the strike lasted five months and was marked by much turmoil and a demonstration

general strike. In the final settlement the company agreed to maintenance of membership.

But even after the status of the union has been assured, the
union security provisions persist, and they have persisted after the enforcement of the National Labor Relations Act outlawed gross opposition to union organization by employers. The reasons for the continuation of union security may be found, first, in the force of tradition.
Union security is regarded as an advance for the union. To give it up
might be interpreted as a setback—this no union leader would be willing
to risk. Perhaps more important is the fact that union security makes
easier the job of holding the union together. If the union member's
attachment to the union is virtually guaranteed by the fact that his job
depends upon it, and if the payment of dues is guaranteed by the same
sanction, the union leadership is relieved of some of its most arduous
tasks. From the point of view of the ardent rank-and-file member, the
closed shop and the union shop provide some assurance that there will
be no "free riders" or "hitchhikers" who will get the benefits of unionism
without making some contribution to its upkeep.

The closed shop in conjunction with the "closed union," that is, a
union which closes its doors to new members, virtually means regulation of the effective labor market in order to reduce the consequences
of more workers than jobs. During the long depression, the closed shop
and the closed union were common; for example, in the unions in the
building trades, metal trades, men and women's clothing trades. The
unions argued cogently that there were not enough jobs to go around
for their own members, why therefore open their membership books to
make for more unemployment.

The effect of demands on an employer are substantially reinforced
if the union leaders speak with authority that comes with representing
the kind of solidified organization in the plant which union security
provides. The not infrequent employer tactic of cutting down demands
by charging that the union representative does not actually speak for *all*
or the greater portion of employees is thus minimized.

Union security persists because many employers favor it once they
have hurdled their initial antipathy to unions. Union security makes it
possible for the employer to hold union representatives to a much
greater degree of accountability for the actions of their membership.
The businessman who deals with a union representative is accustomed
to deal with men in other aspects of his business who can make binding

commitments. The ability of union spokesmen to make such binding commitments is facilitated by union security provisions.

Finally, the absence of a powerful motivating ideology in the later years of the labor movement has eliminated the force of the class struggle idea that union security enforced through the employer is somehow not in accord with canons of union morality; that the union without aid from the "class enemy" must use its own power to get workers to join and to hold them once they do join.

When the Ford Corporation came around to the point where it finally decided to bargain with the UAW-CIO, it agreed to a closed shop and the checkoff even before the union negotiators had an opportunity to make out an aggressive case. One of the reasons Ford did so was that in this way it felt it could count on the union to be fully responsible for committing *all* Ford workers. In the postwar strike upsurge of 1945, it taxed the union leadership with its inability to live up to this responsibility. Early in the defense period, Henry Kaiser negotiated a closed-shop agreement with the AFL metal trades unions in his Pacific Coast shipyards simply because of his conviction that he could build ships more efficiently that way.

With the exceptions stated, there is hardly a union which does not have, or aspire to have, agreements in which union membership is a condition, in one variant or another, for getting a job and holding it. From the so-called conservative building trades and teamsters to the Socialist-sired needle trades unions to the Communist-sympathetic maritime unions, the closed shop is accepted as a matter-of-course goal. The ideas of newspaper reporting as a "profession" and the freedom of the press have prevented the American Newspaper Guild from pressure for the closed shop and instead have asked for a "guild" shop, which is really another word for a union shop. The exigencies of political life have effectively checked any movement for a closed shop in the unions functioning in government employment. The closed shop is forbidden by law on the railroads but that is because the railroad unions wanted it that way in order to block the company unions. By virtue of the way in which the Railway Labor Act is constituted, union membership for railroad workers is practically indispensable anyway, and some of the railroad unions are beginning to change their minds on the closed-shop issue.*

---

* See concluding section of Chap. VIII for effect of Taft-Hartley law on union security.

"Industry-wide" Collective Bargaining

So-called industry-wide collective bargaining is, in any accurate sense of the term, most commonly multiemployer unit collective bargaining; that is, with one exception, namely, the coal industry, the multiemployer unit will fall substantially short of covering a whole industry over the nation.

This type of collective bargaining is one of the devices by which the union seeks to minimize uncontrolled variations among employers in the terms of the collective agreement in the market area within which the industry sells its product or service. Something of a prod to market-wide collective bargaining was given by the National War Labor Board of World War II by its utilization of a conception of wage patterns, labor market-wise or industry-wise.

Market-wide bargaining is not only a way of achieving *uniform terms,* it is also a way of implementing the union's enforcement of the terms. In the apparel industries it is not uncommon for the employers' association to find its strongest support among the unions, since otherwise the policing of the agreement without the aid of an employers' association would be immeasurably more onerous. As a result of multiemployer bargaining, the New England trucking industry in co-operation with several Teamsters locals has organized a Fair Trade Practice Board. "The most important contribution which the board has made to [union] locals has been to enable them to enforce their contracts" is the judgment of a competent observer. Further, "In past years employees frequently violated their contracts" but the unions could not cope with the problem in any feasible way. Now "the board has provided machinery by which locals can effectively ascertain the extent of suspected violations of the contract and obtain redress for them."

Although most unions will ask for multiemployer collective bargaining once they are beyond the initial organizing stages, the actual achievement of it will have to wait for the maturing of the collective bargaining relationship, which for the unions means weathering the ordeal of survival. The Flint Glass Workers (AFL) and the Operative Potters (AFL), the classic unions in the field of industry-wide bargaining, waited fifteen years before they achieved a national agreement. Multiemployer bargaining in the men and women's clothing industry is so much a matter of course today that it is frequently forgotten that it took several years for both unions to bring even one local market under single collective agreement.

Multiemployer collective bargaining is frequently achieved in fact long before, if ever, it is achieved as a matter of form. In the steel industry, the agreement with the U.S. Steel Corporation virtually becomes the model for the rest of the industry even though other individual agreements are signed. Even when a master corporation-wide agreement is signed, the detailed application to individual plants of the corporation may be left to be determined by supplemental agreements settled locally, as in the agreement between the Rubber Workers (CIO) and the United States Rubber Company.

There is no unanimous union sentiment for multiemployer bargaining. The Air Line Pilots (AFL) held out adamantly in 1946 against bargaining with the air transport industry as a unit presumably because they felt they could do better bargaining with each "airline at a time."

The executive board of the Hosiery Workers (CIO) was subjected to considerable internal union criticism during the 1945 negotiations. Of the thirty-one demands which different groups within the union had caused the board to make on management in the industry, only nine were incorporated in the final agreement. The executive board called upon the union's policy convention to "set policy for the National Board so as to avert any exaggerated notions among the rank and file members back home in respect to what they are going to get." [27]

APPRENTICESHIP

The institution of apprenticeship is another way in which the unions seek to control the hiring of workers. In the nature of apprenticeship, it is an avenue which is obviously open only to unions of skilled workers. Several union interests can be recognized as influencing the role of apprenticeship. First, the union tries to prevent the particular labor market from being disorganized by a cheap and excessive supply of labor. This is essentially a restrictive device, a consequence of the chronic excess of workers over jobs. While the threat of flooding the labor market was not serious during World War II, there was no appreciable difficulty experienced in getting the crafts to relax considerably their apprenticeship requirements. Eric Peterson of the Machinists—a union long in the forefront in developing apprenticeship standards—puts the idea this way:

It is obvious that unless some consideration is given to the number of indentured apprentices in a shop or city, the trade will be overcrowded. The result of such overcrowding is equally obvious—an oversupply of skilled labor, and a lowering of wage standards for those who are employed. It was this fact that brought about the insertion in the Grand Lodge Constitution of a provision for a ratio of one apprentice to every ten journeymen employed. Our union, during the war period and in order to assist the war effort, relaxed this ratio. Now that the war has come to an end, in the post-war period every local lodge must see to it that the situation in its locality is thoroughly studied and a definite policy established so that the supply of machinists and the demand for them are balanced.[28]

Secondly, there is a genuine interest among union craftsmen in maintaining the skill standards of the craft. This is evidenced by the considerable amount of technical material always found in the pages of such union journals as those of the Carpenters, Electricians, Lithographers, to cite only a few. Many unions like the Printers and Electricians conduct ambitious vocational education programs for their members. The traditional formulation of the idea of apprenticeship as vocational training is well put in the following by a correspondent to the *Machinists Journal*.

If we are to maintain the quality of craftsmanship that is vitally needed to uphold our position in American industry, we must maintain standards of apprenticeship training through the post-war era that will assure us the development of highly skilled journeymen. Unless we do this, our craft will gradually deteriorate through a series of operations to specialists.[29]

Frequently the apprenticeship requirements go beyond limiting *generally* the supply of skilled craftsmen but seek to limit the supply in particular. This is achieved by specifying requirements of color and kinship. The Plumbers' and the Electricians' agreements with the respective national contractors' association specify qualifications which in effect discourage Negroes from acquiring apprenticeship status. In a few apprenticeship programs, either formally or informally, the applicant for indenture must be recommended by a member of the union or be a relative of a union member: for example, the Brewery Workers, the Stone Cutters, and the Lathers.

A close relative of apprenticeship, but without its training values, is the permit system. The "permit" men are not full-fledged card-holding members of the union, but are allowed to work during peak employment periods when sufficient union members are not available for jobs. The permit system is designed to relieve the pressure on relatively scarce jobs during slack periods. Brewery workers, construction trades, motion-picture operators, upholstery workers, the maritime unions (who call then "trip card men") are cases in point.

The Upholsterers explain the permit system in these terms:

A local union may issue Temporary Working Cards to non-members *In Peak Seasonal Periods* instead of accepting new members who later will find themselves out of work because of the seasonal trade they may be employed in and to *avoid the necessity during slack periods* of dividing the work among more members than there may be work for in the respective craft, trade or industry.[30]

Since the issuance of permits can be a lucrative business, some unions like the Chicago Moving Picture Machine Union have issued permits at the expense of jobs to the regular union members.

Health and Welfare

What is now encompassed in demands for health and welfare funds, namely, provision for the cost of medical care of one kind or another, has traditionally been part of the benefits of membership which the older unions have offered. While these union benefits were feasible for the unions of the relatively high-wage craftsmen, they were not for unions of low-wage workers, who had to seek other means. Even so it was not until a few years before the outbreak of World War II that health benefits financed in whole or in part by employers through collective bargaining became more common. A significant exception is the Street, Electric Railway and Motor Coach Employees Union (AFL) whose collective bargaining achievements in this field date from 1926.

An important contributing factor to the recent growth of these programs has been the government's wartime wage stabilization policy which minimized the utilization of the normal channels of wage increases. The unions, therefore, turned to the so-called "fringe" benefits, one of them being group health insurance, as an indirect wage increase. Under the heading of "Six Basic Reasons for Group Insurance," the Electrical Workers (CIO) list "WLB [War Labor Board] Approval Unnecessary."[31] The Upholsterers (AFL) make the same point. "Social Security programs are legal, do not constitute a wage increase, are permissible under the wage stabilization program."[32]

The view of health benefits as a wage increase is given a higher validity by the Miners Union, which demanded at the 1945 wage conference a royalty of 10 cents per ton for these purposes; "such royalty shall be deemed partial compensation in equity to the mine workers for the establishment and maintenance of his ready-to-serve status, so vital to the profit motive of the employer and so imperatively essential to public welfare." [33]

Figuring also in the union's calculation is the conception that "workers want these benefits as part payment for their labor and not as a grant bearing the stigma of charity." [34] Julius Hochman, author of these words, is following through on the conviction that it is not sufficient from the union's point of view that these benefits be dispensed unilaterally but that the union as a matter of right should have a major voice in the administration of the program.

The fact that the union is involved in these programs can serve as an added inducement which organizers can utilize in persuading workers to join the union. In many instances the union has initiated health programs through collective bargaining where none had existed before; for example, the Labor Health Institute of the St. Louis Department Store Workers (CIO).

The inherent hazards in certain industries impel unions to seek health benefit programs. In the case of the Miners, John L. Lewis has charged that the operator-controlled program is a "harsh, systematic, sordid, brutal exploitation of the mine worker," the enforcement of state safety laws has been characterized by "willful negligence" resulting in "major disasters." [35]

Health protection as a conception of the purpose of collective bargaining has undoubtedly exercised some influence. "Our union," writes Samuel Wolchok, president of the Department Store Workers (CIO), "since its inception has maintained that it is not enough for a union to concern itself only with the economic plight of its members, but must be equally concerned with the social and physical welfare of their constituents as well. . . . Fully 55 percent of our membership are covered by insurance plans or have actual facilities available for treatment when they become ill." [36]

There is wide variation in the administration and financing of these plans. The unions, as David Dubinsky says, "have no particular philosophical objection to employer participation in the administration of health and welfare plans. We have both. In practice we have found,

however, that most employers prefer not to be a party to such administration." [37] As to financing, the plan may be exclusively supported by
the employer, as in the case of the New York Men's Clothing Workers,
or financed jointly by employers and workers, as in the case of the
Chicago Men's Clothing Workers. The insurance risks may be under-
written by a special purpose enterprise, as the Dress Industry Health
and Vacation Fund in New York, or by a private carrier, the Prudential
Insurance Company and the Associated Hospital Service of New York
in the case of the United Furniture Workers. In short, to use Mr.
Dubinsky's term, there is no union "philosophy" of health and welfare
plans.*

Work Rules

The work rules, or, as they are frequently termed, restrictive practices,
of unions range from the simple refusal to allow foremen to do direct
production work to the more elaborate agreements with employers to
regulate trade practices in a particular industry. The work rules are,
of course, inherent in the typical scarcity of jobs, and faced with such
urgent problems no union is above some device or program to minimize
the effects of unemployment among its members. This is the substance
of the argument of President Petrillo of the Musicians. No union
leader has been more publicly identified with these so-called restrictive
practices than James C. Petrillo, president of the Musicians' Union. Let
Mr. Petrillo give his side of the story:

In February, 1945, the International Executive Board ruled that members
of the American Federation of Musicians shall not play for Television in any
form until further notice.

I believe it necessary to give an explanation of the Executive Board's
action:

The introduction and development of Television presents the same threat
to employment of musicians as did the change from silent to sound movies.
As Television progresses from one stage to another, it is apparent that
movies will play a great part in its future, and that it is possible to produce
the majority of Television programs in "canned" form, thus eliminating
all radio employment. You all know, through bitter experience, that when
the Vitaphone and Movietone were installed in the theatres of the United
States and Canada, we lost the employment of 18,000 musicians almost
overnight.

* See concluding section of Chap. VIII for the effect of the Taft-Hartley law on
health and welfare funds.

employer representatives regulated labor and trade practices; Northwest Teamsters striking enterprises which do not maintain "fair" prices.

The range of functioning union tactics and policies with respect to work rules is influenced in large degree by the ability of the union to cope with the situation, rather than by any preconceived philosophy of social progress. This is well illustrated by the policies of the Painters (AFL) to the use of the spray gun. The issue arose most recently at the 1946 convention of that union and the chairman of the committee charged with formulating a nation-wide union policy characterized the various attitudes as "hot, cold, and indifferent." As the chairman reported:

The category classed as hot . . . being in a great majority, expressed an opinion as favoring a national code of regulations and stressed that spray painting is here to stay, regardless of any opposition, and should be controlled by the International District Councils and Local Unions.

Those placed in the category of cold are the group expressing themselves as opposed to a national code of regulations and, while in a minority, declared their opposition based on the statement that in such localities there are no spray jobs which the District Council or Local Unions cannot successfully combat.

The final category, i.e., "the indifferent," being the group that expressed themselves as being neither for nor against a national code of regulations but rather taking the stand that "I don't care so long as they don't bother me" attitude. This was an extremely small minority.[39]

The test which suggests that the work rules of unions arise fundamentally out of relative job scarcity is indicated by an appraisal of union policies in the wartime full employment situation. The unions agreed to substantial relaxation of work rules when it was clear that the jobs of the members were not being endangered by an influx of single-skilled workers. Government-sponsored programs of job dilution and single-skill training encountered no opposition and in many instances the unions actually participated in the development of these programs. The railroad unions, at the request of the Office of Defense Transportation, undertook to re-examine and modify the so-called full-crew laws which the railroads contended meant the employment of useless workers. The Teamsters agreed to staggered deliveries and "carry your own bundles" campaigns.*

* See concluding section of Chap. VIII for effect of Taft-Hartley law on work rules.

Unorthodox Terms

The extent to which unions in general seek to strike out for terms not normally within the area of collective bargaining is not so much influenced by ideologies as by a conviction that these problems have a direct bearing on employment and wages. The Barbers concentrate considerable effort on the maintenance of consumer prices for barbershop items such as haircuts and shaves. Without price maintenance of this sort, the Barbers feel that maintenance of union wage standards would be impossible. The Mine, Mill and Smelter Workers tie their wage rates to the price of copper, which has a decided bearing on the profitability of operations. Here is a reality of the economic environment which despite the militant radical origins of this union cannot be ignored in the collective agreement.

So-called taxes on payrolls for health and welfare funds found in collective bargaining agreements are actively supported by unions as diverse in ideological backgrounds as the Musicians, the Miners, Men's Clothing Workers, the Textile Workers, the Upholsterers, the Women's Garment Workers, and the Department Store Employees. The common circumstance which generated this demand was the search for ways in which the hazards of employment in their particular industries could be minimized.

Ideological motivations may sometimes spur union leaders to make unusual demands in collective bargaining, but even where these motivations function the demands have considerable grounding in the practical realities of wages and hours. Walter Reuther of the UAW-CIO undoubtedly was giving expression to a deeply felt economic philosophy when he made his demand on the General Motors Corporation for wage increases contingent on there being no price increases.

Foremen

Apparently the interest of foremen in securing the right to bargain collectively with management is a reflection of the kinds of motivations that operate for workers in general.

Just as mass production industry unionism sought to establish its right to bargain collectively before it went after wages and hours, so the foremen make this their initial point of attack. A foremen spokesman put their problem this way: "We have no grievance procedure other than standing on your two feet alone to argue with whomever you have the opportunity or whomever happened to be there in authority at the time." [40]

The organization of foremen into unions stems immediately from the contagious effects of the upsurge of union organization among rank-and-file workers. It has also been largely self-organization. Foremen's Association of America, the major organization in the field, grew from one chapter at the Ford plants to the point where, by the end of 1944, there were 148 chapters with more than 30,000 members. This measurable growth was achieved without the employment of one paid organizer. As Robert Keyes, one of the founders of the foremen's union movement, says:

Our original idea was to form a group in just our division of the company for the protection of our rights. We . . . had no idea that our movement would spread all through the Ford plants. . . . Before we realized what was going on, our original handful had increased to thousands. . . . Then . . . we began to get inquiries from foremen in other large Detroit corporations.[41]

The increasing extent to which the foreman's authority has been circumscribed by the movement toward technological and personnel rationalization is the long-run element in the organization of foremen.

It is unlikely, however, that this factor alone, without the growth of rank-and-file unionism, would have been enough to stimulate the wholesale development of foremen's unions. Frederick Harbison has recorded the temper of frustration that is possibly typical of the foreman in large-scale nationalized industry. Says a foreman of a sheet metal department:

It's just pressure—pressure—pressure all day long. The general superintendent comes down in the shop and tells us we've got to get this order out by noon tomorrow. Some job evaluation engineer comes down and tells us our rate structure is all screwy. Then some monkey from the cost department puts his nose in here and gives us a long talk on the company's cost control system. Then Callahan comes down here and tells us we've got to know all about the Wagner Act and that we haven't got any business telling a fellow to go to h— — — just because he belongs to a union. Then there are the new workers which we're supposed to train, and the training director of the company comes down here and tells us how to train them. In order to get along in this shop, you have got to be a lawyer, a cost accountant, a teacher, a production expert, and above all, an "example of the rest of the boys." We're always on the receiving end. They're either telling you to do something or bawling you out for not having it done already. All that talk about the "grass roots of management" which Mr. Jones was blurbing about this evening is just plain bunk. We are told what to do, we're on the receiving end, we're not a part of management—we're just stooges for the brass hats up there in the front office.[42]

There is no evidence that the current demand of foremen for collective bargaining has been motivated by the rank-and-file unions as a way of making inroads on management's prerogatives, by organizing a class of employees normally regarded as part of management. For one thing, there is still considerable difference of opinion among rank-and-file unions as to the desirability of admitting foremen into their own unions. The vigor with which grievances have been prosecuted by stewards against organized foremen in several instances has been noticeably weakened by the fact that foremen were "union men" even though in a different union. The membership rolls of the Foremen's Association of America are the authority for the fact that the majority of its members are old foremen and not recently upgraded foremen, minimizing the possibility that interest in collective bargaining by foremen has been caused by an infiltration into the foremen's ranks of former active rank-and-file unionists.

There is little evidence that the fact of foremen bargaining collectively has any necessary effect on plant discipline or on the efficiency of production. The only concrete evidence I have seen is to be found in the testimony of the general counsel of the Jones and Laughlin Steel Corporation before a 1947 Senate Labor Committee to the effect that "since unionization of supervisors started in our coal mines the number of accidents per thousand man days worked has gone up and the number of discipline slips has gone down." [43] In the considerable discussion that has taken place on the subject, the opposition of management appears to be based mostly on ideological grounds rather than on any practical experience that as a matter of fact there has been a discernible impairment of productive efficiency. This would seem to hold true whether the foremen are in a union of their own or are members of the union to which the rank-and-file workers belong. In the latter, the long experience of the printers and the building trades with foremen suggests that the unions have been more concerned with bringing foremen into their fold as a way of protecting employment standards of the rank-and-file workers than to improve the working conditions of the foremen as such.

The management attitude that probably offers the most fruitful appraisal of why foremen want to bargain collectively is that of John Bugas, Ford personnel director, who says, "We would like them [the foremen] to feel that they are [a part of management] but if they don't and want a contract, okay." Whether the present contract is renewed, Bugas says, depends upon whether the union lives up to it. If it doesn't "it won't get another from Ford." [44] In April, 1947, however, Bugas ended the contract with the Foremen's Association, concluding "that it hasn't worked under test." [45] *

If there is one overriding consideration which motivates the unions' attitudes with respect to the terms of the collective agreement it is fear —fear of there not being enough jobs to go around, fear of unjust discharge, and fear of unequal treatment—in short, insecurity. The available evidence on the character of the economic and social order seems to indicate that this fear of insecurity is rather well grounded in the realities of earning a living. During the war, when the elements of economic insecurity in the environment were offset by full employment, many of the practices arising out of this fear reaction were drastically modified. The working conception of society created by this fear reaction on the part of workers and their unions, and which is shared by other economic groups, was perceptively stated a generation ago by a discerning student of labor affairs, Robert Hoxie, who said, "So far as workers are concerned, there is no society as a whole and no long run but immediate need and rival social groups." [46]

* See concluding section of Chap. VIII for effect of Taft-Hartley law on supervisors.

CHAPTER VI

COLLECTIVE BARGAINING

(Continued)

COLLECTIVE BARGAINING MAY BE THOUGHT OF AS HAVING THREE SIG-nificant stages: the process of negotiation, the formulation of the precise terms of the agreement, and the process of administering the agreement. The terms of the agreement were discussed in the previous chapter. Negotiating and enforcing the agreement are treated here to-gether because these are essentially problems in human and social relationships.

THE PROCESS OF NEGOTIATION IN COLLECTIVE BARGAINING

The conception of a national labor movement policy in negotiating collective bargaining demands is still in its elemental stages. Historically, the AFL, as such, has not sought to exercise significant influence on its affiliated unions in this respect. The autonomy of the international unions is still more than a slogan, it is a functioning reality. The re-lationship of the CIO to its affiliated unions is for the most part sub-stantially the same, but here and there signs appear that the CIO, and Philip Murray particularly, will provide guidance and counsel on collective bargaining issues in which individual unions are involved. This would hold more true of the newer unions like those in auto-mobiles, electrical products, and rubber.

The economic report commissioned from economist Robert R. Nathan in 1947 by the CIO could not in itself be regarded as an attempt by the

CIO to set a "wage policy" for individual CIO unions. As President Murray indicated at the time, "Each union must exercise its own degree of freedom in these matters."[1] The Nathan report maintained the thesis that American industry in general could raise wages by 25 per cent without increasing prices. But it was the first time that either of the national federations had attempted to delineate the broad economic analysis from which collective bargaining policy would presumably proceed. To be sure, the Nathan report was possibly directed more toward cultivating a favorable climate for bargaining than it was at influencing the bargainers. But it is, nevertheless, significant precisely because it represented a *CIO* project rather than the project of an individual international union.

In January, 1947, CIO policy was seen as one of avoiding large-scale strikes during that year. Mr. Murray met with the leaders of the Automobile Workers and Electrical Workers to give what the CIO president described as " 'mature consideration of the various economic aspects of the over-all situation' of contract demands and industry's ability to pay."[2]

The year before, during the automobile and electrical workers' strikes against the General Motors Corporation, there were reliable signs that Mr. Murray had injected himself or had been injected into these situations. The CIO president had been quoted, according to the Detroit labor paper, the *Wage Earner*, as objecting "to the UAW making so strong a public issue of prices without regard for the position of other industries and the economy as a whole."[3] When the CIO Electrical Workers settled with General Motors for an 18½ cents an hour increase while the Automobile Workers strike was still on for 19½ cents, the union's GM Top Negotiating Committee deplored the fact that "the UE failed even to notify President Murray and secure his approval before announcing the settlement jointly with the Corporation."[4]

The greater involvement of CIO in the collective bargaining affairs of its international unions is part of and is explainable by the same general trend that we observed in connection with the whole area of CIO-international union relationships—in large degree an extraconstitutional arrangement.

Anybody's opinion is valid as to whether there is something called an art of negotiation and, if there is, whether it has anything to do in itself with the outcome of the negotiations; namely, the collective agreement. There is probably no way of verifying independently whether good union negotiators can rescue a bad situation, or the reverse, whether bad negotiators can worsen a good collective bargaining position. Two generalizations may be made about the process of negotiation. One is that there are different kinds of negotiators and negotiations; the other is that negotiation is horse trading, and proposal and counter-proposal.

One kind of union negotiator comes to the collective bargaining conference all set to thump the table, another makes his point serenely; still others alternate between serenity and toughness, as the occasion demands. Sometimes the union bargaining committee is chosen to represent the diverse temperaments that have their special purposes at a negotiations conference. When the table thumper has issued his ultimatum, the situation is "rescued" from a state of impasse by the committee member who specializes in "pouring oil on troubled waters."

Sidney Hillman had the reputation of being a suave bargainer. A sympathetic biographer says about Hillman, "If he is compelled to fight, he does it in the field, not in the conference room."

Always remember [Hillman once said], most people are wedded to formulas. They will fight for words when in terms of reality they would be willing to make concessions. There is no use in arguing about the formulas and words. That is meaningless and makes everybody stubborn. Let them have their formulas, and take real concessions in exchange. They will be just as happy and you will get something genuine.[5]

Julius Hochman of the ILGWU is of an opposite sort. Hochman has a flair for the sensational, according to Stolberg.

Once a manufacturer lost his temper with Hochman on some minor point in a contract. "For God's sake," [he] yelled, "why are you holding things up just for a drop in the bucket?" Without a word Hochman poured out a glass of water and shook into it a drop of ink from his fountain pen. "Go ahead," he said, "drink it, it's only a drop."[6]

For all this acting, Hochman is a "superb negotiator! He knows the industry, he understands the psychology of collective bargaining and above all he knows his dress manufacturer."

Negotiations in the auto industry are usually acrimonious. After a particularly heated exchange between Walter Reuther, leader of the UAW-CIO-General motors activities, and Harry Anderson, GM's director of industrial relations, Reuther told the GM representatives:

"Frankly, you are not going to make any automobiles until this is settled, and you can go through all the contract cancellations you want. [This is a reference to the fact that GM had just denounced its agreement with the union.]

"We worked damned hard at this job," Reuther continued, "and I think you guys have treated the General Motors workers like they weren't worth a minute's consideration. A corporation that has the money you have, and you fellows sitting on top and enjoying every damn decent thing of life, everything money can buy and all [this] security and when a bunch of workers asks for their share of it, you thumb your nose at them and tell them to go to hell and refuse to conciliate, refuse to bargain, refuse to arbitrate.

". . . You are asking for a fight and, brother, you are going to get it, and if it's the last thing we do, brother, we are going to sweat this thing out to the bitter end." [7]

Collective bargaining is the union's chief business and, by and large, it is to its interest to bargain in good faith. Occasionally, for strategic purposes, the union sets forth an initial demand on a take-it-or-leave-it basis, which is not collective bargaining in good faith. In several cases the International Typographical Union has maintained that its "laws" are unilaterally determined by the union itself and not subject to collective bargaining. In two strikes against newspaper publishers in New Jersey, the ITU informed the National War Labor Board, which had intervened,

that the terms and conditions under which its members would work are subject to the unilateral determination of the union's Executive Council through amendment of the union's "laws" . . . that its members will not work and the newspapers will not be published except under terms satisfactory to the union.[8]

ITU President Randolph declared in another place that the publishers

have not been asked to accept them. The Union has prescribed them. The usual form of collective bargaining has been discontinued in such cases. The more widespread becomes that policy the more widespread will collective bargaining as we know it be in the discard.[9]

The mechanism through which the union's side of the negotiations are carried on ranges from John Lewis's famous meeting with Myron Taylor in a hotel room, which constituted the first U.S. Steel negotiations, to the large conference type represented by such unions as the Miners and Steel Workers.

Unions normally, however, carry on their negotiations through a bargaining committee rather than through a single individual. First, because the committee can be more representative of the various interests within the union which need to be taken into account if the resulting agreement is to gain popular acceptance. Second, because there is strength in numbers and consequently a committee can put up a more formidable psychological front than can a single individual.

Invariably a representative of the international office participates in local negotiations, for the reasons that the international has a decided interest in maintaining, wherever relevant, certain uniform standards throughout an industry or segment of an industry, and that the international representative is usually less inhibited in dealing with employers than a committee composed of plant workers is likely to be. Most frequently the agreement negotiated by the committee is subject to ratification by the membership concerned. Most agreements are also subject to ratification by the international union.

Several influences have tended to make the content of negotiations more complex. Collective agreements are tending toward a greater inclusiveness in the terms of employment. Government intervention in labor problems has also introduced more technical problems in the subject matter of collective bargaining. The sheer bulk of factual material, therefore, that needs to be mastered by the union negotiators requires the assistance of technically competent economists to work with the union representatives. It is exceedingly rare to find high-level negotiations which do not involve systematically prepared data as part of the subject matter of the negotiations.

It is difficult to make out whether this increasing use of facts in negotiations has actually introduced a considerable area of agreement in collective bargaining negotiations. In large part, what has probably happened has been that the character of the negotiations has become more sophisticated, and the controversies now center on the *interpretation* of the facts rather than on hearsay and folklore of the industry. In the General Motors-United Auto Workers negotiations, important facts in dispute concerned such matters as size of take-home pay, average weekly hours worked, methods in computing profits, and expectations of the volume of production. There was no noticeable abatement, however, of the bitterness between the parties as a result of the use of facts.

The extent of popular participation varies inversely with the size of the geographical area for which the bargaining is being conducted. The responsiveness of the local committee to the sentiments of the local membership is obviously much greater than is a top-side international negotiating committee. With the tendency for the area over which negotiations are carried on to expand, responsiveness to popular pressures is likely to become progressively weaker. In large part, this may well be an inevitable consequence of the increasing concentration of industrial control and its accompanying big unionism. It is nevertheless true that the sense of responsibility and accountability to the membership on the part of the union negotiators exercises a certain restraint on their capacity to make binding commitments—a restraint, by the way, which few management negotiators are able to view patiently and understandingly.

The vitality of popular control of union policy, not the formal mechanism through which negotiations are carried on, is the real index of the reality of democracy in collective bargaining. Potent rank-and-file sentiment in such unions as the Auto Workers, the Hosiery Workers, the Printers, to cite a few outstanding examples, makes for representative collective bargaining. In all these unions the occasions on which the rank and file turn down the recommendation of its committees are not infrequent. Because of the local character of construction work, there is a considerable amount of membership participation in the building trades union negotiation in the smaller communities.

The other generalization about collective bargaining negotiations is that, as in all other kinds of arm's-length bargaining, both parties come in asking for more than they hope to get. The negotiations constitute the process whereby each side whittles down its asking price.

The process of offer and counteroffer may be embellished by something which is frequently called "negotiating strategy" designed to affect the attitude of the employer's representatives. An ILGWU officer once facilitated a settlement by depositing a substantial amount of union funds in the bank in which the clothing manufacturers carried their accounts. This stratagem was designed to impress the employers with the size of the union treasury and the union's ability to withstand a strong siege. Richard Leonard, director of the UAW Ford Department, was criticized for bad negotiating strategy because he virtually conceded on the vital issue of union responsibility before the company had made any commitment of significance to the union.

Making the Agreement Work—the Steward

The union's job of collective bargaining doesn't end with the negotiation of the agreement. The agreement is the charter, as it were, which sets forth the basic terms of the union-management relationship. Like all charters, however, it needs to be enforced and interpreted if it is to be effective. As a matter of practical expediency, the major share of responsibility for enforcement lies with the local union.

In this scheme of things the shop committee and/or the business agent is the key figure. In mass production industry, with its large employee units and extensive departmentalization, the enforcement responsibility rests largely with the committee. In the building trades particularly, given the casual nature of the employer-employee relationship and the prevailing craft autonomy, the business agent is most prominent. In other situations like clothing, for example, the committee and the business agent will complement each other.

The handling of workers' grievances on the job is perhaps the single most important function of modern unionism. No union can afford to let down on this vital phase of union functioning. It is easy to see why this should be so: grievances are matters which affect individual workers in a more intimate way than anything else in modern industrial life.

The typical method of handling grievances is through a graduated procedure of one sort or another. The individual worker takes his grievance to his departmental committee. The departmental committee attempts to settle it with the foreman. If no settlement is reached, then perhaps the chief steward of the plant will take it to the general superintendent. If this fails, it may go to the local president, who will discuss it with the vice-president in charge of industrial relations. If this step fails to yield a settlement, it may then be submitted either to an impartial umpire or perhaps to a bipartisan board or a combination of the bipartisan board with an impartial third person to settle deadlocks. Somewhere after a grievance passes the first stage it may come to the local union meeting for recommendations as to further action. The variations are in the number of steps that exhaust the grievance remedies, the presence or absence of a provision for an impartial umpire, and the kinds of disagreements between the union and the management that are allowable grievances.

The most prolific sources of grievances are wage inequities, improper classification, and seniority. As noted in our discussion of the terms of the collective agreement, the grievances are usually conceived with problems of *relative* status, that is, the worker's pay in relation to what somebody else doing the same work is getting.

The Steel Workers Union has made a systematic attempt to develop an "intelligent and constructive" handling of grievances by its stewards. Two cases, involving this union, including one which the union lost and one which the union won, may convey an idea of the general process. Both cases were judged by a joint committee of union and management.

The facts in one case as brought out at a hearing were as follows:

Five hot-blastmen employed by the Jones and Laughlin Corporation asked for an increase from a rate of 76¢ per hour to 90¢ per hour on the grounds that (1) "their work is a matter of great importance regarding the quality of iron produced"; (2) "the ability required by a hot-blastman, regarding efficiency, in comparison to other jobs throughout the mill are few and far between"; (3) "the nature of their work requires them to regulate the heat on the furnaces, look after blowpipes, to take care of dust catchers, disintegraters and help with cut-backs." The company countered that it was already paying 5¢ an hour higher than the going rate and that it had previously given rate increases to this classification on the order of 15¢. The labor-management committee hearing the grievance "found that no inequality existed and the matter of request for an increase in wages was a question of future negotiations; therefore, it was agreed that the Company's denial for an increase in wages was proper and in line with contract and, therefore, held accordingly."

The other case

involves ten (10) men working in around the pig machine, working in the Blast Furnace Department sculling iron ladles, breaking up and loading scrap. On days when they are pigging iron some of these men are required to operate a stationary crane, known as the tilter, which tilts the ladles in pouring iron into the pigging machine.

The records of the Company show that on a number of days the pigging machine is used in which the tilter crane is operated. It has been the practice of the Company at times when necessary that the electrical repairmen or cranemen operated the tilter and were paid eighty-seven (87) cents per hour. Of late the men working in around the pigging machine were required to operate the tilter at the rate of seventy-two and one-half (72½) cents per hour. The Company stated that it paid 87¢ per hour for this work when the tilter was used the full day, but on such days electrical repairmen or regular cranemen were used and paid 87¢ per hour for the full day. On days when the tilter was operated only three (3) hours, men from the pigging crew were used and paid at the rate of 72½¢ per hour.

The Union argued that inasmuch as the Company recognized the 87¢ per hour rate for a full day established the rate of 87¢ per hour for work of operating the tilter and could not reduce this rate for hours that were less than a full day's work. It was also found that the pigging machine did not operate every day and that there was no one carried as a regular tilter operator.

It was, therefore, agreed that eighty-seven (87¢) cents per hour would be paid to men operating the tilter crane for the actual hours worked.[10]

The grievances detailed above would be typical in mass production industries like autos, rubber, and electrical products, where the borderlines between occupations or job classifications are not too sharply defined. Grievances of this sort could obviously not arise in an industry in which occupational lines are drawn sharply by the jurisdictional interests of the unions, as in the printing or construction trades. The ILG dressmakers will have a different order of grievance dealing largely with the problem of setting "prices," which are really wage rates for various occupations on many different styles. Being a seasonal industry, the ILG will also be concerned with problems of equal division of work.

The central union person in the handling of grievances in mass production is the shop steward. This job is indeed a difficult one. On the one hand, he must think in terms "of the people who have elected me and who expect me to get something for them."[11] On the other hand, he is confronted with urgings that "he must not push complaints which are obviously unfounded,"[12] or that "grievances should be settled on their merits and not permitted to become political issues."[13] But every worker who brings an alleged grievance to his steward believes earnestly that it is obviously well founded. The steward is, therefore, put in the position where, on the one hand, his constituents expect him to be their lawyer no matter how outrageous the grievance may be and, on the other hand, there is the need to develop an effective working relationship with supervision, which requires some rejection of unworthy cases.

This dual responsibility of the shop steward is given substance with great acumen and insight by a "chairlady" in a millinery factory. It is quoted at some length because, aside from the industry background, this is an extraordinarily typical situation. There is at least one "Sally," the protagonist of the following saga, in every shop unit to make the workaday life of the steward a trying one.

The psychology angle is probably more important than all the rest of [the chairlady's] know-how, for she has to know the emotional reflexes of her boss, how to soft-soap him about his grandchildren and his business acumen, how to get him into a good mood to listen to reason, and also how to be sharp and strict when he won't listen to reason. And after she gets through with him, she must also be a student of psychology to sell the price settlement to the girls.

That's where Sally comes in. No price settlement has ever satisfied her. Believe it or not, there were at least two cases in which Sally got exactly the prices she asked for her hats, and still she grumbled and let it be understood that she had been sold out by the chairlady and price committee. According to her idea, it should have been the duty of the committee to recognize that she had made a mistake, and they should have jacked the price up as soon as they saw the boss was willing to grant it. Since the committee didn't do so, it was proof positive that the whole shop was in cahoots with the boss to gyp her.

How was one to tell her that the boss nearly burst a blood vessel when he heard what the committee wanted for Sally's lot of hats? How could anybody persuade her that the chairlady had to use all her talents for negotiation and bargaining to bring the boss about to an agreement?

"Take the damn hat out!" he shouted at first. "Throw it out of the shop. Ya think I'm running a charity here? A hat like that, I'll lose money on it, if I have to pay 76 cents just for trimming—"

That was his first reaction to Sally's bid when the chairlady and committee proposed it to the boss. It was only after the girls placated him with other numbers, cut the prices on their own work, and showed him that even if he priced Sally's items exactly as she wanted them, he would still make a profit, that he simmered down and finally consented to continue those items. As it worked out, the chairlady and the girls on the committee actually made a sacrifice on their own work in order to create harmony in the shop, but Sally wouldn't recognize that. She didn't accuse the chairlady of betraying her; not in so many words, at least, or she would have been slapped down for the insult. But her looks showed that she was full of suspicion, and the suspicion became a well founded conviction when she glanced toward the hats on which the chairlady was working and wanted to know the price she was getting for them.

"What some people won't do for a measly couple of pennies," she would remark to nobody in particular, but for everybody to hear. "Playing up to the boss," she would mutter under her breath.

The pay envelope at the end of the week would show that Sally made more money on her hats than the chairlady and most of the other girls, but that, of course, was because Sally was such a fast worker, a better milliner than anybody else in the shop, and not because she got a better lot of work and better prices. That was Sally's argument, at least, and nobody could persuade her that she wasn't sold down the river with the price settlement.[14]

The quality of day-to-day collective bargaining on the plant level may be combative or co-operative. The combative relationship may stem from the "hell-raising" temperament of management or of the plant union leadership or of both.

In a collective bargaining situation where management has recognized the union for the first time there is frequently a tendency for the new steward to "feel his oats" and to seek opportunity to assert his new-found authority, which may take the form of "telling the foreman off." At least in the initial period, the steward's constituents may feel that he is not representing them faithfully unless he is aggressive and combative.

The effect on the union leadership of combative management policies is discerningly put by Philip Murray: "The point is that when companies oppose unions, the unions elect as their leaders belligerent and wilful men. No other type could survive."[15] When a college professor asked a local steel union president whether the union tries to live up to the "letter of the contract," he received this reply:

"Look, buddy, a contract to us is just a foot in the door with a company like Tindale. I don't care what the company agreed to in that contract, it's trying to kill off the union. They used to employ spies not many years ago; now they are trying to kill off our union by 'cleaning up their back yard.' They never give the union credit for anything, you can bet your boots on that. They are fightin' us and we're fightin' them and we're going to continue to fight them until they change their stripes."[16]

Where union leadership is imbued with the need for co-operative relationships, another kind of union-employer association develops. A Chemical Workers (AFL) business agent relates how he tried to bring about mutual understanding in a newly organized plant which hinged on the union guidance provided the in-plant union committeemen:

We agreed that any chairman or committeeman who had a grievance would make absolutely no effort to settle it on the spot, but would immediately get in touch with the business agent. That procedure had a number of rather important effects. One was that they didn't make any snap decisions which would have been colored by their closeness to the situation, and possibly by the lack of training and experience. Another was that they had the advice and critical assistance of someone who stood a little bit out of the immediate picture and wasn't so intimately and personally concerned with the issues at stake. The third thing was that by working with a trained and experienced agent on every grievance that came up, they gradually began to get some training along with their experience so that by the end of two years those people were thoroughly and intimately trained.[17]

A UAW-CIO spokesman got at one of the most pressing problems for the steward in his relations with management, particularly noticeable under wartime exigencies:

What are you going to do when you have educated your stewards to the point where they can carry out their duties efficiently and intelligently and the supervision or the management, taking advantage of the war situation, simply leans back and says "no" to every grievance or to most every grievance that comes up? Or when they give them the run-around, when they stall? [18]

The sequence of responses of the steward and the grievance committee to work rationalization schemes like incentive systems, time study, and job evaluation runs something like this: first, opposition; then, when the union goes along grudgingly with the installation of one of these schemes, opposition gives way to mystification, and the final reaction in the chain is jockeying for position with the management technicians. The opposition stems from the conviction that systematic scientific management has only one purpose and that is more work for less pay, in a word, "speed-up." The mystification arises from the steward's feeling that invariably the program is presented by the management's engineer as a neat and complicated system and rarely is it constructed with the genuine co-operation of the union. For example, the average shop steward might find it difficult to understand this formula which is used by the U.S. Steel mill in Gary, Indiana, to calculate the earnings of a shear inspector:

$$\text{Total Earnings} = (1.2 \times S \times R_b \qquad \$.10 \times A \qquad D \times Rg) \times \frac{\text{Actual ult. yield}}{\text{Std. ult. yield}} \; [19]$$

Jockeying for position on a catch-as-catch-can basis means opposition to procedures which will result in downward rate changes or pressure for upward rate changes, as the situation demands.

The sense of frustration a union committee frequently experiences in these situations is given some point in the story of the union grievance committee that was being overwhelmed by a pageant of charts and graphs put on by company engineers. For two hours the committee listened and became increasingly unhappy on account of the members' inability to argue with the engineers in their own terms. Finally, the union committee asked for a recess and when it was over the previous committee had been replaced by a new group. The new committee turned out to be made up of semiliterate workers who hardly understood English. As the session went on, it became clear that the engineers were having no effect on the new committee. The workers were calm enough but the genial blankness which their faces clearly portrayed suggested that the company's high-powered presentation was completely wasted. When the company concluded its argument, one of the members of the union group rose, banged on the conference table, and proclaimed, "No give da raise—no producsh!" with which he marched out of the room followed by his colleagues.

The position of the stewards in a time-study situation is fraught with hazards in both their relationship with management and their relationship with his constituents. On the one hand, because the stewards frequently lack the necessary technical training, the result may be that, as Gomberg points out, they "become the management's hostages for the acceptance of many technically questionable practices." Vis-à-vis the union rank and file, "case after case has occurred in which the membership has turned on the union's time study steward and demanded to know whom he was representing:" [20]

From the perspective of functioning democracy, the handling of grievances between the union committee and supervision is a demonstration of popular participation at its best. The workers' representatives are highly responsive to their constituents; the workers, being close to the problems, are well informed about the issues and the units for which grievances are handled are small enough so that the element of individual personality is not submerged.

THE BUSINESS AGENT

The business agent or his equivalent is typically more important in highly competitive and relatively small-scale industries like clothing, construction, and metalworking job shops than, say, in steel, autos, or rubber. The stewards and the shop committees are of greater importance in the larger scale industries. The fact, however, that many stewards in large plants or departments devote practically full time to their jobs as stewards gives them a certain resemblance to the business agent, although, because of the concentrated nature of the area of their operations, the stewards are probably held to a greater degree of accountability by their membership.

Whether or not a local has a business agent depends upon its size. If its membership is 2,000 or more, to strike an approximate figure, it will probably be able to afford a business agent. The business agent is the union's main contact with the employer in the enforcement and interpretation, and frequently the negotiation, of the agreement. The Electricians set forth the business agent's job in this way, and it is typical of business agents in the building trades generally:

He is the contact man between the members and the employers. He keeps a vigilant eye on all shops and jobs to see that no violations of working agreements occur, and when disputes arise settles them as quickly as possible. He has full supervision over handling of jobs for unemployed members and sees that work is distributed fairly. In company with business representatives of local unions of other crafts, through the Central Labor and Building Trades Councils, he is active in promoting the general union activity of his community. He is held responsible by the International Office for the protection of the jurisdiction of the electrical workers in his territory. An important part of his duties is the handling of the union office, and maintaining accurate statistical information relative to hours and wages of the members.[21]

One source of the business agent's competence is the fact that he is able to devote full time to union business, acquiring in this way a seasoned skill and knowledge of conditions prevailing in the whole community. The closed shop, and the fact that the business agent is the guardian of the closed shop, put him in a strategic position in his relationship with the local union membership because the business agent in these situations becomes the employment exchange for the local—

frequently an efficient employment exchange. The building trades unions and their business agents were the major recruitment agency for construction labor during the war, meeting government demands for manpower in the Canal Zone among other places. On the West Coast, the union halls took over the employment service function for the construction industry at the request of the manpower authorities. The multitude of work rules and the fineness of jurisdictional lines (much of the business agent's time is devoted to the latter) put him in an influential position in dealing with the building contractor or subcontractor. The casual nature of construction employment makes difficult, if not impossible, the operation of an on-the-job workers' committee.

In the situations in which construction trades union officials turned racketeers, the closed shop, jurisdiction, and unchecked authority over the union membership were the vehicles through which the labor racketeers operated. Joseph S. Fay, a vice-president of the Operating Engineers (AFL), admitted receiving $40,000 for protecting the contractors of the Delaware Aqueduct Project in New York State "from outlaw strikers." The contractors were perfectly amenable to pay for this service on the part of Fay, which was to protect the jurisdiction of Local 60 of the Common Laborers' Union over the job from being taken over by Local 147 of the Sandhogs' Union, particularly since "the rate for the sandhogs," according to Fay, "would have been much higher than the laborers." To carry out his side of the bargain, Fay also brought James Bove, Local 60 business agent, into the arrangement. Bove secured a ruling from the Laborers' international headquarters to which both locals were affiliated that Local 60 was entitled to the jurisdiction. Nevertheless, the Sandhogs picketed the Aqueduct job and Fay provided "counterpickets," whose duties were defined by Fay as preventing the pickets from picketing.[22]

Martin Parkinson and William J. McGeory, business agents in the Operating Engineers and the Steamfitters respectively, were convicted in New York State courts of extorting $200,000 from contractors in return for protection against demands for wage increases for workers on the job.[23]

ARBITRATION AND IMPARTIAL MACHINERY

Impartial machinery for the settlement of disputes which the union and management cannot settle between themselves alone is becoming increasingly common in collective agreements. There are unions which are traditionally associated with such impartial machinery; notably, the streetcar employees, the printing trades, the garment trades, and of course, under the law, the railroads. The available evidence suggests that effective impartial machinery is a later stage in the seasoning and maturing of collective bargaining relationships between management and labor. It cannot be successfully superimposed over all kinds of union-management relationships.

Impartial machinery works in the garment trades, as is evidenced by the fact that only a small proportion of the disagreements between unions and management ever gets to the impartial chairman. This means that down along the line employer and union representatives have been able to settle the vast majority of their differences without outside intervention because, by and large, both sides are willing to live by a set of common rules. In decided contrast is the impartial machinery in automobiles, which is invariably bogged down with a large backlog of cases and where a relatively high proportion of the disputes initiated at the lower levels reaches the impartial umpire. This means that unions and management have *not* been able to compose their differences without outside intervention and refuse to reach joint understandings on a day-to-day basis.

Many of the unsuccessful impartial agencies in industries where labor attitudes are still in the boiling or simmering stages were imposed as a wartime urgency by the War Labor Board, and did not grow out of a maturing of the collective bargaining relationship.

Unions, like employers, are in favor of arbitration if they can get more out of it than they could by expensive and exhausting tests of power. Similarly, unions are opposed to arbitration in particular instances if it appears on balance that they stand to lose more than they would otherwise.

Union leaders on occasion find the impartial machinery useful in "taking the rap" of rank-and-file criticism for an unpopular but inevitable decision. An arbitrator of wide experience has related how a union leader had privately conceded beforehand that a decision ordering a wage reduction was inevitable but that he (the union leader) would be forced to attack the decision (in the sharpest invective), which he did. Disciplining workers for participating in unauthorized stoppages also is more palatable when administered by the impartial chairman than when the union leadership itself is forced to do it.

A proceeding before an impartial chairman can serve as an opportunity to develop a line of economic reasoning which would be out of mood in the frequent rough-and-tumble atmosphere of collective bargaining if it is the kind of case that can successfully lend itself to such treatment. Undoubtedly one of the factors that motivated the UAW-CIO in asking for arbitration in its dispute with General Motors was that the idea of ability to pay would be more persuasive to an arbitrator than to the company. An arbitration award can rescue the union from an awkward or desperate strategic position. The CIO Department Store Workers were in the last ditch of their struggle against Montgomery Ward when they proposed the arbitration of their dispute.

There is a large segment of opinion among rank-and-file leadership that the union can not get a fair deal from arbitration. This hostile opinion was particularly widespread in arbitration proceedings sponsored by the War Labor Board, and therefore bound by the stabilization policy of the board. In these proceedings, arbitrators were under obligation to turn down many union demands which otherwise, the unions felt, might have been granted.

Both the UAW-CIO and the Typographical Union have viewed with alarm the growing authority of arbitrators, although it must be recognized that these protests occurred in a war context. A UAW regional director, from the background of a relatively new experience with arbitration, asserts that

our Unions are giving arbitrators more and more power, more and more jurisdiction. In many cases the arbitrator holds the fate of our unions in his hands. Time after time our representatives are discharged while on grievances that arise between Management and Labor. It is high time we took away the arbitrators' power to dismiss these people. Dismissal of our people should be our responsibility and ours alone. We ought to guard this responsibility as fully as management guards theirs. *One never hears of a management representative discharged by an arbitrator. Management protects its spokesmen. We should protect our representatives just as jealously.* [Emphasis in the original.] [24]

From the background of a long experience with arbitration the president of the Typographical Union declares:

The International Typographical Union pioneered in substituting arbitration for economic strife, but after twenty years of standardized arbitration policy, the American Newspaper Publishers Association discarded the international arbitration agreement because they could not set aside the historic and vital laws of the union as the basis of union shop operation.[25]

The ITU has stood firm against making its "laws," as they call their shop rules, subject to arbitration.

Many unions, particularly those not too well situated financially, are critical of the expensive fees charged by arbitrators. The Northwestern Union of Telephone Workers (unaffiliated) voiced the conviction that "exorbitant arbitration fees might adversely affect the whole institution of arbitration." [26]

Further in opposition to arbitration is the argument that it puts a brake on direct action, out of which the unions feel they could get more from management. The argument is based on the probably valid assumption that the pressures of direct negotiation can be more persuasive in some respects than logical arguments before an arbitrator. This is especially true when the issue in dispute involves technical considerations, and management, with its fuller command of the engineering aspects, appears to make out a stronger case before the arbitrator.

LABOR-MANAGEMENT CO-OPERATION

Labor-Management Co-operation, in upper-case letters, has ceased to have much vitality. In this context, Labor-Management Co-operation was essentially a synthetic product. The two most publicized schemes— Naumkeag and the Baltimore & Ohio—were thought up, as it were, by social-minded engineers and encouraged by progressive managements. The Naumkeag experiment ended in a strike—the B. & O. program, as such, is no longer of consequence in union-management relations on the road.

In this current period, union-management co-operation is not of the formal variety but has grown out of the maturing of effective collective bargaining. Many of the unions engaged in union-management co-operation would not recognize their relationships to their managements if it were designated as Labor-Management Co-operation because their kind of co-operation grew by bits and pieces, and out of a pragmatic adjustment to the day-to-day tugs and pulls that characterize collective bargaining. Union-management co-operation exists to a high degree in the building trades, for example, because the unions are strong enough to persuade the contractors to come to some working agreement on a wide range of issues—not only wages and hours but materials, processes, and working rules, without erupting into open warfare, on the practical basis that this is the only way in which even a small measure of equilibrium in the industry can be achieved.

In the apparel industries, characterized by a union leadership with a somewhat more ideological bent, union-management co-operation is a real thing because here too the unions, as the strongest single element in the industry, virtually imposed "co-operation," again, as in the building trades, out of the sheer economic compulsion of "stabilizing" a chaotic industry. This stabilization is being achieved by imposing responsibility on contractors for the working conditions of their subcontractors, by controlling the "runaway" shops, even by regulating style piracy, and by seeking to enlarge the industry's markets.

The impetus to systematic union-management co-operation in the full-fashioned hosiery industry came from the threat of industry relocation in nonunion areas. The Hosiery Workers agreed to embark with the employers on a "rehabilitation" program by which the cost position of unionized establishments would be improved enough to compete with nonunion areas. The union agreed to reductions in piece rates in return for management's installation of modern equipment. The reductions permitted in the piece rate were not uniform but varied with the ability of the company to pay and its willingness to introduce new machinery. To implement the program the union undertook to check on the ways in which the employers were modernizing their methods and machines by suggesting improved lighting and plant layout.

In short, the evidence is irrefutable that union-management co-operation in these days grows out of the economic realities of a given industrial situation and that it is a vital force only where the union is strong and is accepted by management.

Factors Affecting Collective Bargaining

The basic influence on the terms of the collective agreement and its enforcement is the extent to which the union has been able to control the potential and actual supply of labor from which the employer or group of employers recruits workers. Over the long pull, the area of working conditions that is subject to union participation is extensive in the railroads, garment trades, construction trades, automobiles, steel, to cite prominent cases in point, because the unions in these industries have been successful in organizing the largest numbers of workers in their industries into powerful cohesive organizations. The area of union control or participation in control is small in white-collar employment, southern textiles, agricultural processing, because the unions in these industries have not been able—for a variety of reasons—to organize the greater number of the workers into unions. Thus, the unions in the former group of industries have been able to secure normally the closed or the union shop and to exercise control over a wide range of job rules, to single out one index of strong unionism. The unions in the latter group of industries are for the most part still struggling for existence and do not have the power to insist on or enforce stringent terms of employment on management. In short, this rule almost always holds irrespective of other considerations—the stronger a union in terms of its ability to organize its appropriate constituents the greater the inroads it makes on the prerogatives of management.

While the power of union organization determines the extent of these inroads, the kinds of inroads are determined for the most part by the peculiar character of the industry itself. The garment union's insistence on equal division of work is inherent in the seasonality of the apparel industries. Seniority is of no consequence to the construction and maritime unions because of the casual nature of the employer-employee relationship, but union hiring halls with hiring on a rotating basis are important. Seniority *is* relevant in mass production industries because there are many people doing the same kinds of work. Seniority is not an important problem in the printing trades because, except for the larger shops, not many workers are doing the same kinds of work.

The degree of competition in industry affects the significance of collective bargaining. In industries populated by small-scale, highly competitive enterprises the collective bargaining will perform a direct stabilizing function and will assume a greater responsibility for protecting the competitive position of the unionized employers; to wit, the apparel trades and their attempts to regulate subcontracting and introduce technical efficiency into the industry, the barbers' insistence on price regulation; construction unions' attempts to control competition by out-of-city building materials companies, and the Hosiery Workers' "rehabilitation" program. Generally, this kind of stabilizing function of collective bargaining is less important in monopolistic or semi-monopolistic industries such as steel, autos, or rubber.

The considerations of union strength and industry economics are essentially longer run influences. Over the shorter run, the bargaining position of unions in collective bargaining is obviously influenced by the factors affecting the contraction and expansion of employment, notably the cyclical aspects. In the downswing of the business cycle, even well-organized unions like those in hosiery, railroads, men and women's apparel were forced to accept wage reductions. While the construction unions stuck to their wage scales, it was common knowledge that during the depression the wage scales were not enforced. The sloughing off of the wartime employment boom made it expedient for the Ford Company to press for a "union" responsibility clause in its agreement with the UAW-CIO. The point need not be labored that during periods of expansion unions seek wage increases and extension of their controls over working conditions.

At all points in the process of collective bargaining the element of union leadership stamps its imprint. There is no doubt, for example, that the idea of price-wage relationship as a valid subject in the UAW-General Motors negotiations stems from Walter Reuther's own awareness and conception of union purposes. There is some evidence too that the Musicians' policies in connection with FM broadcasts and foreign broadcasts has much to do with the outlook of James Petrillo on these matters. On the lower and less glamorous level of collective bargaining, the temperament of the business agent and the shop steward will have something to do with the outcomes.

It is probable that the Communist party ideology will on occasion influence collective bargaining. Perhaps the most potent effect of this ideology was demonstrated in the incentive wage issue, which was one tenet of Communist-controlled union policy. The Electrical Workers (CIO) advocated incentive payments more vigorously than any other union because it was motivated by the party line. Not that it would not have accepted incentive payments if there had been no Communist influence, but the added zeal put into the advocacy arose out of ideological considerations. And the same can be said for the so-called left-wing group in the UAW-CIO during this period.

Employer attitudes are an important conditioning factor in the orderliness or disorderliness of the collective bargaining process. Only altruists of a high order among employers voluntarily accede to collective bargaining. The *normal* employer is pushed into collective bargaining either by the sheer strength of the union or by government intervention or by a combination of the two. Recognizing the inevitability of union participation, the employer learns to live with it and work within the framework of the union and all that it brings with it. Under such circumstances, union-management relationships can evolve to the point where they are orderly and frequently even cordial.

Henry Kaiser is a striking illustration of this kind of employer attitude. Harry Morton, Kaiser's attorney, talking before a convention of the AFL Metal Trades Department, recalls that

Kaiser was not always the idol of the working men. He was at one time as tough as any employer in the United States. . . . Kaiser's people built Boulder Dam, an open shop job. A few years later, they built Grand Coulee, the tightest closed shop you ever saw.

Morton says further:

We did not get religion just because we like you people. I am speaking of management now. We learned this: the cost per yard of concrete poured at Grand Coulee was less than it was per yard of concrete in Boulder Dam. The cheaper job was the closed shop, the union shop. The more expensive job was the open shop job. This is your beginning and reason for us getting religion, and when we got it we went all the way.[27]

Alexander Prinz, a Cleveland women's clothing manufacturer, offers another illuminating experience of this kind of evolution of employer attitudes. For more than twenty years the Prinz-Biederman management had fought unions tooth and nail. It employed every means at its command to keep its employees away from the union—by keeping wage levels and work hours on a par with those existing in other Cleveland cloak factories, by guarding its employment rolls from infiltration by active union members, and finally by organizing an employees' benefit association modeled along the lines of a company union. Despite these activities to keep the union out of the plant, the cutters were brought into the union fold and then the management realized that it was only a matter of time before the whole plant would be organized. At that point it decided to negotiate an agreement, and the amicable union-management relationship now existing is attested to by the fact that the company president has frequently served as the spokesman for both employer and union elements in the industry.

At the other extreme is the employer who believes that in fighting the union he is fighting a holy cause. The opposition of this type of employer to the unions is not only economic, it is moral and even religious. President Baer of the Philadelphia & Reading Railroad was the archetype of this employer attitude when he uttered his famous dictum during the course of the 1902 anthracite strike:

> The rights and interests of the laboring man will be protected and cared for not by the labor agitators, but by the Christian men to whom God has given control of the property rights of the Country.

The idea of union busting as a moral crusade is evident in much of Sewell Avery's opposition to the organization of Montgomery Ward by the CIO Department Store Employees' Union. In testifying before a Congressional committee in 1944, Avery quoted with manifest approval a letter written about twenty years before, which declared that "the rule of the closed shop, and the law of the Constitution cannot both exist and be obeyed. The question for each American is this: Which of them do you stand for?" [28]

Avery believes that union officials are "if not racketeers . . . then unioneers." [29] When asked how to improve the selection of War Labor Board members, he replied, "Would you give me the opportunity to fill the positions? I would guarantee it would be done without difficulty." [30] Referring to public reaction to the government seizure of the Montgomery Ward store, he said, "There was an indignation that was very deep, and that I hope is going to travel from one end of the Nation to the other, that we may save it." [31]

The *Spotlight* is a mimeographed paper of Local 20 of the union organizing the plant. Avery sued the union as the publisher of the *Spotlight* for a million dollars for causing Ward's employees "to fear, distrust and dislike the plaintiff." Also sued have been Marshall Field's Chicago *Sun* and *Business Week* for allegedly uncomplimentary remarks about the practices of Montgomery Ward.[32]

It is not unreasonable, therefore, to see a causal relationship between this attitude of righteous indignation against unions and the kind of collective bargaining it can generate. Samuel Wolchok, president of the CIO international organizing the Montgomery Ward workers, testified that Avery offered a grievance clause in a proposed contract according to which grievances would be processed up the line of management authority without any corresponding participation by the union, with the final settlement of grievances left to the president of the company. Wolchok says he asked Avery for the final submission of a grievance in case of disagreement to an "impartial man on the likelihood that management might occasionally be in the wrong" to which the chairman of the Board of Directors of Montgomery Ward replied, according to Wolchok, "We do no wrong." [33]

Mr. Avery's attitude is not an isolated one, even a decade after the passage of the National Labor Relations Act. The same passionate righteousness is evident in the opposition employers like Ernest Weir, whose town of Weirton it is still precarious for a CIO organizer to enter. If genuine collective bargaining ever gains a foothold in Montgomery Ward or Weirton Steel it will have to live down a long and bitter history, for unions and management in these kinds of circumstances are not disposed to bury the hatchet at once—the distrust and tension linger on.

In large measure, collective bargaining in many of the mass production industries has been something less than amicable because of the violent background of labor relations. It is not easy for the Auto Workers, for example, to forget that the General Motors Corporation spent $400,000 over a period of two and one-half years for the services of the Pinkerton Detective Agency to destroy their union, that Harry Bennett (who as head of the Ford Service Squad was reputed to be the chief of the world's largest privately owned secret service system) told [a New York *Times* reporter] that half the members of his staff belonged to the Union." [34] The Rubber Workers can recall that Sherman Dalrymple, their president, was violently beaten up in Gadsden, Alabama, when he sought to organize Goodyear workers.

This systematic terrorism was the reflection of an employer attitude to unions and an attitude which penetrated to the lowest rank of supervision. To many foremen and superintendents the unions are still interlopers, and to the union members and stewards the heritage of bitterness is still potent.

One large determinant of the collective bargaining process yet remains to be mentioned, the role of government. Collective bargaining on any widespread scale would have been impossible without the National Labor Relations Act. State and federal minimum-wage laws bolster the unions' wage demands. Almost as important in strengthening the bargaining position of the unions has been the impact on employers of the realization that the Roosevelt administration was decidedly sympathetic to unions. Foreshadowed, as this is being written, is a weakening of the unions' bargaining position with the accession of the Republican party to Congressional power.

THE STRIKE

THE STRIKE IS THE UNION'S MAJOR SANCTION IN BARGAINING WITH EM-
ployers. Approximate bargaining equality can be achieved only if the
union is in a position to exercise an effective choice between working
or not working, and the strike is the collective act of refusing to work.

There are no longer unions or union leaders of consequence who act
on the belief that the strike has a complete validity of its own divorced
from the particular strategic purpose it is calculated to serve. This pragmatic approach to the strike stems from the realization that successful
unionism cannot be perpetuated by purposeless striking. The strike
is therefore more or less a weapon to be held in reserve as a last resort,
and the ultimate *threat* of strike becomes the functioning vehicle
through which union demands are realized.

STRIKE PURPOSES

In the period of the upsurge of unionism in the middle and late
thirties, union recognition was the major strike demand. Section 7a of
the National Recovery Act and the National Labor Relations Act put
the demand for recognition on a firmer footing, and as a consequence
spurred the unions on to a wave of "recognition" strikes to compel big
industry to accede by force what it had been unwilling to do by peaceful
agreement. Large-scale strikes in textiles and in the San Francisco
longshore industry in 1934, shipbuilding and Pacific Coast lumber in
1935, rubber in 1936, automobiles in 1937, and in "Little Steel" also in

1937—the bitterest and perhaps the bloodiest of all the strikes of that turbulent period—were waged for one purpose: the right of the union to be recognized as a union and to be bargained with as such.

The strike for wages and hours characterizes a period of fast economic change—rapid expansion or decline in employment, increase in the cost of living. Immediately after World War II, the country was in the throes of a large number of industry-wide strikes in steel, electrical products, autos, meat packing, mining, railroads, and urban transportation. Many of these strikes, particularly in the reconverted war industries, were caused by the reduction in take-home pay as the transition from war to peace cut hours of work and stimulated job downgrading. Sharp increases in the cost of living also were part of this background of strikes. For another group of industries, the fact that the workers felt that the war stabilization policy had kept down their wages provided them with a strong motive for striking for higher wages once the urgency of war had been dissipated. Within recent years, the only rapid rise in prices and cost of living occurred in a wartime situation. The urgency of the war blunted the strike movement that would have otherwise inevitably followed. On the upswing of the business cycle, the strikes are organized because the bargaining power of the union is stronger when job opportunities are increasing.

On the downswing of the business cycle, strikes against wage cuts flare up. Contraction is normally not a propitious time for successful striking, for it finds the union at its ebb in bargaining power, but in many of these strikes union leaders may be powerless to stop these "desperation" strikes because they stem from the highly charged temper of the rank and file of the membership. When the Hosiery Workers Union, in the depression thirties, accepted a substantial wage reduction, a rash of insurgent strikes broke out in the industry culminating in a march of 5,000 workers on the city of Reading.

Strikes designed to enforce rival jurisdictional claims are not infrequent. As has been noted in another connection, they are most common among the building trades unions, which have a high degree of jurisdictional consciousness. Strikes of this sort are not unknown among other unions. In the strike of airline mechanics the UAW-CIO, the Transport Workers—another CIO affiliate—the Machinists, and District 50 of the Miners were involved, each against the other. The motion picture industry on the West Coast in 1945 and 1946 saw an AFL jurisdictional strike between the Conference of Studio Unions, composed of several AFL locals primarily in the building trades, and the Moving Picture Machine Operators.

In the garment industries, strikes have been called to strengthen the enforcement of an agreement previously concluded when it appears that certain employers are attempting to "chisel" on the agreement. The strikes are frequently called "stoppages" in order not to fall under the ban on strikes which the agreement specifies. Many of these stoppages are actually spontaneous walkouts on the part of the workers with no guidance or direction from union officials.

During the war, the protest strike, or walkout, developed in several cases, particularly in the mass production unions. These walkouts were essentially "quickies" and rarely lasted more than a few hours or involved more than a small number of workers in a particular plant. They were always undeliberated and unplanned. In an important sense these walkouts were a way in which the workers "let off steam" from the tensions and fatigue generated by working long hours, living in congested overexpanded wartime communities. Moreover, many workers were convinced that management was taking advantage of labor's no-strike pledge to stall on the handling of day-to-day grievances.

These kinds of strikes were started typically by what appeared to be trivial incidents. A foreman struck a worker and immediately the entire department stalked out. Or the management fired an active union steward for smoking in the toilet during working hours, or the infinite number of grievances which an incentive system can provoke. They may be trivial to the outsider, but to the worker who was affected they were likely to be the culmination of a mounting number of disagreeable incidents, and what seemed to him management's arbitrary ban, say, on taking a two-second "drag" on a cigarette was the straw that broke the camel's back.

The pattern of the wartime quickie walkout unfolds something like this: Reprimanded by the foreman, the worker tells him where he can go and proceeds to collect around him a score of other workers who feel the same way and they march out. Pretty soon a band-wagon movement sets in and the whole department walks out. In two or three hours a much-harassed union officer succeeds in getting hold of the leaders of the "outlaw" walkout and persuades them to call it off, which they do, feeling considerably better for having asserted their personality in what was otherwise an oppressive situation.

A correspondent of the CIO Department Store Workers relates another typical incident surrounding a protest walkout incited when "the company had instituted a new pay system without consulting the union."

The company's new pay system resulted in inconveniences to workers who cannot keep banking hours.

There was here an underlying grievance which the workers could not stomach. That was a grievance the union brought when the company contended the union supported the proposition of rejecting a worker with a weak heart.

The union had defended this particular worker and therefore became agitated when the company attempted to place guilt on the union for rejection of the worker.

The company's high-handedness in inaugurating a new pay system was the last straw of many previous ones.

So there was a strike.[1]

The Rubber Workers, plagued by these "quickies," attempted to deal with this problem when it upheld the action of a local union president in suspending four members for provoking a walkout to bar the employment of Negro women. President Dalrymple said at that time, "If you want officers with responsibility but no powers—if you want a union that permits stoppages and slow-down then get those kind of officers—but I'm not one of them." [2]

Part of the stock in trade a union offers to an employer in return for a collective agreement is its capacity to control the in-plant actions of its membership. There is an obvious and serious weakening of the union's bargaining power in relation to management if it permits any extended number of wildcat strikes. At the same time, a union in which the leadership is highly responsive to local sentiment cannot be too harsh in meting out penalties to outlaw strikers. First, because the strikers may feel there is ample justification for their action since effective and speedy adjustment of a grievance was not possible in any other way. Second, because in the eyes of the local membership the union leadership is taking the side of management as against the workers.

Also in the nature of gripe strikes are walkouts protesting the employment of Negro workers. In peacetime, Negro workers unaided make little headway in securing employment in industries from which they are normally barred. In World War II, the efforts of the Fair Employment Practices Committee particularly and the manpower shortage in general forced the employment of Negroes in wartime industry production jobs. The impact of this practice on southern white migrants into war industry manifested itself in brief walkouts in aircraft plants, on the railroads, and in the construction trades.

Another kind of strike which arises out of government intervention in labor relations and is, therefore, accentuated in wartime, when there is a great deal of government intervention, is the strike protesting an action or a decision of a government agency. This strike is against the government rather than the employer. In 1944 there were 436 strikes "registering dissatisfaction of one party or another with" a decision of the War Labor Board.[3] Also, 353 strikes occurred while cases were pending before the board. It is a fair inference that a large proportion of these were designed to accelerate the board's action. A spokesman for the Alabama State Federation of Labor relates a typical incident. A dispute concerned with wage inequities for the over-the-road truck drivers was presented to the WLB by several teamsters' locals in the South in November, 1942. The case was heard in January, 1943. As of November, 1943, "that was the last anybody in the South had heard of the case" at which time a strike broke out in protest against the delay. The union charged that the War Labor Board "are the ones who stopped that production more than anybody else." [4]

The strike against a government agency persisted in the postwar period while wage controls were continued. After outdoing the rival CIO maritime unions in securing wage increases, the Sailors' Union of the Pacific and other AFL unions called a strike against a decision of the Wage Stabilization Board (successor agency to the War Labor Board) which had disallowed the increase as against national stabilization policy. Subsequently, the director of the Office of Economic Stabilization approved the increase, overruling the Wage Stabilization Board.

The National Labor Relations Board also has been the point of attack in strike movements. When a board trial examiner found in his intermediate report that the Western Electric Employees Association was dominated by the company, the association called a protest strike. In rulings on the unit question, the NLRB has found itself the strike target by a few unions whose claims were rejected.

The sympathetic strike is an expression of two kinds of influences— "logrolling" and union morality. From the logrolling point of view, a craft union setup as in the construction industry demands some sort of working agreement that union members of one craft will not work with nonunionists in whatever craft they may be. Union workers may also refuse to work with materials made under nonunion conditions. The sympathetic strike *sanction*, if not the actual strike itself, is therefore one of the devices that make craft unionism workable in industries where there are many craft union jurisdictions. From the point of view of union morality, a good union man never crosses a picket line no matter whose picket line. The most systematic and businesslike use of the sympathetic strike is in the building trades unions. A residential building contractor decided to construct a suburban New York housing development with nonunion labor. The construction job was picketed by the local Building Trades Council. As a consequence, the union electricians of the public utility refused to cross the picket line and electric power lines could not be installed in the housing development.[5] Although there was much bitterness between the railroad engineers and the trainmen, on the one side, and the rest of the railroad unions, on the other side, the nonstriking unions honored the 1946 strike of engineers and trainmen and refused to man the emergency trains operated by railroad executives. Even the newly organized telephone operators in Washington, D.C., engaged in a variation of the sympathetic strike when they refused to handle incoming or outgoing calls from the strikebound hotels in that city.

Union workers may frequently refuse to work on materials transferred from a strikebound plant. The printing trades unions all over the country, and the Photo-Engravers particularly, conducted over a period of weeks what they called a "struck work" embargo to ensure that the striking Donnelly Printing Company in Chicago could not effectively farm out its work.[6]

Picket lines are not always honored by nonstriking labor organizations. The justifications the union formulates for permitting its members to go through a picket line are varied. Daniel Tobin recalls "that when a dispute arose not long ago in a certain branch of the [newspaper] trade in Chicago, that the Teamsters remained loyal to their contract and their members continued at work." [7] Rival unionism may cause disregard for a picket line, as happened when the CIO Electrical Workers ordered its members to pass the picket lines of the salaried workers at the Westinghouse Springfield (Massachusetts) plants,[8] or when the AFL Seamen's Union condemned the East Coast Longshoremen's asserted "rank and file" revolt as a "Commie putsch." It should be added that Harry Lundeberg, the leader of the AFL Seamen, is intensely anti-Communist.[9]

The demonstration strike is designed to dramatize in the public mind and to the employer the strength of the union forces and the urgency of particular issues. This kind of strike has no set demands and is called for a preannounced duration. Underlying the demonstration strike is perhaps a feeling of frustration and helplessness to do something more pointed toward the desired end. At the same time, the demonstration strike seeks to reinfuse weary strikers with the spark and enthusiasm that a well-staged strike of this sort does so well.

A three-hour demonstration during which both AFL and CIO unions stopped work was organized in Stamford, Connecticut, to support the strike of the Machinists against the Yale and Towne Manufacturing Company and to protest the use of Connecticut State Police "to break through" the union's picket line in front of the company's plant. A crowd of 10,000 people gathered in front of the Stamford Town Hall and heard union spokesmen proclaim the solidarity of labor. Placards were carried singling out for attack W. Gibson Carey, President of the company and a former president of the U.S. Chamber of Commerce, for his determined open-shop stand.[10]

Less dramatic was the one-week strike called by the Department Store Workers (CIO) against Montgomery Ward, largely because the success of a longer strike was dubious. At the same time the union recognized the need for an expression of protest against Sewell Avery's opposition to the union and for some effort to bolster the sagging morale of the Montgomery Ward union members. As Samuel Wolchok put it, "Such a campaign of economic attrition—a campaign of short strikes—will dramatize our last request for arbitration. We want to impress the average man—the average citizen—in the United States with Mr. Avery's labor policy and his entire doings toward labor as a whole: with his reactionary methods in dealing with labor." [11] After the strike, the union declared it resulted in "unprecedented wage offers by the company" and the strike morale of the Ward workers augured "well for any future action" by the union.[12]

Farthest removed from what may be considered the normal scope of union demands is the political strike. The strike conducted by the National Maritime Union and other maritime unions including the Longshoremen headed by Harry Bridges against delays in bringing back overseas servicemen was of this character. These unions planned a 24-hour demonstration stoppage on all shipping except the ships at sea and those engaged as troop carriers and relief ships. One specific demand which the strike wanted to popularize was aimed at the Maritime Commission for a "certified list of troop carriers and relief ships" [13] on the basis of which the maritime unions would set up manpower priorities in the ports.

The difference between the political strike and the demonstration strike is that the latter is directed toward clearly recognizable union objectives whereas the political strike has nothing much to do with the job.

In the period that is the major concern of this book, the United States has had one clearly recognizable general strike, and at least one near-general strike, if we define a general strike as a "strike of a majority of the workers in the more important industries of any one locality or region." [14] In this sense, the San Francisco 1934 strike was clearly of that magnitude, and the Minneapolis Teamsters' strike almost became one.

These strikes started out like any other strike. The Longshoremen were striking against the "Blue Book" system in the San Francisco longshore industry, which was another term for the then-prevailing employer-controlled open-shop hiring hall. The Minneapolis teamsters demanded a written agreement and union recognition.

Both strikes took place in 1934 as labor was awakening from its big sleep. In both San Francisco and Minneapolis the organized employer forces, the Industrial Association and the Citizens' Alliance respectively represented attitudes and policies of bitter union antagonism. The union leaders, Harry Bridges and the Dunne brothers, were able, shrewd, tough-minded, tough-muscled left-wingers, stemming from the most volatile element in the labor movement, the longshoremen and the teamsters. In the rank and file of both groups there was an underlying distrust of what they considered to be the "labor skates" who made up the official hierarchy.

Given this setting, these strike situations contained their own irresistible dynamic. The need for tying up the San Francisco waterfront dictated the inclusion of *all* the maritime crafts in the strike movement, as well as the teamsters. The employer forces met this threat with the standard weapons in the antiunion employer's arsenal—systematic strikebreaking and violence with the direct assistance of the constituted forces of law and order. The clashes between the strikers and the strikebreakers made for a tension which arrayed the whole community on one of the two sides. The unions, like the teamsters, machinists, painters, transport workers, saw in a possible defeat for the longshoremen a serious setback for the whole West Coast labor movement and came quickly into the battle arena. Police brutality was another target against which the general strike was aimed. So there was a general strike in San Francisco for perhaps two days, after which the nonmaritime unions began to fall off. In Minneapolis, a strike leader said later:

Only by all sections of the trucking industry *acting together* did we have a chance to win anything for any one of them. We knew very well that would tie up the city. And although what we were striking for was the right of collective bargaining guaranteed to us by law, we knew that if we failed the Citizens' Alliance would succeed in pinning prison sentences on all of us.[15]

In San Francisco the favorable results of the general strike were more evident in the building of a powerful longshoremen's union on the West Coast than in any immediate significant gains. The Minneapolis team-sters, with the aid of a sympathetic Farm-Labor administration in the state, were able to gain union recognition and a written agreement. In both cities, however, the strikes generated a bitter antiunion element which, at least in Minneapolis, was a contributing factor to the subse-quent displacement of the Farmer-Labor government by a more con-servative group.

San Francisco and Minneapolis provide these useful insights into the purpose of the general strike: Although the igniting spark of the general strike may be the demands of a single union, the issues and tensions set in motion by these demands are of such a character as to cause other labor elements in the community to come in as reinforcements lest an adverse resolution of these demands cause irreparable damage to the whole labor movement in a community. A long drawn-out general strike will always end in at least immediate defeat for the unions—the hope of the unions must lie in a quick settlement.

Racketeers who gain control of a union have utilized the strike weapon as a lever for extortion. Willie Bioff muscled in on the Moving Picture Machine Operators' Union and used his power to extort sizable amounts of money from the motion picture producers threatening damaging strikes if the bribes were not forthcoming. In general, however, racketeering strikes flourish more in industries marked by a large number of small-scale enterprises, notably the building trades, dry cleaning, the fish mar-kets, and small retail establishments.

STRIKE STRATEGY AND TACTICS

As in other aspects of union functioning, the strike involves both strategic and tactical considerations. The strategy of the strike embraces the questions of timeliness and the nature of the purposes for which the strike is to be fought. The tactics concern the day-to-day improvisations in the conduct of the strike.

Manifestly, a strike is called when production is likely to be at its peak, when the loss to the employer is greatest, and when, therefore, the bargaining power of the union is greatest. It is for this reason that the incidence of strikes is heaviest in periods of expanding economic activity, all other things being equal. In the auto industry, strikes were called when a new model was put into production. In other seasonal industries—clothing, construction—immediately before the season's peak is when strikes are likely to be heaviest. The Pittsburgh department store employees threatened a strike in 1945 immediately before the Christmas rush. Generally, the unions seek to have their agreements with employers expire at about the peak period in their respective industries.

"Divide and conquer" epitomizes another aspect of strike strategy; that is, striking one employer or group of employers at a time. This was the announced strategy in the automobile strikes of 1945, when the UAW struck the GM plants at the same time that it continued negotiations with Ford and Chrysler and concluded an agreement with the new Kaiser-Frazer Corporation.

The timeliness of a strike may also have something to do with the temper of the times. In the period since 1933, the nation has experienced two strike *waves,* the wave of union recognition strikes in 1937 and the wave of postwar strikes in 1945-1946. The major generating force of the 1937 strike wave was the validation of the National Labor Relations Act and with it the realization on the part of the unions that for the first time government could be utilized as a positive force on the union's side, and that employers could no longer break strikes by sheer brute force. In the postwar strike wave, maintenance of real earnings in the face of a rapidly rising cost of living was the chief issue and the belief that public sentiment was committed to high wages made it possible to call strikes for wage increases of a magnitude that would have been inconceivable before the war. So far-reaching was the strike wave following World War II that before it receded it had engulfed groups in the working population for whom organized striking had previously been thought of as fantastic. Teachers, telephone workers, electric power and gas utility employees, railroad workers, municipal employees, who had always conscientiously abstained from exercising the strike weapon, were now part of the industrial turbulence that swept the country. By the same token, strikes during wartime were not timely, all other considerations aside. John L. Lewis was the one leader who was able to utilize wartime stringencies as a basis for what must be regarded as two successful strikes.

The attitude of government is taken into account in strike strategy. The facts are clear that prior to the Roosevelt administration a large and powerful corporation or industry could successfully break any strike if it wanted to badly enough. Imported professional strikebreakers, hired provocateurs in the strikers' ranks, the use of the constituted forces of law and order to break up picket lines, company-inspired "citizens' committees" and vigilante groups, and the injunction were commonplace weapons in the arsenal of the antiunion employer. And this characterization held up for practically every important mass production industry—automobiles, rubber, steel, coal, electrical products—as the hearings of the La Follette Committee documented at great length.

The validation of the National Labor Relations Act and the sympathetic attitude of government generally to labor organization tended to deprive employers of the grosser forms of union opposition during a strike. Moreover, the act, in making union recognition by an employer mandatory if the union was chosen by a majority of the workers in a secret election, minimized strikes which stemmed from an employer's refusal to recognize the union. In the same way the NLRB, by setting standards of collective bargaining procedures for employers, made it easier for agreements to be consummated without strikes, rather than *after* strikes.

That there was practically no violence in the strike wave of 1945-1947 can most certainly be attributed to the fact that employers conceded in advance the ability of the unions to stop production, which condition in turn evolved in particular from the greater union security which the NLRA had made possible.

The tactics of the strike are designed first of all to keep the struck facility from operating; secondly, to condition a public sentiment favorable, or at least not hostile, to the strikers.

The strike tactic calculated to be most effective in achieving the major objective of preventing the plant from operating is the picket line. Mostly, the picket line is organized to exercise a moral and physical deterrent on those who want to get into the plant in order to carry on production. A picket line, like other mass and crowd phenomena, generates its own tensions. To be sure, the union seeks to keep the morale of the picket line high by songs, slogans, and coffee and sandwiches. When the strike is in its early stages and the enthusiasm of the picket line is high, the atmosphere and mood of the participants is gay and almost like that of a picnic. In a large strike, this atmosphere will hold if there is no attempt made to break up the picket line. If the picket line is attacked, then the strike is not a picnic because then the picket line becomes the symbol of the struggle, and the strikers fight hard to protect it. The tensions and violence generated when an attempt is made to break the picket line is graphically told by Sidney Garfield, an AFL Chemical Workers business agent who describes a strike which he directed in Chicago in 1940:

We had about twenty-five people out of one-hundred-fifty or so that we could really depend on and who were down every day for picket duty and so forth, and we just threw a picket line around the Company. Things have to be planned a little bit in a situation like that, so I split the gang into two groups. One group was posted right in front of the Company door and the other group down at the street car where the people who were coming to work got off. When this second bunch met anybody coming to the plant they just caught them right then and there and asked them, "Are you with us or against us?" and there wasn't anything in' between—it was either yes or no, and if the answer was no and they were against us, Wham! There was fighting then and there and a lot of people were hurt.

The group down in front of the door of the Company was the same way. They had one great big fellow there who was a wild character. He was really violent and I had to kind of keep control of him, but whenever things got going he was always in there with both fists flying. One of the supervisors tried to get five girls into the plant by hooking his arms into theirs and walking up to the door with them. This wild man cut in front of him and when the supervisor said, "You can't hit a man with glasses on," he just took the glasses off and handed them to him and then pasted him. The supervisor put his glasses on and just turned around and staggered away.[16]

Conflict involving the attempts of the forces of law and order to break the picket line occurred in the course of the Republic Steel Strike in 1937, which was filmed by a newsreel sound cameraman and the description "comes from a person who saw the [film] several times and had a particular interest in studying it closely for detail. Its accuracy is beyond question." A long straggling line of pickets numbering about three hundred parade across the field leading to the plant gates. They are led by bearers carrying American flags and behind them are placard carriers with slogans "Come On Out . . . Help Win the Strike," "Republic vs. the People," and "C.I.O." The spokesmen for the line argues with the "police officer who appears to be in command" insisting on permission to continue through the police line of about three hundred. "The spokesman's expression is serious but no threat of violence is apparent." The police officer refuses to let the picket line through. "Then suddenly, without apparent warning, there is a terrific roar of pistol shots, and men in the front ranks of the marchers go down like grass before a scythe." The police then charge on the marchers with riot sticks and tear gas grenades and the "ground is strewn with dead and wounded." [17] When the casualties could be counted it was found that "ten marchers were fatally shot. Seven received the fatal wound in the back, three in the side, none in the front." [18]

At the Kearny, New Jersey, plant of the Western Electric Company during the strike conducted by the unaffiliated Western Electric Employees Association, "1,000 non-striking executives, supervisors, and maintenance employees" made "a mass dash" to break through a union line composed of forty-two pickets and hand-to-hand fighting ensued. Earlier in the morning, the picketing was peaceful as "hundreds of individual non-strikers were turned away by the pickets." The union president charged that "the morning battle was the result of a well organized plot by management to incite a riot." The violence would not have occurred, he said, if the nonstrikers had not used "football tactics" to press their entrance into the plant. The union president said that top management and maintenance would be allowed to enter the plant but to permit supervisors to get in would mean the restoration of production, and that only a small picket line would be maintained unless there was another mass attempt to enter the plant. In that event the union would put 1,000 pickets at each gate.[19]

In the strike of the International Association of Machinists against the Yale and Towne Manufacturing Company "management representation won the right . . . to enter the plant without union passes but as they passed through they were checked against a list by union officials, who refused admittance to foremen and other personnel who might theoretically be used in any production work. The union in that sense maintained full control over those entering the buildings." [20]

Violence on the picket line is rarely a premeditated union plan of action. In 1915 the U.S. Commission on Industrial Relations made the classic statement on this subject, which can be said to hold true today: "All experience shows that if no attempt is made to operate the plant, violence and disturbances requiring the police are practically unknown." [21] A comparison between the strikes of 1934-1937 and the 1945-1946 strike wave is illuminating in this connection. On the whole, the strikes in the former period were of much lesser magnitude because the mass production industries were not as well organized but strike violence was frequent in maritime, autos, rubber, and little steel. Nation-wide strikes in these industries (except possibly maritime and motion picture production) during 1945-1946 were accompanied by little or no violence. The difference can be attributed to the fact that management granted in advance the ability of the unions to shut down the plants and, therefore, made no attempt at productive operations.

The sit-down strike reflected not a philosophy but a tactic of expediency by which the strikers made certain that the plant could not operate. When it became clear that the sit-down strike provoked considerable public opposition even in circles sympathetic to labor, the tactic was dropped. In the automobile strikes of 1937 and the rubber strikes of 1936, where it was given a wide application, the attitude of management toward the unions and collective bargaining was one of violent and systematic opposition. As Homer Martin, the president of the UAW during the sit-down period, put it:

A strike can only be effective if and when it brings about a cessation of production. It is an absolute interference on the part of workers with the right of the employers to make profit. . . . A sit-down strike concerns itself only with making the stoppage of profits more effective, and the courts in granting us the right to strike did grant us the right to stop profits.[22]

The sit-down strike was undoubtedly effective in compelling the auto and rubber industries to deal with the unions. It was accompanied by surprisingly little violence compared to the strikes of the period, and apparently little damage to property. The backbone of the sit-down strike was the workers recruited from the hill and mountain country of the South—a stock of Americans theretofore not commonly associated with militant labor tactics. For years these workers resisted the blandishments of union organizers. When they finally flocked into the union they brought with them an indigenous toughness and an attitude of "we've been pushed around long enough, now it's our turn."

The events leading up to the greatest of the sit-down strikes, that of Fisher Body Number One plant in Flint, Michigan, is set forth in this ballad which the strikers set to the tune of "The Martins and the Coys."

> Now this strike it started one bright Wednesday evening
>   When they loaded up a box car full of dies.
> When the union boys they stopped them,
>   And the railroad workers backed them,
> The officials in the office were surprised.

Chorus

> These 4,000 union boys
> Oh, they sure made lots of noise.
> They decided then and there to shut down tight.
> In the office they got snooty,
> So we started picket duty,
> Now the Fisher Body shop is on a strike.

> Now they really started out to strike in earnest.
>   They took possession of the gates and buildings too.
> They placed a guard in either clock-house,
>   Just to keep the non-union men out,
> And they took the keys and locked the gates up too.[23]

Rose Pesotta, an ILGWU organizer lent to the UAW in this strike, gives a vivid account of the sit-down in this same Fisher plant. Provided with an escort of two strikers, she got into the building through an open window.

Brilliantly lighted, this vast plant was heavily guarded inside and outside—to keep strikebreakers and other interlopers from entering, and to protect the building and its contents. Especially did these strikers guard the company's dies. No liquor was permitted on the premises, and smoking was prohibited on all production floors. Forty-five men were assigned to police patrol duty inside. Their word was law.

Production being at a standstill, a long line of Fisher bodies hung from the motionless conveyor-belt, as if frozen in space. But throughout the building there was ceaseless movement and watchfulness. One section had been fitted up like a hotel lobby, with soft cushions from car bodies to sit on.

Newspapers and periodicals of varied political shades, labor papers, and mystery magazines were among the reading matter in evidence.

Having organized an orchestra and a chorus, they staged nightly concerts, broadcast through a loud speaker from the window to audiences outside in automobiles and on foot.[24]

In 1937 the automobile industry could not have been organized except by the use of the sit-down strike. It is also clear that the determined, and on the whole successful, effort of Governor Frank Murphy to resist the use of organized force on the part of the forces of law and order played an important part in the effectiveness of the sit-down.

In a large strike, an elaborate organization and mechanism is set up to make the cessation of work effective and continuous. In the Minneapolis Teamsters' strike the central strike headquarters was an old garage. The garage served as "barracks, commissary, hospital, auditorium, squad car assembly, and staff headquarters for the strike committee." According to Charles Rumford Walker, who investigated the strike at first hand, "the brain core of military operations was the dispatchers room" where "men stood all day at four telephones which poured forth information to them and registered calls for strike help from all corners of the city." Picket captains were under instructions to keep in touch with headquarters every ten minutes. Messages like "Truck attempting to move load of produce from Berman Fruit under police convoy; have only ten pickets; send help" and "Successfully turned back five trucks entering city at —— Road North. Am returning cars 42 and 46 to headquarters" were written down and given to the dispatchers, who were responsible for the allocation of pickets.[25]

There are other activities in the larger strikes which are carefully planned. Picketing is rigidly scheduled. A commissary to dispense hot food to the pickets is set up. Material and financial aid is doled out to needy strikers' families. A fund-raising campaign may be organized to raise money from sympathetic outsiders. Legal aid is immediately available to protect pickets who may be arrested.

The conduct of a strike becomes much more complex if several unions are involved because responsibility for strike tactics is divided and the weakening or defection of one group will endanger the successful outcome of the whole strike. This was the situation that prevailed in the bitter strike against the long-time open-shop Donnelly Printing Corporation by the unions in the printing trades when International President George Berry ordered the pressmen back to work without consultation with the other unions involved in the strike. The defection of the pressmen had the effect of virtually breaking the strike.

Strikes are conducted not only on the picket line but in the forums of public opinion—the halls of Congress, the press, and the radio. Indeed in some strikes the public opinion sector of the strike becomes strategically more important than the picket line. This holds particularly true where the union has already assured the cessation of production and management recognizes this condition as an accomplished fact by not attempting to operate the struck facility. In these situations, which prevailed in the automobile, electrical products, railroad, and steel strikes during 1945-1946, the picket line ceased to be a protective device and became merely a token demonstration.

The emphasis of strike strategy in the industries cited above shifted to the public sector as the unions sought to impress government and the people at large with the justice of their demands. The public appeal utilized by Walter Reuther in an attempt to bring community sentiment on the union's side of the General Motors strike was the idea that "we want to make progress with the community and not at the expense of the community." [26]

The Steel Workers' Union used paid radio time before and during the strike to explain its position to the public. Churchmen, economists, persons prominent in public life went before the radio microphones and supported the steel workers' demands as just and essential to the economic health of the nation. The steel union, however, did not make as much of the wage-price relationship as did the UAW.

The Railroad Engineers and the Trainmen, led by A. F. Whitney, called a strike in May, 1946, which was lost not on the picket line but before the public. Heretofore, the prime factor in the strike strategy, particularly of the operating unions, was not to strike. Although there is no legal ban on strikes in the railroads, it had been previously realized by the railroad unions that public sentiment would not support a wholesale railroad strike considering the dislocating consequences to the nation's economy. The Engineers and Trainmen were forced to return to work because it was impossible to withstand the pressure that was being exerted against them, particularly since, unlike the mass production industry strikes, it was the unions that turned down the final government settlement offer and not the management. Moreover, again unlike the striking meat-packing and oil unions, the railroad unions ordered the strike notwithstanding the fact of government seizure. These were obstacles which could not be overcome by the Engineers and the Trainmen.

The coal miners, without a deliberate public relations campaign, were able to engage successfully in several crippling strikes. The essence of Lewis's skill as a strike strategist seemed to be that he was daring without being reckless, at least until the coal strike of 1947. Somehow Lewis settled just short of the time when it seemed drastic punitive action would be applied.*

The strike is, in the main, a form of predetermined union high strategy aimed against the employer and designed to bring him to terms. In rare situations the strike has been used for purposes other than as a source of pressure against employers. As a strategic device, the strike, small or large, is consciously planned for a time, place, and occasion when it will be most effective and its tactics are accommodated to the demands of the situation.

* See concluding section of Chap. VIII for effect of Taft-Hartley law on strikes.

CHAPTER VIII

UNIONS, GOVERNMENT, AND POLITICS

THE UNION'S INTEREST IN POLITICS AND GOVERNMENT STEMS FROM precisely the same motives and compulsions that characterize its other activities. Naturally the expression that these motives take is suited to the peculiar medium of politics and government as a way of achieving union purposes.

WHY UNIONS TRY TO INFLUENCE GOVERNMENT

First, it is an obvious point that unions are interested in encouraging government measures which will make for more jobs in their industry. The building trades unions are constantly urging upon local and federal government large-scale public works programs. For example, Harry Bates of the Bricklayers, as chairman of the AFL Housing Committee, is one of the most ardent spokesmen for the large-scale housing program embodied in the Wagner-Ellender-Taft General Housing bill. The shipyard workers have been in the forefront of the labor organizations agitating for a powerful navy and merchant marine.

On occasion, this pressure for favorable government action for more jobs is consciously aimed at government action against competing workers or competing jobs. The interest and the activity of the building trades unions in behalf of municipal building codes is in part the craftsmen's interest in promoting the use of safe materials and practices. It is also designed to compel the use of materials or restrict the use of ma-

142

terials which otherwise would deprive their members of jobs. Pressure on the federal government of this restrictive character is typified in support of tariffs which would inhibit foreign competition. The Textile Workers (CIO) have opposed reduction in textile tariffs in the United States. The Miners and the railroad unions have opposed the construction of the St. Lawrence Waterway, which would, it is held, adversely affect the volume of traffic carried by the railroads and, of course, for the Miners it would affect the consumption of coal by the railroads.

This is the approach also of the Painters, who advocate legislation either banning or severely curtailing the use of the spray gun. Louis Weinstock, an officer of the Painters' Union, who also happens to be a well-known Communist party member, asks rhetorically:

Who can be opposed to a campaign initiated by our International from one end of this country to the other to create such legislation that will make it almost impossible in certain localities and on certain types of work to use the spray gun? [1]

Unions favor legislation which will increase wages directly or indirectly and reduce hours of work. For the AFL as such, this attitude is of relatively recent origin. Until the New Deal came to power the AFL opposed government measures designed to affect wages and hours (except regulations for women and minors) believing that these ends could better be achieved through collective bargaining. For the period with which we are concerned, however, union support and indeed encouragement of all measures which set minimum wages and maximum hours is practically unanimous.

Some unions will press harder for certain kinds of wage and hour legislation than others. For example, as this is written, the amendment to the Fair Labor Standards Act to raise the national minimum wage to 65 cents an hour is under consideration. The Textile Workers (CIO) is perhaps the union that is working harder for this legislation than any other for the understandable reason that the southern textile workers, who are the least organized, stand to benefit most from such legislation. The Department Store Employees (CIO) are also pressing for the extension of minimum-wage regulations to the relatively low-wage mercantile employees.

In this respect it is significant that there is no substantial fear that statutory action to raise wages and reduce basic hours will compete with the union's stock in trade to workers. On the contrary, the union's calculation is that such action will bring the low-wage employers closer to the average and thus weaken the extent to which they can undersell unionized employers; particularly since the low-wage employers are frequently the most difficult to organize. It is also worth noting that the more effectively an industry is organized the more the union gets out of government regulation. This influence was clearly operative in the wage and hour features of the NRA codes where the better organized industries got the best labor codes and the most effective enforcement (in what was on the whole a spotty enforcement record), since the unions constituted themselves an enforcement agency.

Maintenance of health and safety standards provides another field of government action which commands practically universal support by unions. The Miners, operating in an industry with high accident rates, has fought over the years for adequate federal and state inspection laws. The activities of the mine inspectors are given much prominence in the *Miners' Journal*.

A large area in which unions have sought to influence government policy in one way or another is in the cultivation of sympathetic attitudes on the part of government toward union practices and activities. In an elementary way, it takes the form of the newly arrived organizer visiting the local mayor and police chief in order to minimize possible hostility on the part of the forces of law and order.

Although the National Labor Relations Board was subject to attack by both AFL and CIO for particular decisions, there has never been any question of their support of the underlying assumption of the act that government has a basic responsibility to protect the right of workers to organize into unions of their own choosing. Indeed, it is possible that, if the labor support had not been forthcoming, the National Labor Relations Act would have been amended out of existence long ago. Similarly, all union forces have been actively mobilized against federal legislation designed to weaken the unions—proposals slanted toward compulsory arbitration, outlawing of the closed shop, "cooling-off periods" in labor disputes.

Influencing government, particularly the federal government, can become part of the union's total strategy in collective bargaining with the employer. Thus, the strike upsurge of 1937, as well as the postwar wave and its accompanying wage demands, would not have been prosecuted with the same zeal if the union leadership had not felt it could count on tacit and even direct assistance from government. Walter Reuther's willingness to present the UAW-GM case before a fact-finding panel was undoubtedly predicated on the belief that whatever came of the panel would be to the union's advantage. Similarly, in the steel dispute, Philip Murray's compliance with President Truman's request by way of calling off the strike for the time originally set must have been on the basis that he felt the government was favorably disposed toward the union position. This is what Sidney Hillman must have been thinking about when he said in the spring of 1946 that the CIO had won its strikes by "political action" as well as economic action.[2] It is not unlikely, therefore, that industry's general opposition to government-sponsored fact-finding and compulsory arbitration was due less to a hostility to the principles and more to their conviction that government intervention of this sort would generally favor the unions.

The facts of a chaotic industry, economically speaking, impel unions to seek government intervention to "stabilize" that industry. Always responsive to the interests of the coal miners, Senator Guffey sponsored, under the urging of the UMW, a bill which fixed coal prices as well as established a labor relations mechanism in a coal labor board. The Textile Workers Union too sought to introduce order into the highly competitive economics of its industry through the enactment of the Ellenbogen bill which would have set up a "little NRA" for the textile industry. In general, the AFL, as such, was moderately sympathetic to the aims and administration of the National Industrial Recovery Act. The needle trades unions had been enthusiastic supporters of the NRA.

There are unions which, in the very nature of the field in which they function, must necessarily turn to government for the effectuation of their objectives. The railroad unions, dealing as they do with a public utility, subject to close regulation by government of all levels of jurisdiction, pay considerable attention to the influencing of government policy. As much as anything else, the railroad unions are powerful political pressure groups. In state legislatures, these unions have been active in behalf of full crew laws and railroad safety legislation. Nationally, the railroad unions were powerful enough to secure protective labor relations legislation in the Railway Labor Act nine years before comparable legislation was available to other workers in the National Labor Relations Act. Railroad workers also have their own old-age insurance and unemployment compensation in the Railroad Retirement

Act and the Railroad Unemployment Insurance Act. In all this legislation the railroad unions were the main motive power behind the legislation. The rail unions went further along the path toward government intervention than any other important labor group, when they excited considerable interest in the public ownership of the railroads in the form of the much-debated Plumb plan immediately after World War I. One of the master minds of the rail union's political strategy is Edward Keating, editor of *Labor*, the organ of the railroad unions. Keating once quoted J. J. Pelley of the Association of American Railroads as saying in connection with the debate on the second Railroad Retirement Act, "Will you kindly tell me when the railroad boys are going to permit Congress to adjourn?" [3]

Even more dependent on government action than the railroad unions are the unions in public service employment. Deprived ordinarily of the most important sanction of collective bargaining—the strike—these unions must rely extensively on government action rather than on the more normal union activities. The unions in the postal service are continually active in behalf of favorable legislation and are an important political power in the halls of Congress. The metal trades unions have been successful in securing legislation forbidding time and motion studies in the naval shore establishments. The Teachers' Union has been vigorously active in behalf of federal aid to education, and in the state and local governmental bodies for increased salary schedules.

UNIONS AND NATIONAL POLICY

The range of union concern with government up to this point, we have been suggesting, has been an outcome of the practical necessity of running a union in a society in which government plays an increasingly important part in economic and social affairs. When we get into the field of union interest in broad national policy, it is likely that the ideological roots of unions and union leadership affect the extent to which activitiy is undertaken in these fields. In more specific terms, it may be said that CIO unions are more prone to take a position and agitate for legislation which is further removed from immediate job problems than are the AFL unions. In turn, within the AFL, unions like the International Ladies' Garment Workers have a broader range of interest in governmental affairs than do most AFL unions. The explanation is not hard to find. The CIO unions rose to power as part of a wave of reform—the New Deal. Intellectually at least, unionism to them is of a piece with the other segments of the New Deal. The mainstay unions in the AFL, notably the building trades and most of the metal trades unions, on the other hand, stem from an environment which was not as sympathetic to broad programs of social reform. On the contrary, many of these unions experienced conflicts with Socialists and, in later years, Communists, which has had the effect of hardening them against what they regarded as "causes."

The CIO Political Action Committee is as good an example as any of the broader range of the CIO's political interests as compared to those of the AFL. The keynote of the PAC campaign was in terms of support of Roosevelt policy, not of labor policy as such. The candidates who received PAC support were those who were supporting the President or, at least, his general policies with particular emphasis on foreign policy. As Sidney Hillman said at the 1944 CIO convention, following by only a few weeks the presidential election of that year, "When we organized [PAC] last year and announced a program, it was not a narrow labor program."[4] Or in another place in the same address, "Our program was not a program for labor alone."[5] Whatever support candidates received from the AFL and its individual unions was on the basis of the candidate's voting record on issues of immediate concern to organized labor and not foreign policy particularly.

Within the past few years, however, there has been a discernible change in AFL attitudes with respect to taking stands on public issues not too immediately related to union affairs. In part this tendency has evolved because of the AFL's recognition that an articulate expression of opinion on matters of broad public policy is expected from them by people sympathetic to labor. Another factor in this expanded interest is to offset the notion that the CIO is the only organization that speaks for labor in these matters, although on national policy there is little disagreement between AFL and CIO. Finally, the AFL has become increasingly aware of the relevance of issues of national economic policy to the health of its unions. The AFL has recently added a Social Security Department to stimulate interest and action among its affiliated groups in pending legislation, and to make its point of view effective in government councils. In the spring of 1944, the Postwar Committee of the AFL held a national forum on problems of postwar adjustment in which there were sessions on world organization and full employment. AFL spokesmen like Matthew Woll have been increasingly articulate on foreign affairs.

How Unions Influence Government

The most common mechanism to influence government policy is through legislative representatives, or, put more invidiously, the lobbyists. Like every other group which has vital stakes in government action, labor organizations maintain full-time representatives in Washington and in the state capitals. Perhaps the most effective labor lobby is that of the railroad unions. Much of the legislative strength of the railroad unions arises out of (1) their limited legislative objectives and (2) their strength in the rural sections of the country. The strength of the rail unions among legislators from rural constituencies, which is where the major opposition to labor legislation stems from, grows out of the fact that the railroad shop is frequently the single largest industrial enterprise in many of the rural communities and railroad labor is, therefore, the only labor group of importance in these constituencies. Such legislators are, therefore, more responsive to the pressures of the rail labor group than they are to labor groups in general.

The results of this superior political position of the railroad unions are not difficult to detect. As Keating puts it:

No legislation affecting the railroads can be put through Congress until it has the support of railroad labor. That was amply demonstrated when this last transportation act was put through. That act was a great thing for the railroads but they couldn't put it through without the support of these organizations and they know it.[6]

Both AFL and CIO, as well as many international unions, maintain permanent legislative organizations in Washington. The job of the labor lobbyist is like that of any other lobbyist, as far as the mechanics of the job go. It involves keeping track of what is happening to legislation, providing technical assistance in drafting and promoting legislation, pressuring legislators to vote labor's position, and organizing pressure from back home put on wavering legislators.

The CIO, in this as in other aspects, tries to be more sensational in its lobbying. In October, 1945, for example, the *CIO News*[7] reported that delegations from nearby states aggregating 2,000 CIO members "marched" on Washington, visiting their congressmen and senators "to find out how they stood on unemployment compensation, full employment, and the 65 cent minimum wage bill." The *CIO News* carries on its back page a score card of bills before Congress under the heading "Keep Your Eye on Congress" and presents, in tabular form, the title of the bill, "what it does," "where it is," and recommended action such as "wire or write to your congressman to oppose."

Electoral activity is another way in which labor unions seek to influence government policy and action. There is no *fundamental* difference between AFL and CIO or among the affiliated unions with respect to electoral activity. Before the New Deal, there was always an articulate minority which pressed for independent political activity by labor at AFL conventions. This was essentially the Socialist group. Since the New Deal, there has been no serious espousal of independent political action by any considerable group in either AFL or CIO. As this book is being written, the disappointment of some CIO unions with the Truman administration has stimulated a light flurry of talk about a third party, but all responsible elements in the CIO have disavowed independent labor political action.

There is, however, a significant difference in degree as between the various kinds of electoral activity engaged in by labor. The older unions in the AFL, notably the building trades, carry on their activity for the most part not as organized labor but as part of the existing political parties. Dan Tobin of the Teamsters heads the Labor Committee of the Democratic party. William Hutcheson of the Carpenters is Tobin's opposite number in the Republican party. The central bodies on the state and local levels "reward their friends and punish their enemies" by passing resolutions and occasionally by permitting favored candidates to address their meetings, but there union identification with electoral activity ends. In the local communities, the officials of the older AFL unions are active in the precinct work that is the heart of American political activity. There is evidence that, despite certain offsetting tendencies, the CIO is moving in a direction of this kind of electoral activity too. R. J. Thomas and Philip Murray were delegates to the 1944 Democratic convention. Sidney Hillman was charged with being the power behind the failure of the convention to nominate James Byrnes for vice-president, as the phrase "Clear it with Sidney" has memorialized.

Within the AFL, the unions with Socialist traditions have not become completely reconciled to assimilating themselves in the old political parties. The International Ladies' Garment Workers leaders made a clean break with the idea of independent political action when it became active in the American Labor party in support of Franklin D. Roosevelt's second campaign in 1936. The American Labor party was, in fact, set up for the purpose of getting a kind of support for Mr. Roosevelt which would feel uncomfortable voting for him under the Democratic emblem. When a coalition of Sidney Hillman and Communists and Communist sympathizers captured the American Labor party in New York State, David Dubinsky was the most important factor in setting up the Liberal party. Except for minor offices, the Liberal party has supported candidates of the major parties. In all instances, the political activity was vigorous and it differed from the traditional electoral activity only in this respect, in that it was *labor* activity.

Much the same can be said by way of characterizing CIO electoral activity. Starting with Labor's Nonpartisan League in 1936 and currently the Political Action Committee, the CIO supported old party candidates, predominantly Democratic, nationally and locally. The distinctive flavor of CIO came from the energy that was put into the electoral activity, the systematic public relations "techniques" that were used to influence political attitudes, and the unvarnished identification of its electoral activity as "labor" activity.

The CIO Political Action Committee was organized in the summer of 1943 because "the deplorable record of the 78th Congress has brought sharply home to labor the dire results of its political apathy in 1942." [8] In broad conception PAC reflected the high-powered administrative temperament of its moving spirit, Sidney Hillman. More perhaps than any labor leader of comparable importance, Hillman had always demonstrated a great capacity to think in wholesale terms about any project in which he was involved. And from its very inception PAC operated with a sweeping magnificence in all aspects of political activity visible to the naked eye.

It utilized "public relations" techniques on a scale and of a kind completely unprecedented in American labor political action. Some sense of the large-scale public relations operations of PAC in the 1944 elections may be gleaned from the fact that it distributed, or at least printed, 85 million copies of campaign literature which included 2 million copies of pamphlets, 57 million copies of leaflets, and over 400,000 posters. PAC had a women's section, a Negro section, a students' section, a church section, a radio section, and a press section. To this output must be added the considerable output of individual CIO unions.

By way of personal contact with the voters PAC urged intensive use of house-to-house canvassing. "In any political campaign," according to *What Every Canvasser Should Know*, a CIO-PAC publication, "you may have mass meetings, radio speeches, leaflets, newspaper ads. . . . But all of them put together would be wasted without the quiet talk of neighbor to neighbor about the issues and the candidates." [9]

The first objective of PAC strategy was to get citizens to register on the theory that progressive candidates could win only when a relatively high proportion of the prospective voters were eligible to vote. After registration, PAC through the CIO international and local union committees aimed to elect its friends and defeat its enemies. Between the 1944 and 1946 elections there was no evidence that CIO-PAC as such sought to engage in extraelectoral activity such as lobbying, except as individual CIO unions carried on their normal lobbying activities. The CIO-PAC was distinctly conscious of the attacks on the propriety of unions engaging in political action and much of its literature sought to justify political action both to its own membership and to the public at large. One leaflet compared political action to collective bargaining:

> The only alternative to a collective bargaining contract, good or bad, is no contract at all. Likewise, the alternative to taking political action is to take no political action and to leave the control of politics up to undemocratic political machines. [10]

In the 1944 elections many sources both friendly and unfriendly credited CIO-PAC with an important contribution in electing President Roosevelt. After the 1946 elections PAC received a decided setback as the vast majority of the candidates whom it had supported were defeated. The PAC placed the blame on the reactionary turn of the Truman administration. Others expressed the judgment that the PAC "kiss of death" was one of the elements in the rout of Democratic legislators.

Much of the zeal that characterized PAC activity in 1944 was absent two years later. The response of CIO members to contribution appeals was extremely disappointing, reflecting a state of mind which foreshadowed heavy defeats even in districts and states heavily populated by CIO members—Michigan, for example. In varying degrees the same elements which were sources of PAC's strength in 1944 were noticeably lacking in 1946: PAC association with a great and popular personality,

the cohesiveness generated by a wartime situation, and the availability
of the loyal Communist party members and their followers, as the spark
plugs in the local election precincts.*

The railroad unions have much the same notion of the character of
political action as has the PAC. To quote Mr. Keating:

> It hasn't made any difference to them [the railroad unions] whether they
> were Republicans, or Democrats, or independents. They judged them on their
> records and then supported them not merely by passing a resolution but fre-
> quently by sending organizers into their districts.[11]

A traditional way in which unions have secured labor participation
has been to require the designation of people from its ranks in the agencies of government as *quid pro quo* for its political support. In the
local communities craftsmen's licensing boards—plumbers, electricians,
motion picture operators, etc.—commonly include active union officials.
In the states, the labor department is likely to be headed by an important union leader. At one time or another, the labor department
head in Rhode Island was a president of the State Federation of Labor;
in Michigan, a president of the Michigan CIO Industrial Union
Council; in Kentucky, an officer of the Brotherhood of Railway Trainmen. In the federal government, at least two of the secretaries of labor
were union officials, William Wilson and William Doak; currently there
is an assistant secretary of labor recruited from AFL ranks and one from
CIO ranks. In many instances the trade union movement provides the
only source of experienced personnel for government affairs and such
agencies would naturally include a large number of officials with origins
in the trade union movement.

As the unions have grown in influence and size, another way in
which they have sought to affect government action is through direct
labor participation in government administration. This is a reflection as
well of a normal desire for status and recognition. The union's concern
with labor participation, in turn, has been determined by the increasing
scope of governmental functions in matters related to union problems.

The most common form of labor participation in the making of government policy has been through so-called advisory committees to
governmental administrative bodies. The unions wanted advisory committees because they thought they could in this way influence the ac-

---

* See concluding section of Chap. VIII for effect of Taft-Hartley law on political
action.

tions of government agencies. The government administrators wanted advisory committees either because they honestly wanted advice from the union representatives or because they felt the need for some symbol of popular participation in policy making which might take the heat off them for unpopular measures.

The advisory committee mechanism reached its peak in wartime administration and functioned with varying degrees of effectiveness. In the Office of Price Administration and the War Manpower Commission, the advisory committees exercised a moderate influence on policy because the members were well informed and were supported by a full-time staff on the payroll of the respective agencies. The presence of full-time labor representatives made it possible to maintain a continuous and knowing appraisal of agency policies and to feed the advisory committee members with information which otherwise they could not have obtained. Because the advisory committee members were not on a government payroll and represented influential organizations, it was possible for them to bring to bear some pressure on administration of these agencies. In the War Manpower Commission, for example, the advisory committee was able to exert considerable influence against the adoption of compulsory measures in recruiting and holding manpower. It was also true that in both the OPA and the War Manpower Commission, the administrators were not unreceptive to the ideas which the union representatives had to offer. In the case of the latter agency, union representatives were especially active in the regions and areas in connection with appeals from rulings on certificates of availability. On the vast majority of issues considered by the advisory committees, there was a unanimous union opinion.

Labor participation through advisory committees was casual when the union representatives were made up of high-level union officers who met infrequently and had no time or opportunity to give the study and care that the job required; nor was the agency administrator particularly concerned that there was no genuine participation by the unions. The Office of War Mobilization and Reconversion under James Byrnes contained within it an advisory committee made up of representatives from labor, management, agriculture, and the public. Many policies of major importance were undertaken without adequate consultation with the advisory committee; notably, those relating to national service legislation. Another element in the ineffectiveness of this advisory committee was the fact that, for example, AFL and CIO labor representatives were

Philip Murray and William Green. With no full-time personnel in the agency, these men were much too occupied with a multitude of other problems to be able to give their jobs the attention they required.

Another kind of labor participation is evidenced where the unions are given responsibility for a phase of the administrative process, such as in the Office of Labor Production and the Office of Manpower Requirements in the War Production Board. The heads of these offices were men who were chosen by virtue of their standing in, and recommendation by, the AFL and CIO respectively. These offices were set up not because of an awareness that there was a job to be done in the WPB and the labor unions were the best qualified to do the job but rather because the AFL and CIO were influential enough in the highest councils of government so that a demand on their part for some sort of recognition in the WPB had to be listened to with respect.

Both AFL and CIO were more interested in the symbol of participation in administration than they were in utilizing labor participation to put through a set of policies positively advocated by the unions. Only on the rarest occasions did the highest levels of authority in the AFL and CIO show much concern with WPB policy and those were situations in which the issues were rather directly related to union problems, such as national service legislation and the extent of permissible civilian production. The men from industry who controlled WPB policy regarded the labor offices not as impersonal administrators of a necessary WPB function but as partisan advocates of a labor point of view. As a consequence, the labor offices were seldom in on the ground floor of policy making and whatever functions were carried on by them were acquired by a process of elbowing themselves in, in hostile territory.

The fact that the unions achieved the status of an equal partner with employers and government in the War Labor Board was inherent in the purpose of the WLB—namely, the establishment of a mechanism and procedure in which labor-management disputes could be eliminated without the sanction of overt compulsion. But labor's functioning as an equal partner was sharply circumscribed by the charter of authority within which the WLB operated: wartime wage stabilization policy with its emphasis on minimizing wage increases. There was no discernible difference of consequence between AFL and CIO representatives in the WLB and most split decisions found all labor members invariably voting on the same side of an issue, except issues in which opposing claims of AFL and CIO were involved. In the major conflict on the board, the validity of the Bureau of Labor Statistics cost-of-living index as a statistical underpinning for the Little Steel formula, R. J. Thomas, then president of the UAW-CIO, and George Meany, secretary-treasurer of the AFL, issued a joint report.

The differences between unions with respect to the utilization of political action and the political apparatus of the state are differences in degree and articulateness. This is another way of saying that (1) no union can function in modern society without seeking in one way or other to influence government; (2) some unions utilizing government do it as part of a systematic philosophy; while others just do it as a matter of run-of-the-mill union activity. Although there are differences in temperament and technique and emphasis in utilizing government, there is little evidence of much difference in the substance of what the unions seek to get out of government. On federal and local domestic government policy there has been a remarkable unanimity of opinion among labor groups.

THE TAFT-HARTLEY LAW

With the passage of the Taft-Hartley law, also called the Labor-Management Relations Act of 1947, the character and temper of union attitudes and functioning will undergo substantial reorientation. Although this is being written shortly after the overriding of a presidential veto and, therefore, the full impact of the law can hardly be foretold with any precision, it may be safe to hazard a few general observations on how the aspects of union functioning considered in this book will be affected.

From a historical perspective, the Taft-Hartley law marks definitely the end of an era of federal government sympathy toward the labor movement which began with the passage of the Anti-Injunction Act of 1932—the Norris-La Guardia Act. By the same token, is marks governmental support of the ascendancy of the management interest in the collective bargaining relationship. The bent of this legislation was foreshadowed in large measure by the growing state anti-union legislation, the presidential appeal against the striking railroad workers in 1946, and the upholding of the injunction against the miners in 1947.

The union's task in organizing workers will be more difficult because the new legislation broadens the kinds of things management may say against unions. Management can balk union organization by demanding elections for bargaining representatives under terms more favorable to it than in the past. So-called independent or single-plant unions will be more powerful in contesting the organization drives of the AFL and CIO unions.

Since the Act intends to make it more difficult for guards, professional employees, and craftsmen to be part of the larger units, there may well be a deemphasis of all-inclusive industrial unionism. Jurisdictional strikes and secondary boycotts are unfair labor practices and are as well subject to injunctive restraint.

Offsetting the statutory provisions designed to lessen inter-union rivalry are those provisions which will encourage such rivalry: NLRB certifications of majority bargaining representatives can now be challenged annually; the craft unit as the appropriate bargaining unit now gets greater weight attached to it by the National Labor Relations Board.

Aspects of internal union administration become subject to federal regulation. The outlawing of the closed shop, the stringent regulation of the union shop, the ban against "excessive" initiation fees will alter the relationship of union officers to large sections of their membership with respect to discipline and financing. Information with respect to other details of union administration are required to be filed with the Department of Labor, although this will not make much difference since such information had been quite generally available before. In general, the lawyer in the union will occupy a more strategic position than he has ever occupied before. In general, control of leadership over rank and file activities will be greater because of the potential damage suits against the union likely to result from undisciplined actions of union members.

Certain significant features of the terms of collective bargaining—notably union security provisions and union rules—are either eliminated or regulated. Less important in the general run of collective bargaining terms, the administration of health and welfare funds will need to comply with specified legal requirements, to wit, bi-partisan administration, impartial settlement of disputes, and the acquisition of legal trust fund status. The extension of the collective agreement of foremen and supervisors will no longer be a subject of bargaining if management is not disposed to concede it voluntarily. Work rules of the "stand-by crew" variety are outlawed in the so-called "featherbedding" provision.

The *process* of collective bargaining is specifically subject to court influence in a way to reduce the informal settlements of disagreements. Grievances arising out of the interpretation of an agreement may conceivably be open to formal litigation by way of damage suits which either management or the union can initiate. The process of renewing agreements must now conform to provisions of law. In short, the rule of give-and-take of the conference room will have to give way to the rule of legal punctilio of the court room.

The union's capacity and effectiveness in the use of the strike weapon is drastically curtailed in a variety of ways. Large-scale strikes are now subject to injunctive proceedings. Strikes in connection with the expiration of an existing agreement may not be called without waiting periods. Jurisdictional and secondary boycott strikes are virtually outlawed as well as strikes protesting NLRB certifications. The use of mass picket lines and the reemployment rights of strikers are circumscribed in ways to lessen materially the strategic effectiveness of the strike in bringing an employer to terms.

In the union's political activities contributions and expenditures in support of or in opposition to aspirants for federal office are banned. This provision has been interpreted to apply to such support or opposition expressed in union publications financed by dues payments. Although the law's provisions are aimed to discourage union political activity, the ultimate result may well prove to give the rank and file union member a stake in politics which the ambitious activities of PAC in the past could never command.

The extracurricular activities of unions—specifically, workers' education, public relations, and research—will as a consequence undoubtedly be mobilized as they have never been before to seek repeal of the Taft-Hartley law and to solidify the union membership against the divisiveness between rank and file and leadership which the law seeks to promote.

Since there is much question of the constitutionality of the provision which in effect deprives unions with Communist leaders of their rights under the Taft-Hartley law, it is not possible at this writing even to suggest what the consequences are likely to be. The upsurge of anti-Communist sentiment within the ranks of many CIO unions, however, may well be abated in the face of what many anti-Communists will regard as a greater danger.

Union leadership will not be receptive to plowing new fields of co-operative relationships. It will revert increasingly to fighting (as we have heard in Sidney Hillman's words) "from a sense of outrage against exploitation" rather than from a "sense of social and industrial responsibility."

Generally, the whole range of union functioning and attitudes will be marked by turbulence, toughness, and bitterness. How much fury will be generated by the new law depends on whether the prevailing management strategy will seek to use the Taft-Hartley law as an instrument to break the unions. Aided by a depression of major proportions, the movement to undermine union power could be substantially accelerated.

With the best of management intentions, however, there will be little opportunity to cultivate that reflectiveness and long-run vision which may be regarded as the indispensable ingredients of stability. The net effect of the Taft-Hartley law can be to provoke the assorted and diverse interests which prevail in the unions to think and act more like a *movement* than they have ever done before.

EXTRACURRICULAR UNION ACTIVITIES

THE ASSORTED ACTIVITIES DISCUSSED IN THIS CHAPTER HAVE THE COM-
mon characteristic that they are not now part of the main stream of
union activities. As the heading suggests, they are regarded by the
unions as only incidental to their main purposes. However, the extent to
which these activities are tangential to the main union business will
vary from union to union. With a few unions, some of the activities
are integral phases of union functioning.

WORKERS' EDUCATION

Unions may carry on workers' education activities to develop a sense
of loyalty to the union, to the labor movement, and to progressive ideas
in general. When this approach to workers' education functions it
means, of course, that the union leadership itself must be responsive
to these motivations. This attitude is most common, therefore, to that
leadership which has brought a broad social and economic ideology
to its union activity and we find this motivation for workers' education
figuring prominently, for example, in the International Ladies' Garment Workers' Union with the strong Socialist traditions of its leadership, and more latterly the Auto Workers and the Textile Workers.

The ILG is perhaps the pioneer and has been the most persistent
evangelical force in promoting workers' education of this kind. Miss
Fannia Cohn, secretary of the ILG Educational Department, who has
been in the forefront of workers' education for many years, has for-

mulated this philosophy of workers' education in terms like these: "Workers' education should interpret the world upheaval as an historical phenomenon. It should analyze the clashes of ideas involved in this revolutionary struggle and should critically evaluate economic and social values from a national and international point of view." [1] Stemming from such an outlook, workers' education in the ILG had, consequently, emphasized classes in history, economics, and current events as part of its program. The ILG also sought to extend this kind of workers' education through its sponsorship of Brookwood Labor College, a resident labor school, which ceased functioning in 1938, but which probably exercised an important influence in shaping the outlook of the newer generation of union leadership coming into prominence after 1933. But for practical purposes, before the New Deal the ILG stood alone among the unions in providing substantial support to ideological workers' education. Later, Mark Starr, ILG educational director, became the most influential evangelist for workers' education within the labor movement and outside of it.

The influx into the unions of millions of workers with no attachment to unions—ideological, sentimental, or otherwise—has shifted the orientation of workers' education toward a somewhat more practical purpose. The Textile Workers (CIO) has been among the most effective practitioners of this more current emphasis. "The core of the [educational] department's work," reports the TWUA executive council, "has been its efforts to aid the more effective functioning of the local union leadership to obtain a better understanding of its problems in the TWUA and in the labor movement at large." [2]

Training of shop stewards has been the major point of concentration in these newer educational programs because

the steward body has aptly been called the nerve structure of the union, and unless it functions well the whole of the union suffers. To function well, however, shop stewards must know their duties. . . . None is born with this knowledge. It is acquired by experience, by study and through discussion of common issues raised in meetings and classes.[3]

The approach of the unions to steward training is highly matter-of-fact. In keeping with this matter-of-factness, the union steward training will take into account the situations in which workers will occasionally press unjustified grievances. Noticeably underemphasized is the symbol of the "boss" as a scheming, profit-hungry figure, which is a conception marking the more public union utterances.

Many unions have compressed the advice to stewards in a pocket-sized pamphlet. The style is terse and breezy. Invariably there are cartoon illustrations to highlight the major points.

The manual will generally open with a statement noting the importance of the steward's job and putting it as the very core of union functioning in collective bargaining. "The shop steward is the cornerstone of the local union" is the statement that opens the steward's manual prepared by the CIO Department of Education and Research. "Without you, and your fellow stewards," it goes on to say, "the best contract can be a dud. You give it life. You make it work. The smartest union leader cannot build the union alone. The most efficient business agent cannot make it run smoothly without your help."

A more elevated note is sounded in the steward's manual developed by an AFL federal local:

As a shop steward, yours is the job and the opportunity to make this industrial democracy function. You represent your fellow workers in the shop. You are the non-commissioned officers in the union army. You keep the union running smoothly and efficiently. As you carry out your duties effectively, you will represent your fellow unionists well, and the union will have value and meaning for them and will flourish.[4]

After the motivation, the manual sets forth the canons of "good stewardship." The CIO formulation is fairly typical:

KNOW YOUR CONTRACT

Know your contract! . . . To know if the company and the union are living up to their agreement, you must know what's in it. Unless you know what it says, you cannot tell a worker if he's right about it. And you certainly can't discuss it with management. . . .

KNOW YOUR DEPARTMENT

Understand each process thoroughly. Know which jobs are paid for by the hour and which by the piece. . . . Know the men in your department! You will soon learn which ones present grievances which are usually just; which ones are always beefing. You will find out which members are short-tempered or argumentative; which have upsetting outside problems; which ones present thoughtful ideas. . . .

KNOW YOUR GRIEVANCE PROCEDURE

The contract usually provides four or five steps for settling a grievance. This is much the way our judicial system carries appeals from lower to higher courts. Know these steps and be sure to keep within the time limit set for each of them. . . .

IS IT A GRIEVANCE?

Perhaps a worker complains about unfair distribution of work, while the facts show him to be mistaken. Or else he may feel entitled to promotion, although the seniority clauses in the contract prove him wrong. If the worker was mistaken in his facts or attitude, it is better to discover this yourself than to be corrected by the foreman. . . .

GET THE FACTS

Getting the evidence does not end with getting the workers' full story. Checking up means checking on the whole situation. . . .

GET IT IN WRITING

The written grievance, signed by the worker, backs up the steward when he argues the case. And the worker takes more care in stating his facts when he has to sign them. . . .

KEEP A RECORD

They can be used to check on whether the company has lived up to the settlement. Records of past settlements may guide the handling of similar future grievances. Thus they build up a valuable addition to the original contract. . . .[5]

The steward's manual will also develop pointers on "bargaining with the foreman." The St. Louis Retail Employees (CIO) advise: "Make every effort to settle as many grievances as possible at the first step." This approach is good strategy "from the union's point of view" and "makes for smoother industrial relations."

Here are some suggestions to the steward:

1. Follow the Rules of the Game. . . .
2. No Horse Trading. . . .
3. Positive, Not a Defensive Approach. . . .
4. Be a Good Listener. . . .
5. Stick to the Point! . . .
6. Disagree With Dignity. . . .
7. Keep a United Front on Your Own Side. . . .
8. Be Prompt. . . .
9. Don't Make Empty Threats. . . .
10. Follow Through. . . .
11. Finally, Keep Up With Your Cases! . . .[6]

When the unions go beyond the steward's handbook in their educational program, it may take the form of a weekend institute. The Textile Workers (CIO) Educational Department runs its institutes "at an isolated spot where the students are closely associated with one another." This union has found such isolated spots in "labor schools, church conference grounds, colleges and state universities and at a resort owned by one of our joint boards."

The program of the institute includes such courses as Making Your Union Work, Collective Bargaining, Labor History, Textile Unionism, Labor Economics, Public Speaking, and Parliamentary Law. The basic teaching method used is "classroom instruction. However, the teaching is completely informal and the discussion technique is used throughout." Some use has been made of "workshops." For example, in the collective bargaining course, "mock grievance and arbitration hearings are conducted." [7]

On the whole, the CIO unions have given greater support to this kind of workers' education than have the AFL unions. There has been, however, a considerable upsurge of recent interest among AFL unions in this direction; notably in several state federations like Kentucky and Colorado and in the Pulp and Sulphite Workers, which has given vigorous sponsorship to a series of zone conferences. The characteristic workaday turn which these conferences are giving to workers' education is illustrated by the subjects under discussion. In the session on "Running a Local Union" the conferences considered such problems as financial management of a local, handling local meetings, local records, and reports to headquarters. Under the heading "Daily Relations with Management" there were panel discussions on the handling of grievances, improvement of management in relationship to the union and "What should a local expect from an international representative?" [8]

Within the past few years, for the most part, the universities have developed programs of workers' education designed to train union officers. The University of Wisconsin pioneered in this field twenty-five years ago with a somewhat greater emphasis on the broader aspects of unionism. The Trade Union Fellowship at Harvard University has been at once the most ambitious and the most publicized program enlisting union support. AFL students have predominated in the Harvard program. In keeping with current trends, the emphasis has been on the "efficiency" aspects of union functioning rather than on ideology.

There is an enormous output of printed literature on the part of the newer unions designed to give the union member a sense of direction and enthusiasm for the things that are of importance to the union. This output is uniformly attractive in make-up and style, and all the attention-getting devices are utilized to make this literature accessible to the average member. Whether it is actually read by the workers for whom it is intended is a question which has not been given an authoritative answer. Much ingenuity has also been displayed in utilizing film strips and radio in making the ideas of unionism attractive to the rank and file of the membership.

Under the heading of workers' education, many unions have embarked on recreational programs which seek to reach the union membership that cannot be reached in any other activity outside of the shop. Here again the motive is to give these workers a sense of oneness with the union and to develop a sentiment of loyalty based on something more than the material benefits that belonging to the union provides. Unions operating in industries with a previous history of employer paternalism, like the telephone industry, attempt to sever the remaining extracurricular ties which the company has maintained through "old-timers'" dinners, picnics, and other social events, by organizing counterattractions but under explicit union sponsorship.

For many unions promotion of a workers' education program is a way of garnering laudable public comment on the statesmanship of the union leadership in educating its members. The participation of several unions in the university-sponsored workers' education programs has undoubtedly been motivated by this consideration.

Now, workers' education of the kind here outlined is far from being widespread. The vast majority of unions do not give substantial support to workers' education. In fact, only a relatively small minority of the workers who are members of unions have these programs available to them. For the most part, with the exception of the International Ladies' Garment Workers' Union, and the Workers Education Bureau, the AFL educational agency, such education as there is is of recent origin and urged by these unions which have strong attachments to New Deal outlook, and whose leadership has an active interest in issues of broad public policy.

Indifference or opposition to the kinds of workers' education outlined above by the bulk of union leadership in the United States is not something which it proclaims publicly. From informal discussion with union leaders who are thus disposed, it is possible to construct a composite union attitude which is something on the following order:

Education is not the job of a union—it is the job of the schools, and labor has always fought for adequate public education. When one of the classes is started, the first thing you know it becomes a forum for disgruntled elements to denounce the union administration. There is no reason why we should subsidize this kind of opposition to our leadership. The large majority of our membership doesn't want it anyway. Why, one time when we started a class, five workers showed up the first week and the next week only one showed up, and he was the local Communist. When they do attend these classes, all of these Johnny-come-latelies come to union meetings and think they know everything there is to know about running a union. No sir, our job is running a union and getting more money and shorter hours for our members—we don't have any time to play around with this nonsense.

Many AFL unions with strong craft ties have shown substantial interest and support in vocational education. The International Brotherhood of Electrical Workers has recently given an endowment to Marquette University to provide courses in electronics to its members. The unions in the printing trades and the barbers, for example, carry on their own vocational programs. Most of the craftsmen's unions work with employers and the trade schools in training apprentices.

RESEARCH

The research department is more often than not the only unchallenged niche of the intellectual in the unions. Research is not a new function in American unions, but its utilization has been accelerated in recent years by the widespread intervention of government in matters which concern the unions, the extended use of arbitration, and the growing technical complexity of the subject matter of collective bargaining.

The typical union research department—and here is one union function which runs true to type—prepares the economic data preparatory to collective bargaining negotiations; some researchers may even participate in the negotiations, as in the Amalgamated Clothing Workers, for example. If an issue is submitted to arbitration, the research department prepares the brief and may even present it, since some demonstration of expertness in matters concerned with cost of living, financial condition of the industry, and wage incentives may influence the arbitrator's decision.

In appearances before government tribunals, the union economist plays an important part. A significant section of the UAW argument in the General Motors fact-finding proceedings in 1945 was presented by Donald Montgomery, who is Walter Reuther's economic adviser. The Mid-West Labor Bureau argued the union's case in the fact-finding involving the Street Car Employees (AFL).

The functions of the typical research department are not normally of a policy-making character, but rather of a technical nature in making presentable the policy developed by leadership. The union leader argues that this is as it should be. Union policy must be determined by the elected officials, not by a hired hand.

A research department is sometimes revered by practical union leaders in the same way that an unschooled parent proudly exhibits his educated children. Many union officers will take great pride in the fact that there is somebody employed by the union who is a "Doctor" or a "college man." This sentiment may stem from the fact that when the union officers are called upon, as they frequently are, to comment on a wide range of public issues, the research director is relied upon to make the presentation.

The role of the economist in the unions, from the point of view of leadership, has nowhere been better put than by President Charles MacGowan of the Boilermakers.

In recent years the task confronting your International Officers has become increasingly difficult because of the remarkable changes made in the field of organized labor and the processes of collective bargaining. For example, the methods used in the negotiation of wages and working conditions, partially because of the enactment of laws and other governmental regulations and the activities of the various agencies of government, has undergone a tremendous revolution in the last few years. In the old days the local committee could handle negotiations and either arrive at an agreement or they called a strike, but with the enactment of the National Labor Relations Act and the Railway Labor Act and other labor laws of a regulatory nature, the situation has moved into an entirely different and alien field.

In present day negotiations we are required to meet our employers who have their lawyers and statisticians to present truck loads of factual information to bolster their claims of inability to meet our demands, so that unless we are prepared to substantiate our claims with counter-statistics and data our case is lost at its very inception. With the result that we are often required to utilize the services of men with university degrees, as well as statisticians, economists and attorneys, to prepare our cases. . . .

It is not sufficient for us to say that we do not like the trend that collective bargaining is taking. These things are facing us every day and we must be prepared to meet them. . . . With this thought in mind it is the purpose of the International, immediately after the first of the year, to establish a research department at headquarters.[9]

Labor's Public Relations

Within recent years the greatest advance in labor's extracurricular activities has been made in the field of public relations. The union's public relations programs seek to serve two purposes: (1) to sell the union's position on a given issue, and (2) the "institutional" purpose of creating a generally favorable climate for the union in the community. Indeed, many of the research and educational activities of unions are directed more toward their effect on the general public than to the problems of union functioning.

A strike is a particular situation which lends itself to the need for a public relations program. The organization of all the important strikes in the strike wave of 1945-1946 contained experienced publicity people. Paul Sifton handled the Washington end of the publicity for the UAW-GM strike. Sifton, an experienced newspaperman, organized a committee of distinguished citizens to hear the case of the GM strikers, which then issued a report favorably disposed to the union's position. Even before the steel strike, the Steel Workers utilized paid network radio time to set forth the union's case for a wage increase. In the Electrical Workers' strike (UE-CIO) veterans who were also strikers sold apples on stands bearing signs, "We are striking because we don't want to go back to selling apples." Expertly prepared advertisements in the large metropolitan newspapers became a common practice; a cartoon in the *New Yorker* magazine depicts a collection of heavy-set, cigar-smoking, board-of-director-type gentlemen listening to one of their number saying, "The need for action is urgent. We can't afford to let the union beat us to that half-page ad in the *New York Times*." There is no doubt that this emphasis on favorable public sentiment yielded fruitful results in the first wave of the 1945-1946 strikes. There were other factors which accounted for the absence of a substantial vigilantist attitude, but certainly of major importance was the systematic way in which the unions went about cultivating community sentiment.

The ILG, as in other matters in this area of activity, is outstanding in the AFL in seeking to influence public opinion in strikes in a professional way. The ILG's *Handbook of Trade Union Methods* illustrates three Boston girls, one of them on a white horse, strikers dressed in the costumes of Knights of the Crusade with simulated shields headed "To All Cotton Garment and Underwear Workers—The Crusade Is On Against The Sweat Shop—Low Wages—Long Hours."

The institutional public relations of unions spring from the desire to be an accepted and reputable group in the community at large and to develop a favorable sentiment toward labor by the community. The educational director of the CIO devotes much of his time setting forth the position of the CIO before church groups over the country, and the pamphlet output of the CIO has much the same general purpose. The Steel Workers employs full time a person who acts as a liaison and interpreter of labor's aspirations to the organized churches. Mark Starr, ILG educational director, devotes a considerable amount of his time talking to and writing for nonlabor groups. The ILG in general is responsive to public relations and undertakes many extracurricular activities with an eye toward its reception by the newspapers and writers in general. To be noted in this connection is the increasing interest in FM radio by unions. The Amalgamated Clothing Workers, the Auto Workers, the ILG have all made application before the Federal Communications Commission to operate such stations.

Within recent times the AFL and some of its affiliates are paying greater attention to the need for stimulating a sympathetic public opinion in their behalf. The AFL Building Service Employees maintains a full-time public relations director who has been noticeably successful in directing public attention to the union and its president, William McFettridge. The AFL Executive Council pointed with pride in 1946 to an AFL series of radio programs designed to "debunk most of the attacks against labor and in creating a favorable state of public opinion toward the American Federation of Labor."[10] The Minnesota State Federation of Labor has organized a public relations department. The Machinists (not, as this is written, in the AFL) is issuing a weekly newspaper aimed for general public consumption.

THE LABOR PRESS

Unions support periodicals of their own to provide the union leadership with an outlet for its opinions, to give recognition to the rank-and-file activists in the union, to air the union's position on all matters, and because it is traditional for unions to have a "journal."

The extent to which the union periodical devotes space to the opinions of union leadership depends in part on the temperament of the leaders. The opinions of Dan Tobin figure prominently in the columns of the *International Teamster* on a wide variety of subjects. In one issue, selected at random, Mr. Tobin delivered himself on the following subjects: "Radicalism Is Sweeping World—Free Enterprise Can Survive Only Ten Years in U.S.," "Tell Congress to Kill BBH Bill," "Chicago Independents Belong in IBT—Division Among Truck Drivers Is Injurious," and "AFL Won't Work with Red Labor—Executive Council Refuses to Change Its Position" (this in even reference to the World Trade Union organization).[11] Most union leaders are less versatile than Mr. Tobin and generally fill only one column. R. J. Thomas used to have something to say in every issue of the *Auto Worker;* Matthew Woll, in the issue which comes to hand, editorializes in the *American Photo-Engraver* on "Labor's Post-War Tasks," "Stalin's International Victories," "Labor Triumphs in Britain," and "A New Charter for John Bull." [12] In a full page in tabloid, the *Fur and Leather Worker,* President Ben Gold ventures the opinion that "though the war is over there is no peace," passes judgment on "Imperialist Exploiters" and "the Rankins and the Bilbos, mouthpieces of the reactionaries." [13]

Traditional features in the older AFL journals are the monthly reports (in considerable detail) of officers, international representatives, and organizers. In the *International Molders and Foundry Workers Journal,* over ten solid pages are normally devoted to these reports. Thus, it is possible to learn that Seventh Vice-President Voit during the month visited Taunton, Massachusetts, where he met Secretary Grosser and set prices on work in a steel shop . . . Cleveland, Ohio, where he appeared before the Appeals Division of the Regional WLB . . . Chicago, "to attend an NLRB hearing on a case where the CIO is attempting a raid on our members" . . . Aurora, Illinois, and attended a meeting of Local Union 137, and "as the month closed, was on his way to Louisville, Kentucky, to take up a matter with Local Union No. 16." [14]

In addition, most of these journals carry detailed correspondence from the locals on many varied topics. In the *Paper Makers Journal* for October, 1945, correspondent Marco Marcoceni of Iroquois Local No. 109 discusses postwar problems, R. J. Amlotte of Cloquet Local No. 128

judges that the proposed amalgamation between the Paper Makers Union and the Pulp and Sulphite local "is a fine step," and George E. Contoes of Border Local No. 247 reports that members had enjoyed the Labor Day outing which featured "an excellent chicken dinner," and cigars, and "Brother Chamberlain's excellent accordion playing of lively jigs." Many of these journals also feature technical information relating to their respective trades. Outstanding in this connection are the *Lithographers Journal* and the *Electrical Workers Journal*.

The labor periodicals which are in newspaper format are more likely to carry news of interest broader than that of immediate union concern. The labor newspapers are published by international unions and by regional labor groups. In addition, both AFL and CIO issue periodical publications. The AFL issues the *American Federationist*, which contains articles of general coverage in a magazine format. The *CIO News* is a weekly tabloid profusely illustrated. A few smaller CIO internationals get out their own editions of the *CIO News*.

From a journalistic standpoint, the general run of the labor press is inferior to the average commercial newspaper or periodical. In part, the lack of journalistic expertness is due to the prevailing opinion in union circles that editing a labor paper does not require a measure of professional competence and can, therefore, be executed by any literate union official who can use scissors and paste pot. An illustrative exception among the "journal" types is the *International Teamster*, which is enlivened by Dan Tobin's forceful comments on everything that moves him. In the international union newspaper type, the *Guild Reporter*, of the American Newspaper Guild, the *Hat Worker* and the *Shipyard Worker* are printed in readable type, attractively made up, and generally carry items and articles which are interestingly written. *Labor*, the weekly newspaper owned jointly by the railroad unions, stands out because of its fresh and vital coverage of Washington news. Among the local labor newspapers, *Kenosha* (Wis.) *Labor*, which is also unusual in that it is a joint AFL and CIO publication, the *Southern California Teamster*, and the *Wage Earner* are outstanding. The last-named is not, strictly speaking, the organ of a union but is published by the Association of Catholic Trade Unionists in Detroit and is indispensable to anyone who seeks to understand the American labor movement.

The American labor press is essentially highly partisan journalism; not only partisan to the labor point of view on public affairs but partisan to the administration in power in the particular union. A few labor papers like the *Guild Reporter,* the *Typographical Union Journal,* and the *Pilot* (National Maritime Union) permit the expression of conflicting opinions within their columns. On subjects that matter, the union journals are, therefore, the organs of the administration in power, and only in extremely rare cases does one get an objective account of a controversial intra-union issue. The extent to which the labor press is partisan to a general labor point of view is attributable to the strong conviction of union leadership that the commercial press is "kept" and cannot be trusted to give fair treatment of union policies. The unwillingness of the group in authority to expose possible points of vulnerability to rival union groups and to employers is largely responsible for the aversion of the labor press to the airing of its internal dissensions for public consumption.

INTERNATIONAL AFFAIRS

The organizations currently involved in the labor aspects of international affairs are the International Labor Organization and the World Federation of Trade Unions. The ILO is a quasi-governmental body, the only surviving legacy of the League of Nations, and soon to be absorbed in the United Nations. The President of the United States appoints the labor, employer, and government delegates to the ILO. The AFL has insisted that it alone is entitled to representation on ILO as the most representative national labor center in the United States and has refused to participate if formal representation is granted the CIO.

The WFTU is the international organization of labor that succeeded the International Federation of Trade Unions. The International Federation of Trade Unions found its origins in 1901 as a by-product of the Socialist International, the international of the Socialist political parties. For a period after World War I the AFL withdrew from the IFTU, only to rejoin in 1937. The IFTU refused to admit the Russian unions on the ground that they were not free unions, nor would the AFL permit the admittance of the CIO.

The WFTU is not a governmental mechanism although it had asked for official recognition by the United Nations. In an important sense, however, WFTU seeks to be an implementation in the field of international labor relations of the interests of the respective governments whose labor movements are represented. This fact is recognized by a section of the February, 1945, Conference Manifesto, which says in part that "By a continuation of the close collaboration and decisive action by which the governments and peoples of the United Nations have brought victory within their reach, our World Conference believes the new and onerous responsibilities which the future will bring, can be adequately met, and all difficulties overcome." [15]

The CIO supported the formation of the WFTU for several reasons. First, as has been observed in other connections, the temper of CIO leadership has been characteristically more "world-minded." Second, the CIO has harbored a deep resentment toward the AFL for keeping it out of international labor conclaves of one kind or another. Third, the spur given to the idea of the WFTU by the Communists within the CIO who supported it because it was also part of Soviet policy.

The AFL has refused to participate in the WFTU for many of the reasons which impelled the CIO to support it. As a matter of policy, the AFL has refused to participate voluntarily in joint movements with the CIO. The AFL leadership is opposed to Communists either domestic or international. Only free trade unions can appropriately participate in a nongovernmental international labor organization, the AFL has argued, and that makes the participation of the Russian unions in the WFTU improper. Finally, it must be recalled that the AFL had never been an enthusiastic participant in the IFTU because of its Socialist complexion, although now that the threat of Communist domination of Europe's labor movements is serious, it is giving its support, financial and otherwise, to the Socialist anti-Communist elements in the European labor movements.

The AFL on its own has in the past few years embarked on a program of international activities which is unprecedented in scope. Under the leadership of Matthew Woll, David Dubinsky, and Robert J. Watt, the AFL program has been vigorously anti-Communist, but it also has sought to give positive aid to the anti-Communist Socialist and Social Democratic elements in the European labor movement. During the war, the AFL sponsored a country-wide tour for Haakon Lie, a Norwegian Socialist leader, in order to raise funds in support of the various non-Communist labor movements. In the postwar period, the AFL is supporting at least two permanent representatives in Europe who have responsibility for maintaining liaison between the AFL and the European Socialist and labor movement. At the 1946 AFL convention much time was devoted to the presentation of representatives of Latin-American labor as well as speeches relating to broad international policy. From the kinds of people who are active in AFL international affairs in the United States and its relationships abroad, it is clear that the AFL is firmly following a policy of supporting the Socialist anti-Communist in the international labor scene.

This policy is significant because in the past radical ideologies of all shades were indiscriminately attacked by most AFL leaders. Indeed, the AFL had refused to maintain its affiliation to the International Federation of Trade Unions between 1914 and 1937 in large part on the ground that

through the issuance of appeals and proclamations the executive body of the international federation had committed the federation to a revolutionary principle, to which the American Federation of Labor is and always has been uncompromisingly opposed.[16]

A major element in the AFL's return to international labor activity has been the gradual perception that something more than a vocal anti-Communist attitude would be required to combat the sway of communism in the world; to wit, a positive program of moral and financial support of the groups who could effectively combat the rise of communism; the Socialists composed the only group who could meet that qualification. To a few leaders in the AFL of Socialist extraction, notably David Dubinsky, this was not a new strategy but its implementation had to wait for the support of a man like Matthew Woll, who represented the major ideological tendencies after World War I in the AFL more authentically than Dubinsky.

INSURANCE AND BENEFIT ACTIVITIES

Provision for some protection against the hazards of death and sickness are indigenous features of the older unionism. In 1887 the Cigar Makers asserted that one of the objectives of unionism was "to provide a system of benefit payments which saves the workers the humiliation and degrading influence that surrounded charity and the poorhouse."[17] Insurance against a pauper's grave was a strong influence in the formation of the early unions. This interest has continued, until today the insurance and welfare activities of the older unions are big business and represent many millions of dollars in investments. In the words of the Electrical Workers (AFL), "the belief that brotherhood and benefits are inseparable has prevailed throughout the life of the union." [18] Moreover, it was difficult for many workers to get regular insurance protection at reasonable rates and they sought a solution to this problem through mutual effort.

The railroad unions and the printing trades unions count their insurance activities as among their major activities. Much of the convention time and of the journals in the railroad unions is consumed by the discussion of insurance problems. The Trainmen provides a standard variety of insurance features: in life insurance a member may choose from full life, 20-payment life, endowment, annuity, and term insurance; as well as disability, accident, and health types of insurance. Alexander Whitney, president of the Trainmen, notes in this connection that "the Brotherhood of Railroad Trainmen owed its start to the deep-rooted desire of railroad workers to protect themselves and their families against the hazards to their life and limb while on the job." [19] The Photo-Engravers provides strike benefits of $25 a week, unemployment benefits ranging from $10 to $25 a week, sick benefits from $10 to $25 a week, and special hospitalization for tuberculosis, $200 death benefits, and a $1,000 life insurance policy. The International Ladies' Garment Workers' Union maintains the Union Health Center in New York to provide prepaid medical care for its members and to administer the medical features of the sick benefit systems of the unions.

The tendency in the newer unions has been against incorporating elaborate benefit schemes in their dues structure, and even some of the older unions have established a "nonbeneficial" category of membership. For the most part the newer unions in the CIO have been organizing production workers rather than craftsmen, and these unions have used their relatively low dues as a selling point in their organizing campaigns. Moreover, these unions grew up in a period when statutory unemployment and old-age and survivors' insurance programs developed, and union-sponsored benefit programs have therefore been less attractive. Strike benefits in the mass production industries would be impossible when it is realized that an industry-wide, or even a company-wide, strike may involve tens of thousands and hundreds of thousands of workers. There has also been a noticeable tendency for collective agreements to incorporate employer-union health and welfare programs.

There are various extracurricular activities which have not been discussed under previous headings. In this connection there may be cited the co-operative housing and labor banking activities of the Amalgamated Clothing Workers, the wartime development of active union participation in the welfare and fund-raising activities of the local community chests. From this latter has evolved on the part of some CIO unions an interest in what is called "union counseling," under which program union people are trained to help their fellow members utilize the social services of the community. This activity served a good purpose during the postwar strike wave when, in Chicago particularly, a functioning mechanism was established to meet the needs of strikers' families for assistance in securing relief and unemployment compensation. As has been observed in the other extracurricular activities, the CIO unions have tended to demonstrate a more considerable interest in these phases of union activities than have the AFL unions.

The contrast between AFL and CIO unions is more marked in these extracurricular aspects than in any other aspect of union functioning. The contrast may be accounted for in large measure by the fact that most of the important AFL unions struck their roots in an era when unionism had little time or opportunity to concern itself with anything more than protecting itself against destruction by a violently hostile environment. The battle for survival generated a certain hardness and cynicism toward activities which could not immediately be translated into increased membership or a better agreement. The CIO unions, on the other hand, found their origins in a period of social reform and its accompanying responsiveness to ideas and the techniques of getting ideas across to the total community.

With the exception of the benefit phase of what we are calling here extracurricular activities, the stock in trade of these other phases—workers' education, research, public relations, labor journalism, and international affairs—is essentially ideas, not action.

Now there is evidence that the AFL unions are becoming increasingly sensitive to the fact that the hold which CIO unions have on liberally disposed labor groups has been induced by the cultivation of these extracurricular activities and that complexities of union functioning in an era of government intervention require some utilization of these devices.

UNION LEADERSHIP

IMPERATIVES OF UNION LEADERSHIP

UNION LEADERSHIP IN THE UNITED STATES IS CHARACTERIZED BY CERtain basic imperatives—a kind of hard core of qualities common to all union leadership. The first imperative is the emphasis on maximizing the favorable position of the union members in the short run; or, more tersely, "more here and now."

More here and now means the maintenance of the maximum possible number of job opportunities for the union membership in the discernible present. It means more pay for less work. It means, too, that since the effectuation of these objectives depends upon the existence of a profitable enterprise, union leadership has a real interest in maintaining an optimum profitability for the business that provide jobs for the members of the union. Optimum in this context signifies the lowest profit consistent with providing the most jobs at the highest pay and the best working conditions during a given period.

General adherence to a political and economic philosophy which may appear to run counter to the dictates of more here and now has nothing to do with the validity of this generalization. Thus, both John Lewis, an avowed Republican, and David Dubinsky, a leader of Socialist extraction, have found it necessary to lend funds to faltering enterprises in their industries. Both the Cigar Makers—the citadel of union conservatism—and the Amalgamated Clothing Workers—with more liberal aspirations—were much concerned with promoting what appeared to them more profitable price arrangements for their respective industries. The Communist-sympathetic National Maritime Union manifests the same concern over protecting its own members in the face of an influx of "green men" who can't find jobs elsewhere—the "trip card men" [1] —as any so-called conservative union shows in taking care of its full-fledged members as against "permit" holders.

Another set of imperatives of union leadership is related to the nature of the union as a democratic institution. Democratic institutions require politicians to make democracy manageable on a day-to-day basis, since nose counting is out of the question in all but the smallest aggregates. The union leader must therefore be a politician, which in the labor movement as in any other democratic enterprise means that he must be accessible, personable, and remember to help his friends and supporters.

The way the international president carries on his work reflects one facet of the political character of the modern union. The union president is invariably accessible to the lowliest of local union officials and even to rank-and-file members in a way that would be fantastic for an important executive of a corporation. If the international office of the union is located in an area of great concentration of union member-ship—like Akron for rubber, Detroit for automobiles, and New York for the garment trades—the president's office is the forum for the airing of every grievance from issues of major union policy to political squab-bles among local union officers. As a result, an international union presi-dent is constantly in the midst of matters of immediate urgency and has little opportunity for what some would consider the orderly administration of union business.

If the local officers and membership cannot come to the president, they insist that he come to them, as the Paper Makers' survey complains:

Some local unions as well as some employers occasionally approve the arbitrary position of demanding that the International President must come to their locality and personally do the job to be done. Granting that they are sincere and the problem serious, the fact still remains that there are many serious problems confronting Headquarters every day. While the President is away, work accumulates. Reports of field men continue to flow in; ques-tions from field men, local unions, employers, requiring his personal atten-tion remain unanswered; important decisions are not forthcoming; the pile of mail and telegrams on his desk mounts ever higher. The net result is that while the President is away from his office handling one local problem, probably ten others are suffering from lack of attention.

The International President should be in a position to devote his time and talents to the overall picture, and not be required to negotiate agreements, settle controversies, organize new locals, handle local complaints, etc.[2]

A further imperative of union leadership, which stems from the political character of unionism, is the fact that leadership almost always works its way up from the ranks. The personal following that is the indispensable ingredient of leadership is not at the beck and call of any Johnny-come-lately, and is only available to the men who have worked their way up within the union. C. Wright Mills, who has made an interesting analysis of the vital statistics of union leaders concludes that "the majority of these leaders have worked as laborers in the industries with which they later dealt as union officials; the majority took their first union jobs with a local." [3]

A few thumbnail sketches of representative figures in American union leadership reinforce this point:

William Green—coal miner, 1889-1900; United Mine Workers subdistrict president, 1900-1906; district president, 1906-1910; member Ohio Senate, 1910-1912; secretary-treasurer United Mine Workers, 1912-1924; member executive council, 1913-1924; AFL president, 1924——

Harvey Brown—machinist apprentice, 1902-1905; journeyman machinist, 1905-1911; Machinists Union business representative, 1911-1921; Machinists Union vice-president, 1921-1938; Machinists Union president, 1938 ——; AFL executive council member, 1940-1945.

William Hutcheson—journeyman carpenter, 1902; union business agent, 1902-1913; international vice-president, 1913-1918; international president, 1915——

Alexander F. Whitney—railroad news agent, 1888-1890; brakeman, 1890-1901; chairman general grievance committee Brotherhood of Railroad Trainmen, 1901-1907; vice-president, 1907-1928; president, 1928——

James Carey—inspector radio manufacturing plant, 1929-1934; assisted in organizing AFL federal labor union, 1933; AFL general organizer, 1934; president United Electrical and Radio Workers (CIO), 1936-1941; secretary-treasurer CIO, 1942——

Reid Robinson—member AFL Newsboys Union, 1919; mine worker, 1926-1933; secretary Butte Miners Union, 1933; president local union, 1934-1935; international president Mine, Mill and Smelter Workers, 1936——

A few union leaders have not come up from the ranks: Donald Henderson of the Food and Tobacco Workers, who came into the labor movement via the Columbia University faculty and radical politics; A. Philip Randolph of the Sleeping Car Porters, whose interest in the union stemmed from activity in the Socialist and race relations movements; Ralph Helstein, who rose to the office of president of the Packinghouse Workers from his position as general counsel to the organization.

The rapid growth of many CIO unions evoked two unusual trends with respect to what Mills calls the career pattern of leadership: first, the comparative youthfulness of the CIO top leadership, the average of which was 42 in 1945 as compared to 55 for the AFL. The second trend is to be found in the fact of leadership transferability, most notably in the case of the Steel Workers where Murray, David MacDonald, Van Bittner, and Clinton Golden had already established their union backgrounds in organizations other than steel and, with the exception of the last named, all in the Miners. This is, of course, a reflection of the fact that John Lewis had put UMW officers in charge of the steel industry organizing campaign.

Finally, among the political imperatives of union leadership is the need, first, to build a following and, second, to maintain it once leadership status has been achieved. The intensity of the pressure to build what in less elegant language may be called a machine varies directly with the level of leadership. Frequently local union leadership may not be highly prized and little effort may be required in getting office and holding it. The Paper Makers' investigation notes:

. . . our locals sometimes have trouble finding a member who will accept an office. There are many reasons why men decline nominations. They may be "too busy," "live too far away," "working wrong shift," or any one of a dozen other alibis. They may suspect an office in the union will hurt their chances for promotion or maybe they would rather be able to criticize the other fellow than have to take some of it themselves. A few sincerely believe they are not qualified.[4]

The Philadelphia correspondent for the *Coopers International Journal* asserts with great feeling:

To those members who at one time or another held office in a local union, the writer can say that he certainly realizes what it means to be an officer and not sit out in the quorum and criticize most anything that officers are trying to do. It is not an easy job to be an officer of a local union.

A little more appreciation on the part of the members would be a great encouragement. Above all, dignity and respect that goes with it is more important than anything else.[5]

Where the president, secretary-treasurer, business agent in larger locals are full-time officials and are therefore paid, the position is somewhat more competitive. Although the salary is not much more than a better paid worker receives in the shop, there is more security in the better established locals and the character of the work has a somewhat higher social status.

The systematic character of the efforts involved in building a following depends, of course, on the extent to which there exist rival groups within the union. In any event, union leadership takes these groups into account. How much account depends on how well organized and articulate these groups are.

Union groups or factions may divide themselves geographically, by national origin, by religious groups, by industry segments, and by ideology. They are either in the form of informal groupings or well-organized and disciplined factions. They may be part of an administration coalition or in active opposition to the administration.

Luigi Antonini's position as first vice-president of the International Ladies' Garment Workers' Union is in part a recognition of his standing with respect to the large Italian membership in the union. Unions with Canadian membership will invariably give this condition appropriate recognition by providing for some representation on the executive board. When the Pulp and Sulphite Workers set up a research and educational department generally, a special section was set up for Canada. Philip Murray, whenever he appoints over-all CIO committees, will see that representation is provided for the anti-Communists, the middle-of-the-roaders on the issue, and the pro-Communist groups. It is a common practice for unions functioning in interracial industrial situations in the South to give representation to Negro members among the various union offices. Probably the only way in which the Hosiery Workers can be kept within the Textile Workers-CIO is to give them virtual autonomy as a group. The fact that Albert Fitzgerald is president of the Electrical Workers-CIO represents in part a concession by the dominant Communist-minded leadership to the strong Catholic group within the union. Union leadership will also maintain its position by playing a balance of power strategy, as did R. J. Thomas who, with no following in his own right, managed to hold the presidency of the UAW-CIO for eight years by neutralizing the opposing forces of Walter Reuther and George Addes.

On the other extreme is the leadership that is in such undisputed control of a situation that the problem of cultivating various groups is reduced to the bare minimum of rewarding friends and punishing enemies. In this category would fall George Berry of the Pressmen, Hutcheson of the Carpenters, the late Sidney Hillman of the Clothing Workers, Lewis of the Miners, and Philip Murray in the Steel Workers.

Thus far we have been discussing the *imperatives* of union leadership—"more here and now," rising from the ranks, and building and maintaining a following. But these imperatives are rarely discernible in union leaders in the simple and unadorned fashion in which they have been described here. Rather, union leadership expresses itself through many kinds of temperaments and personalities; the imperatives constitute the hard core common to all leadership however a particular union leader reveals himself as a total personality.

The "Good Trade Unionist"

Perhaps the most common expression of union leadership is epitomized by what in labor circles is called a "good trade unionist." The good trade unionist makes no pretensions to a co-ordinated philosophy, but does his union job well because he believes it is worth doing for its own sake. The good trade unionist is honest, devoted to his job, and thinks in terms of a labor movement rather than in terms of his own union alone. The union is for him a way of living, although like most other Americans he does many other things. He is pretty much run of the mill, so he doesn't attract much attention outside of his own circle. This kind of union leader rarely gets to be higher than perhaps the president of his local central labor body.

The question "What is a good trade unionist?" was put to a group of organized telephone workers. This is how they formulated the answer:

a. Recognize a picket line.
b. Do not discriminate between color, race, creed, sex, or minority groups.
c. Patronize union labor.
  1. Advertising to other workers the benefits of belonging to a labor organization.

2. Unifying effect in labor movement.

3. Shows spirit of mutual aid.

d. Shows management he profits from unionism.

e. Does not report another worker to employer.

f. Abides by majority decision.

g. Does not carry internal union disputes to public.

h. Keeps union affairs from management.

i. Be sure information about union is complete and correct before released to members.

j. Settle disputes and grievances between members within the union.

k. Organize the unorganized. Every unorganized worker retards the progress of organized workers.

l. Participate in civic affairs.

m. Bring the principles of unionism to the public.[6]

In some degree every union officer has something of the good trade unionist in him. The labor movement in this respect provides a fairly unique phenomenon. Unionism is not the only way of earning a living, but for most of the people who hold paid or volunteer office it is also a cause with values and ethics which are on a somewhat higher plane than those exacted of a purely vocational undertaking.

As a practical matter, the idea of unionism as a cause has its advantages and disadvantages. Its advantages are that it is possible for the organization to command a measure of devotion from its leadership which has little counterpart in more businesslike enterprises. But, by the same token, the practitioners of unionism are held up to standards of social and economic behavior which are normally not applied to more businesslike undertakings.

RUGGED UNIONISM

Further along the gamut of temperamental shades and overtones in which union leadership expresses itself is what might be characterized as "rugged unionism." By and large, the union leadership that takes on this attitude matured in an economic and cultural environment which demanded toughness and hardness if its unions were to survive. It is indifferent to the effects of its actions on what passes for public opinion because public opinion is regarded as manufactured by forces unsympathetic to unions anyway. The major source of strength of the union, according to this outlook, is its ability "to pull its men off the job." The rugged unionist is unimpressed with the relevance of broad issues of national and international policy to the life of the union.

James C. Petrillo, president of the American Federation of Musicians, and before that head of an important Chicago local, typifies this kind of leadership to a marked degree. Petrillo has one consuming interest as a union leader and that is that no place of amusement which can pos‑ sibly use a musician should be permitted to get along without one. In recent years he has spearheaded campaigns to get the radio and record‑ ing industries to contribute toward the cost of the technological unem‑ ployment they create through royalty payments, banning musical pro‑ grams originating in foreign countries, and the presentation of radio musical programs simultaneously over FM and standard stations.

Discussing the foreign radio ban before a musicians' local meeting, Petrillo said:

There's the tariff. The manufacturers' lobby to keep cheap material out of the country. There's the immigration law. The Government, everybody, protects themselves against labor. Why the hell should we be exempt?

You know what happened to Swiss watches. They stopped some from coming into this country. We're trying to see that foreign musicians, in person or by air, don't get our jobs.

For a long time the conductors came from London, all the stars from Europe. They'd stay here several months, make a lot of dough, and then go home. I said, huh, you boys get into the union. There was a hell of a holler from the long‑haired boys about that. Well, what about it?

Then all the Heifetzes, the artists who play in front of the orchestra, didn't belong to the union. They said they didn't need a musician's card. We said, all right, if you don't need a card, go play by yourselves. They're all in now.[7]

Referring to the controversy over recordings, Petrillo said:

The President wired me on that one. The wire said, "Your loss would be the country's gain." I said, if that were true, it would be granted. But it would be a gain for only a few manufacturers. We won that one.

I'll tell you where a lot of these bangs I get come in. There are 900 radio stations, 300 owned by the press. Every time you make a move against radio, the press (not all of it, though) goes for you. You won't hear any musicians saying anything against me.

[The future of the union] looks good. The fact they go out on strike in the recording matter for twenty‑seven months without anyone drawing a string across a violin shows it's a strong organization. That cost some of the big band leaders $100,000 and they did not squawk.

"It's this way," Petrillo said another time, "the average band receives in the neighborhood of $1,500 for a recording. By the time the record has been discarded it has wiped out around $1,500,000 worth of business for living musicians. Can anyone explain why musicians should help destroy themselves? Hey?" [8]

Petrillo is ruthless and hard with his members as well as with employers. Heavy fines and even expulsions penalize members for violating union rules, and he has little patience with democratic procedure. He stays in office because he has been successful in getting higher wages for musicians than anybody else has been able to get. In the spring of 1946 Petrillo succeeded in securing a contract requiring the motion picture producers to increase their employment of musicians by 44 percent, and raising the musicians' annual wage by 33 percent, from $5,200 to $6,916. This increase was the highest negotiated in a period marked by significantly high wage increases.

Dave Beck of the Pacific Northwest Teamsters demonstrates the same single purposeness in the pursuit of his union goals. In the nature of the fact that the Teamsters occupy a strategic position in modern industry, he operates in a much wider arena than does Petrillo. Beck shares with Petrillo the indifference to what the community at large may think of his practices, although the business community regards Beck as a stabilizing influence because he is considered a bulwark against an incipient communism on the West Coast, led by Harry Bridges, and because he uses union action as a device for eliminating what he thinks is unfair competition. An aspect of Beck's philosophy of union objectives, summed up in the following, is clear and pointed:

There are too many filling stations in Seattle. More are threatened. We are going to close some of them. First I advise promoters against starting new stations. If that doesn't work, the Teamsters' Union will simply refuse to serve them.[9]

In action, Beck approaches problems in the same vigorous and decisive fashion. Jurisdictional claims of rival unions, CIO, and businessmen who won't go along with what somebody called "Beck's voluntary NRA" are treated with forceful dispatch. One of Beck's supporters told Richard Neuberger, "Dave doesn't believe in compromise, but neither does he believe in suicide."

The kind of union leadership demonstrated by Beck and Petrillo regards unions as business enterprises without humanitarian trimmings.

Both men are illustrious practitioners and perhaps somewhat more sensational in their tactics, but much of American union leadership in the building trades and the metal trades, say, embody in essence this approach to unionism. Their reasoning, when they think about it in a conscious way, is that their methods are perfectly in accord with the ingenious and determined pursuit of gain that is the hallmark of American business.

Although John L. Lewis of the Miners has fundamentally much in common with Beck and Petrillo, he is in a class by himself because his aspirations are much more ambitious in scope than those of either of the other two. Perhaps Huey Long didn't foretell the future very exactly, but most people who have written and talked about Lewis would agree with the general idea, if not with Huey's precise formulation, when he told a reporter once, "Old Huey thinks this John L. will be the most powerful man in America unless I get there first." [10] Lewis evidently enjoys speculation as to his motives. James Wechsler relates an incident in which Lewis, in an expansive moment, asked rhetorically, "What makes me tick? Is it power I'm after, or am I a St. Francis in disguise, or what?" [11] No answer seems to have been forthcoming.

If Mr. Lewis is in doubt as to what makes him tick, the record seems to provide a more certain answer. The milestones in Lewis's post–1932 career—his leadership of the CIO, the break with Roosevelt, his subsequent isolationism, the defection from the CIO, the determined prosecution of the coal strikes during the defense and war period, the inclusiveness of his District 50 organizational drives, and his return to the AFL —seem to have been pointed in the direction of making John Lewis the center of things. Lewis has never, it can be seen, been one to share the front seat of power and authority, as his leadership in the Miners and the CIO demonstrates rather effectively.

Lewis has followed no consistent pattern in pursuit of power as to where and from whom he has sought his supporters. In building the CIO he established working relationships with men whom he had bitterly suppressed in the Miners' Union—men like John Brophy and Powers Hapgood—and with the Communists. Returning to the AFL, he has found his most cordial allies in Hutcheson of the Carpenters, whom he had engaged in a violent scuffle on the floor of the 1935 AFL convention, and Dubinsky of the ILG, who had left the original committee because he would not tolerate Lewis's one-man rule. The paradox is heightened by the fact that it would be harder to find two men further apart in their conceptions of the purposes of unionism than Hutcheson and Dubinsky.

Lewis employs no public relations counsels to present the miners' side of controversies or to glamorize the head man, himself. Instead, Lewis invests his actions with an element of drama and lets the molders of opinion pick up from there. Important moves seem to be timed not only for their strategic effect but for their dramatic effect. At 10:00 P.M. on Sunday, April 30, 1943, President Roosevelt was scheduled to talk to the people of the United States and denounce John L. Lewis for his studied aim to cripple the war effort by calling a coal strike for the next day. At 9:30 Lewis called the waiting reporters into his office and announced that by agreement with Secretary of Interior Ickes the strike had been called off for two weeks. When an Associated Press reporter attempted to leave the conference after Lewis had revealed that he was calling off the strike, Lewis asserted that no one would be permitted to leave the room until he was through. Only at 9:45, fifteen minutes before the President was scheduled to go on the air, the news of the strike postponement went on the air. James Wechsler, a reporter covering the coal crisis, says that the delay between the actual agreement to call off the strike and its release to the press "was arrogantly deliberate." [12]

In the same pattern of behavior is Lewis's action in calling for a week of mourning in which the miners remained away from the coal pits as a symbol of their sympathy with one hundred eleven of their followers who died in the collapse of the Centralia, Illinois, mine in 1947. The period of mourning coincided with the beginning of the nation-wide strike which would have otherwise taken place if the U.S. Supreme Court majority had not banned it beforehand.

Yet if Lewis has been daring in his manipulations, he does not appear to have been reckless. In all his major strike conflicts during the war, Lewis successfully skirted the kind of punitive action that broke the 1946 strike of the railroad engineers and the trainmen.

There is no indication that Lewis has strayed far from the orthodox path in the terms he has sought to get from collective bargaining. The union shop rather than the closed shop prevails in the coal industry. The demand for a health and welfare fund was of relatively recent origin in view of the hazards of coal mining, which are not of recent origin. Nor, in the area of purely union activities, has Lewis embarked on any substantial programs to improve housing or to set up co-operative stores in competition with the coal company stores. These activities, it is conceivable, Lewis would regard as being outside the union framework.

It would be a serious mistake to conclude that Lewis stands for nothing but a consuming passion for power. The leverage for the power drive has been provided by an effective demonstration that he had the personal equipment, energy, and resources to build a strong rival movement to the AFL where all previous efforts had failed. Moreover, there was no uncertainty in the minds of the miners, or anybody else for that matter, that he could make a successful attack on the wartime wages, hours, and working conditions front when every other labor leader was content with minor skirmishes. In short, Lewis makes a serious bid for power in the whole labor movement because he has been able, in the first instance, to come across with the basic stock in trade of unionism. Under Lewis's leadership "workers in bituminous coal mining made significant gains during the war and the immediate post-war periods. Only two advances in general wage rates occurred after 1937, each of these (1941 and 1946) averaging about 17 per cent. Average earnings and hours of work, however, rose far more than basic rates, and important supplemental gains were made; notably paid vacations, pay for travel time in mines at established rates, and improved standards of safety, health and welfare." [13]

IDEOLOGICAL UNIONISM

Thus far we have been discussing the kinds of union leadership that regard the union as the self-contained bounds of interest and concern. With the ideological unionists, the imperatives of unionism are flavored, tempered, colored, and in a few instances, even modified by attitudes on and philosophies of national and international policy. For the ideological unionist, the scope of the union's interest is much broader than the well-known wages, hours, and working conditions. It comprehends political action, active interest in and support of liberal and humanitarian causes in a way which the "pure and simple" trade unionist looks upon as fuzzy.

On the whole, ideological union leadership is more sensitive to public reaction on particular union issues and will take it into greater account. This manifestation of union leadership will also take greater pains in rationalizing union policy with what are regarded as socially desirable principles of economics. By and large, with the exception of the Communists in the unions (who are treated in the next chapter), ideological union leadership has in recent years been more sentimental than disciplined.

New Deal Unionism

An aspect of ideological unionism is to be found in the social reform temper generated by the New Deal, which conditioned the union leadership born and come of age during the New Deal. Specifically, this means CIO leadership, rather more than AFL, expressing itself in a tradition of loyalty to Franklin D. Roosevelt and a philosophy of slightly left-of-center liberalism.

Philip Murray, president of the CIO and of the United Steel Workers of America, more than any other union leader of consequence, represents the tie between two generations of union leadership; the tie between rugged unionism and ideological unionism. For twenty-five years Murray was a top lieutenant to John L. Lewis and knew as well as anybody could the struggle for survival that was the dominant theme of the union story before 1933. As the pivotal element in the forces and counterforces that have made up the CIO after 1940, Murray has also comprehended what it takes to make unionism function when the theater of operations is the total community.

Murray was literally catapulted into national prominence when Lewis paid off on his covenant to withdraw as CIO president if Wendell Willkie were defeated. Previously, as chairman of the Steel Workers Organizing Committee, Murray had been overshadowed by Lewis's gigantic figure.

Murray's job as head of the Steel Workers has possibly been the easier of his dual responsibility. Unlike any other of the new CIO unions, steel organization had been controlled from the very beginning in 1935 by Lewis, and its top leaders including Murray were men with long schooling in the Miners. The Steel Workers Union was, therefore, exempted from the political jockeying produced by the more fluid situations in the other new CIO unions.

On the collective bargaining front U.S. Steel—Big Steel—came to terms with the union in 1937. Little Steel—Inland, Youngstown, Sheet and Tube, Bethlehem, and Republic—were successful in repulsing the first union offensive in 1937, but succumbed in 1941. The general steel strike in 1946 was of shorter duration and with no lesser gains than any other of the major strikes. In short, both within his union and in dealing with employers, Murray has succeeded in fulfilling the imperatives of union leadership.

It is as president of the CIO that Murray has had to breast the waves of conflict among the constituent unions. There are three recognizable tendencies within the CIO—the anti-Communists, the Murray men, and the followers of the Communist line. In the first tendency would fall men like Walter Reuther of the Auto Workers, Emil Rieve of the Textile Workers, and John Green of the Shipyard Workers. In the center group Van Bittner, Murray's assistant in the Steel Workers and head of the southern organizing drive, Allan Haywood, CIO director of organization, and Buckmaster of the Rubber Workers would be located. In the so-called Communist, or left-wing, faction there are Harry Bridges of the Longshoremen, Julius Emspack of the Electrical Workers, and Michael Quill of the Transport Workers. The late Sidney Hillman and the Amalgamated Clothing Workers have found themselves at one time or another in all three groups. What has emerged from this welter of conflicting forces it is fair to characterize as the "Murray line." The Murray line is applicable to union policy and official CIO attitudes on general public policy. During the war, the Murray trade union policy was one of common-sense adherence to cooperation with the war effort, not quite as obsequious as the Communist line and not quite as belligerent on maintaining normal union prerogatives as some in the anti-Communist group demanded. In the immediate postwar period, the Murray line was against a second wholesale CIO strike offensive to offset a rising price level on the strategic ground that the CIO might be measurably weakened, and was in favor of concentrating on a campaign to reduce prices.

On the political front, since the death of President Roosevelt, Murray has resisted the many pressures to break openly with the Democratic administration. The political activities of the CIO incorporated in CIO-PAC have been brought administratively closer to the CIO as such, reversing the tendency for PAC, under Sidney Hillman, to exist as a more or less self-governing organization. During the war Murray sought to minimize open disagreement with Mr. Roosevelt's policy, but this loyalty did not inhibit him from conducting a vigorous campaign against the then President's support of civilian national service legislation nor from reprimanding the leaders of certain "left-wing" unions who were supporting such legislation as part of their "win the war" program.

Altogether, Murray has come to ideological unionism not so much from a preconceived disposition in these matters as from a pragmatic adaptation to the exigencies of union functioning in a period in which government and over-all economic policy became a crucial factor in union calculations. That the ideology has been of the New Deal brand is possibly explainable in terms of his liberal but devout Catholic persuasion and his practical bent that a union cannot stray too far off the political reservation.

Murray gives appropriate recognition to the fact of contending forces within the CIO. Convention and special-purpose committees appointed by Murray invariably contain spokesmen from all the significant ideological denominations. If the mission is important enough to Murray he assigns one of his own trusted lieutenants, as in the case of the southern organizing campaign headed by Van Bittner.

The chances are that Murray will not assume the offensive in a wholesale purge of Communist followers in the CIO unless the latter should force the issue by way of coming into serious open conflict with Murray on union matters. An incipient purge of this character in his own Steel Workers was, as a matter of fact, stopped by Murray, not because of any Communist sympathy but because in his opinion it would do irreparable harm to the union as a whole. Murray has, in individual situations, threatened or actually carried out punitive action against followers of the Communist line, as in the support of an anti-Communist resolution at the 1946 CIO convention.

In summary, Murray's power and authority in the CIO stem from three sources:

1. He is the undisputed head of the most powerful and stable union in the CIO.

2. He is not "beholden" to any particular group or person within the CIO.

3. He is by far the most astute and ablest leader in the CIO.

SOCIAL ENGINEERING

Union leadership with ideological overtones finds another expression in the kind that has been variously characterized as "labor statesmanship" or "social engineering." The point has been made that all union leadership is concerned with optimum profitability of its particular industry, but the "social engineer" union leader views the problem in a more positive way. In a sense it constitutes a system of union philosophy. The general approach is that the union has a positive stake in maintaining and increasing the efficiency of the industry, that the conflicts of interest between labor and management, while they exist, can be minimized by establishing, adhering to, and developing a kind of collective bargaining common law.

That the apparel industries should have provided the most fruitful economic environment for the growth of social engineering union leadership is understandable. Functioning unionism virtually required, as a condition of survival, a conscious industry-wide view. The union leader who has achieved the greatest public distinction as the embodiment of the social engineering union leadership is, of course, Sidney Hillman, the late president of the Amalgamated Clothing Workers of America.

The beginnings of the organization that was later to be the Amalgamated began in the now famous Hart, Schaffner and Marx strike of 1910 in Chicago, and its outstanding leader was Hillman, then twenty-three years old—he had arrived in the United States three years before. The strike ended with an agreement which proved to be a breeding ground for the civilizing of labor-management relations, popularizing the use of systematic impartial machinery, and other techniques now associated with seasoned collective bargaining. In 1914 Hillman was called to be the president of the organization, which had bolted from the United Garment Workers and which a year later became the Amalgamated Clothing Workers. Hillman was the president of the Amalgamated continuously from its founding until his death in 1946. As George Soule says in his sympathetic biography, "there never has developed in the Amalgamated a party or a candidate in opposition to the administration which was installed at the beginning."[14]

Under Hillman's leadership, the Amalgamated brought under union conditions virtually the entire men's suit industry and raised it from sweatshop levels to some degree of decent working conditions. The Amalgamated was one of the first unions to capitalize on the favorable union climate created by the New Deal.

The key to the coloration that Hillman gave to union leadership is found in observations like these:

There is no chance to bargain efficiently with an employer whose business is not prosperous: labor must be industry conscious.[15]

and

We help the employers for one excellent reason. The clothing workers must make their living out of the clothing industry—just as their employers. Until now labor has fought mainly from a sense of outrage against exploitation. Hence it will fight more and more from a sense of social and industrial responsibility.[16]

In short, what Hillman did was to convert an implicit awareness of every union leader into a philosophy.

These conceptions of union responsibility were implemented by experiments in impartial machinery, union-sponsored research and engineering assistance to employers, labor banking, co-operative housing, and jointly sponsored unemployment and old-age benefit schemes.

The special flavor of Hillman's approach to collective bargaining is illuminated by the following account told to George Soule by an employer in the industry, of how Hillman succeeded in winning for the first time in 1937 a national agreement. As business was improving in the industry, pressure among union members for wage increases was gaining momentum. Hillman tried to check these demands at first, saying in effect, "The time is not ripe. Who knows how long this recovery will continue. We do not want to get caught out on a limb. Let's not have a wage increase that may put too heavy a burden on the industry before we are sure that it will not set back the increase of employment."

When Hillman felt that the improvement was of a character to sustain a wage increase he met with a leading employer in a large market. "The pressure is getting too strong—I can't hold back the members any longer," Hillman told him. "If something is not done we will have trouble. What do you recommend?"

A brief discussion ensued as to whether the increase should be 10 per cent or 15 per cent. Hillman seemed indifferent to the precise amount of the increase, suggesting that this matter could be settled in negotiations. He pressed a more important point. "Don't grant the increase in this city alone. If you do and some other market holds out, it will upset competitive conditions and may bring unemployment here. Instead, call for a meeting of the national association and insist that any wage increase be on a national basis. Insist on a national agreement to protect yourselves."

The employer assented to this tactic and so did strategically placed employers in other large markets. Two weeks later the employers' association demanded that the union negotiate a national agreement. The union agreed. In the negotiations, the union asked for a 15 per cent increase, the association countered with 10 per cent, and the parties agreed to 12 per cent.

There were other facets to Hillman's talents. He guided the political activities of the CIO through the PAC. He was the key figure in CIO's participation in the World Federation of Trade Unions, and functioned in important government positions during the NRA, the National Defense Advisory Commission and its successor the Office of Production Management. In all these activities he demonstrated an administrative competence rare among union officers.

Although his union upbringing was in a Socialist environment, there is no indication that Hillman himself ever seriously believed in social-ism. After 1936, when the Amalgamated endorsed President Roosevelt, Hillman resolutely opposed the idea of third-party movements and used every occasion to emphasize that none of the political movements he was associated with would be permitted to serve as a proving ground for class-conscious independent politics. Despite these articulate at-titudes, it is not unreasonable to infer that Hillman's association with ideologies played an important part in his deliberate bent of thinking in terms of policy and broad concepts.

While he was not an excessively vain person Hillman liked his role as a labor statesman. When the spotlight of public attention shifted to the more dynamic union situations in the mass production industries, Hillman's activities shifted to a larger arena than being the head of the Amalgamated Clothing Workers alone could merit. This seeking for new worlds to conquer was undoubtedly a strong motivation in his participation in the formation of the CIO and his willingness later to take on the labor functions of the National Defense Advisory Com-mission with virtually no support from the CIO or the AFL.

In this larger arena he was not averse to making and unmaking alliances as the situation in his opinion demanded, although Hillman himself maintained a fairly consistent position. He was content to play a secondary role to John Lewis in the first years of CIO. In 1940 he was virtually invited to leave the CIO by Lewis and the Communists when both were taking an isolationist line. After the Nazi attack on Soviet Russia, he did not hesitate to work with the Communists in PAC and in the American Labor party.

SOCIALIST UNIONISM

Union leadership with ideological overtones next shades into what may be loosely termed "Socialist unionism." Few of the Socialist unionists are currently members of the Socialist party, but their roots in the Socialist movement are evinced by more concrete things than the token of membership in a political party. In the case of Socialist union leadership, the imperatives of unionism are tempered by an overlay of sympathetic attitudes to substantial government involvement in economic affairs, not only as a matter of strategy but as a matter of philosophy. There is also a great interest and even participation in movements and causes with broad humanitarian coloring. The idea of a labor *movement* with its emphasis on solidarity exerts considerable influence on Socialist union leadership. In short, to a greater or lesser degree, Socialist union leadership tends to appraise its activities against conscious objectives and purposes which are larger than the objectives and purposes of unionism as such. The practical consequences of Socialist union leadership are more characteristically seen in the extracurricular union activities and political activities than in the main course of union functioning.

David Dubinsky, president of the International Ladies' Garment Workers' Union in many ways symbolizes a whole generation and tradition of Socialist union leadership which has clustered about the "needle trades" in New York City. The tradition was in its heyday during the twenty years or so before World War I. Much of the needle trades leadership, like Dubinsky, absorbed its socialism under the oppression of Russian Czarism, and when it migrated to New York's East Side it established a whole self-contained milieu of union activities and attitudes.

Dubinsky achieved the presidency of the ILG from a position as a vice-president and manager of Local 10, the Cutters Local in New York, which is one of the most powerful units in the international because of the strategic place of the cutter's craft in the process of manufacturing women's clothing. The presidency climaxed eighteen years of activity in the union for Dubinsky.

At the same time that the ILG under Dubinsky's leadership has organized garment workers wherever they could be found and raised their wages, the union has been the most potent influence in introducing a measure of stability and profitability to the women's apparel industry by much the same approach to the economic problems as was utilized by Hillman and the Amalgamated. The attempts at orderly industrial relations in the former, as a matter of fact, antedate the founding of the Amalgamated. What it all comes to is that an intelligent reaction by unions to the same order of industrial problems evokes generally the same kind of response.

Dubinsky's Socialist orientation to unionism reflected itself after 1933 in an attempt to prod the labor movement along progressive steps to an extent exceeding the necessities of maintaining his own position or that of his union.

The decision to participate in the original Committee for Industrial Organizations in 1935 and the substantial material aid which the ILG provided did not stem from any compulsion inherent in the labor problems of the industry—the ILG was well on its way to solid strength through its own effort by 1935. In fact, sentiment within the Executive Board in December, 1935, was so evenly divided on the issue of continuing membership in the CIO that Dubinsky's vote for continuation was the decisive factor in keeping the ILG in the CIO. During this period Dubinsky was cited as saying that "nothing could overshadow the fact that the CIO represented a movement with which the ILGWU has profound sympathy, whose policies we have traditionally advocated for years past, and whose objectives are close to the hearts of our members." [17]

On the face of it the ILG withdrew from the CIO in 1938 because it felt that the Committee was departing from its original purpose, in setting itself up as a *permanent* rival to the AFL. There were undoubtedly other causes which prompted the ILG to break with the CIO. Dubinsky, although nominally part of the top leadership of the CIO, was hardly consulted by Lewis in the formulation of major policy. Furthermore, Dubinsky was much alarmed by the increasing prominence of Communists and followers of the party line in Lewis's entourage.

For two years the ILG remained unaffiliated. Although the fact of affiliation was not a condition of maintaining union strength in the industry, the ideological bent of Dubinsky's leadership is revealed in an observation which he made during this period. "We derived our moral and spiritual sustenance from being an integral part of the entire labor movement." [18] Dubinsky advanced three conditions for the return of the ILG to the AFL: that a one-cent anti-CIO per capita be repealed, that the Executive Council of the AFL divest itself of the authority to suspend or expel constituent unions, and finally that the AFL undertake a vigorous campaign against labor racketeering. Whether, as a matter of fact, these conditions were actually fulfilled is open to question. But the ILG was back in the AFL. As if to mark the return well, Joe Fay, a vice-president of the Stationary Engineers assaulted Dubinsky in the bar of the convention hotel in New Orleans, presumably because of the latter's stand on racketeering.

Dubinsky was one of the founders of the American Labor party in 1936. In 1944 he moved out of the ALP after an unsuccessful attempt to oust the Communist group in the primaries. Throughout his career as an ILG official Dubinsky has fought Communists within and outside of his union with great intensity, and has become the most outspoken anti-Communist in the labor movement. As with many other ILG officials, the bitter antipathy toward the Communists dates from the internal ILG conflict with the Communists in the later years of the 1920's which did everything but destroy the union as a going concern.

The causes to which the ILG has lent financial aid are numerous. Workers' education enterprises, international Socialist and labor movements, Red Cross, Community Chests suggest the scope of this aid. At the risk of some disaffection within the rank and file, considering the large Italian Catholic membership, the ILG gave considerable financial aid to the Spanish Loyalists and the Italian anti-Fascist movements.

Many of the ILG's extracurricular activities have been directed toward making the union a respected institution in the community. Its educational activities and its contributions for worthy and respectable purposes have had as a major purpose to efface the popular symbol of a union as racketeers or Bolsheviks, and to get across generally the idea of the union as a reputable American institution. There is this much difference between Dubinsky and the two generations of Socialist union leadership which he has bridged. The earlier generation were unabashed Socialists and the capitalist standards of reputability were of little consequence to them—indeed these standards had been used as instruments of oppression against the struggle of their unions to exist. Dubinsky cherishes the tradition from which he grew, but he is not displeased to have his union and the labor movement accepted even according to the values of a capitalistic society.

Union leadership with ideological strains of the Socialist variety is also found in Walter Reuther, president of the United Automobile

Workers, CIO. The origins of Reuther's ideology are indigenous to the United States and stem in part from his associations in the American radical movement.

Reuther was an automobile tool and die maker, the most skilled trade in the industry, and ascended rapidly to a union position of top responsibility in the fluid situation existing in the UAW. In his late thirties Reuther became the UAW president and director of the union's General Motors Department.

"Program" is a word that figures characteristically in Reuther's public and private discussions. Paul Weber relates an incident in which Reuther was "having it out" with another high UAW official who was complaining that Reuther did not like him. "'Listen,' said Reuther, 'it isn't a question of whether I like you or you like me. As a matter of fact I don't like you very well. But I will go along with you and support you if you are for the same program I am for. All I am interested in is your program.'" [19]

The so-called Reuther plan for the conversion of the automobile industry into the production of airplanes was Reuther's first major venture into the area of national planning. The plan was supported by a formidable array of data relating to unused plant capacity in the automobile industry.

It was during the GM negotiations and subsequent strike of 1945-1946 that Reuther utilized a "programmatic" approach on a scale probably unprecedented in an important collective bargaining situation. The essence of the union position, which Reuther articulated, was the contention that it was possible to raise wages without increasing prices. Reuther had expressed himself in this fashion long before the GM negotiations began. The idea, without doubt, represented a deeply felt philosophy of union policy. Reuther's first formal presentation of the idea was incorporated in a pamphlet titled, appropriately enough, *How to Raise Wages Without Increasing Prices* published in August, 1945. The factual support for Reuther's position was adduced from data showing the vastly increased profitability of industry at large and GM in particular. From these data Reuther argued that the ability to pay sizable wage increases without raising prices existed and that such a policy was indeed necessary if postwar full employment were to be realized.

The specific demands served on the corporation were embodied in a brief submitted by Reuther and headed, "Purchasing Power for Prosperity." The brief was marked by the application of the professional tools of economic analysis and statistics to the union's case, a technique which has characterized much of Reuther's approach in the espousal of a controversial position.

As has been observed in another connection, the GM strikes, like most of the other important strikes in the 1945-1946 upsurge, were fought not on the picket line—although the union's power to shut down the plants was basic—but in Washington and in the press and over the radio. The union angle which Reuther kept pounding away at was (1) the corporation's ability to pay was the crucial issue; (2) the union was prepared to withdraw its demand for any increase if it could be demonstrated from an authoritative examination of the corporation's books that the increase could not be met without raising prices; and (3) the approach to wage-price policy was indispensable to the maintenance of a full employment-full production economy.

Reuther was fully aware that this fusion of wages and prices in a concrete collective bargaining situation was unorthodox and he made the most of it. When the corporation charged that Reuther's injection of the ability-to-pay consideration was undermining the free private enterprise system, Reuther replied, "All that we have done in this wage case is say that we are not going to operate as a narrow economic pressure group which says 'we are going to get ours and the public be damned' or the 'consumer be damned.' We say that we want to make progress with the community and not at the expense of the community." [20] Later, as president of the UAW, Reuther characterized the union's position in the GM case as rising above " 'unionism as usual' in our efforts to set a pattern of wage increases without price increases." [21] Reuther's unorthodox brand of union leadership asserted itself again when as president he invited the representatives of the leading automobile producers to confer with the union on methods of increasing productivity.

The "basic principles" of labor's long-range program have been succinctly stated by Reuther himself:

First, we must try to get all of American labor to join us in the fight to win wage increases without price increases.

Second, we must employ every possible democratic technique to get community-wide action behind the campaign for full employment and full production.

Third, we must win public acceptance of the principle that it is the responsibility of a democratic government to provide useful, creative employment when private ownership cannot offer jobs to all people able and willing to work.

Finally, we must push a broad educational and organizational program to pool the economic power of workers and farmers in powerful cooperative enterprises that will challenge, and compete with, private ownership.[22]

Despite his concern with broad issues of high economic policy, Reuther has not been insensitive to the imperatives of union leadership. The original demand on GM for a 30-cent an hour increase was at that time rather a daring proposal. When the company offered the UAW the same 18½ cents that had been accepted by the Electrical Workers (CIO), Reuther held out for the 19½ cents recommended by the President's Fact-Finding Board. Indeed, he could hardly have done less, since to have accepted the 18½ cents might have been fatally damaging to Reuther's prestige. The GM strike was settled after 113 days by an 18½ cents across-the-board increase which, with elimination of wage inequities and other concessions, came to, the union estimated, an increase of at least 19½ cents an hour.

More than articulateness is necessary to hold a position of influence in the UAW. Reuther has had to organize his supporters in a more or less cohesive group, particularly since the forces opposed to Reuther have always been well disciplined and organized. This has not been easy for a person of Reuther's disposition. He lacks the temperament that makes for the easy accessibility of the popular leader in a new union like the UAW. Reuther has often been stamped as "standoffish" and intellectual.

Reuther's most important opponent in the UAW is George Addes, the secretary-treasurer, who includes in his following the well-disciplined Communist group. Except for the brief "united front" with Addes in resisting the attempts of Homer Martin (the UAW's first president) to control the union, Reuther and his followers have consistently pursued an anti-Addes, anti-Communist policy. In turn, the Communists within the UAW and the CIO have been Reuther's most vocal opponents. At this writing, the Reuther forces do not control the executive board of the UAW and Reuther is, therefore, in the extremely difficult position of having to act as president of an organization the control of whose governing body is vested in an anti-Reuther coalition.

Evolution of Union Leadership

Union leadership in a given situation follows a recognizable pattern of evolution. In the first stage, leadership is still struggling with the problems of organizing workers and collective bargaining; in other words, with the problems of getting the union established as a going concern. There is little time left for internal conflict and factionalism. From 1935 to 1938 most of the CIO unions were in this initial stage of leadership evolution.

In the second stage, the external pressures are somewhat abated and early fervor wears off. Attention is turned to the control of internal union matters. Identifiable group and factional interests within the union emerge. Contests for union offices develop. Witness, for example, the hotly fought elections in the period 1938 to the present among the Automobile Workers, the Newspaper Guild, and the CIO Electrical Workers—all of them unions who had already passed their early struggles for survival.

In the final stage of leadership evolution, one dominant group (or one dominant leader) has established itself and the likelihood of unseating it becomes increasingly remote if it continues to produce results. Voluntary changes among top union offices in this stage are uncommon and occur only in the face of some unsettling circumstances, as when George Browne's conviction for extortion forced his retirement from the presidency of the Moving Picture Machine Operators Union, or when there is a falling out in the administration, which is what happened when Dan Tracy defeated E. J. Brown for the presidency of the AFL Electrical Workers.

There is no close correlation, inverse or direct, between the unfolding of the various stages in union leadership and the development of effective and successful unionism. There is no evidence to support the romantic notion that when union leadership stabilizes its internal position, it necessarily goes lightly in pressing collective bargaining demands. John L. Lewis, James Petrillo, and Philip Murray are outstanding refutations of the idea that union leadership turns "soft" with age. What may happen is that union leadership gets more "know-how," to borrow a phrase from the other side of the bargaining table, and goes after what it wants with less waste motion.

There is also no rigid conformity in the time span over which this pattern unfolds. The Steel Workers leadership reached maturity comparatively early as a result of its being grafted on from the Miners. On the other hand, the internal factionalism among the Automobile Workers may prolong indefinitely the second stage of leadership. Almost a century of growth in the Typographical Union has not produced a union leadership which is proof against defeat in office. However, generally speaking, the older the union the greater is the likelihood that its leadership will fall in the later stages of development. Because the AFL unions are older, there is a tendency for more of their leadership to fall in the last stage of development than is true in the case of the CIO. It is also worth noting that the idea of the pattern is more valid on the higher levels of union leadership. The closer the union leadership is to the membership functionally the less is the tendency for the leadership to solidify. The shop stewards and shop chairmen are invariably very responsive to their constituents.

The unique forms of expression assumed by union leadership in particular cases should not obscure the large common ground in the most important aspects of union functioning which all union leadership occupies. The fundamental sameness of union leadership is most pronounced in the area of strictly union problems. The diversity of union leadership is most pronounced in the extracurricular aspects of union functioning.

CHAPTER XI

COMMUNIST UNIONISM

HISTORICAL BACKGROUND

WHEN WILLIAM Z. FOSTER FOUNDED THE TRADE UNION EDUCATIONAL League in November, 1920, he became in effect the father of Communist unionism in the United States. For years Foster had been prominent in left-wing union and political activity, and organized the TUEL after the tragic failure of the steel strike of 1919.

When the TUEL was first formed, Foster was not yet an official Communist. He viewed the TUEL as a common meeting ground for the "militants" in the labor movement who could be used to "bore from within" the existing "reactionary" labor movement and ultimately capture it and transform it into a revolutionary organization. As Foster said subsequently:

> Immediately, the newly organized TUEL bumped against the same rock on which its two predecessors [the Syndicalist League of North America and the International Trade Union Educational League] had been wrecked; the dual union attitude held generally by revolutionary elements.[1]

At the point that Foster was arguing out the issue of "boring from within" vs. dual unionism, particularly with the IWW element in the TUEL, he was invited in 1921 to attend the First Congress of the Red International of Labor Unions. The RILU congress was held in Moscow immediately after the Third Congress of the Third International (the political organization of international communism).

Lewis Lorwin, who has written the definitive American work on international labor and political movements, recounts the decisions of this meeting of the Third International:

Taking its cue from Lenin, the Congress approved the N(ew) E(conomic) P(olicy) in Russia and the Soviet policy of making trade agreements with foreign countries and of giving concessions to foreign capital, justifying this policy as a necessary "temporary retreat" and as a method of making "capitalism serve the cause of the proletarian revolution."

The Third International also laid down a policy of

splitting the socialist parties . . . in order to consolidate the newly formed communist parties. But in all other spheres the Communists were to remain within existing organizations.[2]

The Congress of the Red International of Labor Unions followed immediately. Foster seems to be confused in his autobiography on the sequence of congresses and recalls that the RILU congress preceded the Congress of the Third International. Actually, according to Lorwin, the Third International met in June, 1921, and the RILU congress opened in July, 1922. This point is more than an academic quibble since it establishes the fact that the general policy of the RILU had already been laid down by the Third International.

The program of the RILU congress with respect to American trade union work, "in line with its general policy on the union question, declared basically for a policy of boring from within in the United States."[3] Foster quotes the decision of the RILU as follows: "Therefore, the question of creating revolutionary cells and groups inside the A. F. of L. and independent unions is of vital importance. There is no other way by which we could gain the working masses in America than to lead a systematic struggle in the unions."[4] When Foster returned to the United States he joined the Communist party and "took [his] proper place in the ranks of the revolutionary Communist International," namely, the TUEL.[5]

Foster summarized the TUEL program as follows:

(1) categoric rejection of dual unionism,
(2) repudiation of the A. F. of L. policy of class collaboration,
(3) for industrial unionism through the amalgamation of existing unions,
(4) the organization of the unorganized,
(5) for unemployment insurance,

(6) for a labor party,

(7) for the shop delegate system in the unions,

(8) affiliation of the American labor movement to the RILU,

(9) the whole-hearted support of the Russian revolution,

(10) the abolition of the capitalist system and the establishment of a workers' republic.[6]

The campaign for amalgamation made substantial headway considering the relatively small numbers in the TUEL. The fact that the TUEL was articulately anti-dual union did not prevent the AFL leadership from castigating it as a dual union movement, and more. The AFL was effective subsequently in cutting off the TUEL "militants" from organized workers. Foster lays part of the blame for the decline of the TUEL on the organization itself. "The TUEL unskillfully," he says, "made worse its relative isolation from the masses by identifying itself too closely with the Communist Party."[7]

In 1928 three not unrelated events occurred. First, Soviet Russia abolished the NEP and embarked on the first five-year plan. As seen later by Stalin,

the basic task of the Five Year Plan was to change the backward, and, in some respects, medieval technology of our country into a modern technology . . . to transform the U.S.S.R. from a weak, agrarian country, dependent upon the caprices of capitalistic countries, into a powerful industrial country quite able to stand on its own.[8]

In 1928 also, both the Third International and the RILU transformed the policy of the united front and its logical consequence "boring from within" into a policy of "independent unionism," or dual unionism. Losovsky, the chief of the RILU, paid special attention to the TUEL and described its policy as one of "dancing quadrilles around the A.F. of L." and in Foster's words of "making a fetish of anti-dual unionism."[9] Thereupon there followed the changes in political and trade union policy throughout the world where there were Communist movements.

In the United States, the policy of dual unionism was carried out by the TUEL during 1928 by organizing new unions in mining, textiles, and the needle trades dual to the established unions already in the field. In 1929 the TUEL became the Trade Union Unity League, which asserted that "the new Trade Union Unity League has as its main task the organization of unorganized into industrial unions *independent* of the A.F. of L." [Emphasis supplied.] [10] At the peak of activity the sponsors of the TUUL never claimed a membership of more than 125,000 in its affiliated unions but maintained that its real influence was much more widespread than this small number would suggest. The relationship between the TUUL and opposition groups, ranging from the dissident Communist groups to the Socialists to the AFL, was bitter indeed. "Social fascism" was the term invariably applied to people and groups differing from the Communist party and the TUUL line. Foster, as general secretary of the TUUL, was the guiding figure. "A number of sectarian weaknesses" in the TUUL were noted by Foster. "The first was a tendency" to identify the TUUL "too closely with the Communist Party . . . The second weakness was a tendency in the direction of dual unionism." [11]

After Hitler came to power, the keystone of Soviet foreign policy was protection against a Nazi attack through forming alliances with anti-Fascist Europe. Also after Hitler came to power there was a reversal of the Third International strategy with respect to non-Communist groups. Dimitroff, in his keynote speech before the Seventh World Congress of the Communist International in 1935 (the first meeting since 1928) declared:

> In countries where small Red Trade Unions exist we recommend to work for their affiliation with the big reformist unions but to insist on the right to defend their views and on the reinstatement of expelled members. But in countries where big Red Trade Unions exist parallel with big reformist trade unions *we* must work for the convening of *Unity Congresses*. [Emphasis in original.] [12]

In March, 1935, a movement got under way to liquidate the TUUL and, in the words of a TUUL policy resolution, "to wage a ceaseless struggle and agitation for the unification of the remaining unions in the TUUL." [13] Foster, in explaining the reason for the shift said, "the entry of the 1,000,000 workers into the A.F. of L. in 1933-5 at least partly removed many of the glaring evils that had been the original cause of the independent union policy of the TUUL." [14]

In 1939 the Nazi-Soviet pact was signed. In May, 1940, Earl Browder declared that "the War Party of the American bourgeoisie is on the march and Roosevelt stands at its head." [15] Socialism, Browder saw "as the only solution of our problems." [16] World War II, then starting in Europe, was condemned as an "imperialist war" and followers of the

Communist party line in the unions echoed the slogan "The Yanks Are Not Coming."

June, 1941, saw the Nazi invasion of Soviet Russia. During this period "class collaboration" became the official Communist position. In December, 1943, Earl Browder, then the major Communist spokesman in the United States, told a Bridgeport audience that the perspective of the future was one

of expanded production and employment and the strengthening of democracy within the framework of the future—and not a perspective of the transition to socialism. . . . We have to be prepared to break with anyone that refuses to support and fight for the realization of the Teheran agreement and the Anglo-American-Soviet coalition. We must be prepared to give the hand of cooperation and fellowship to everyone who fights for the realization of this coalition. . . . If J. P. Morgan supports this coalition and goes down the line for it, I as a Communist am prepared to clasp his hand.[17]

In the same spirit, during this period, Harry Bridges of the CIO Longshoremen avowed that

only by rejecting the defeatist philosophy that peace must be the signal for industrial warfare on picket lines can we start in an atmosphere suitable for the cooperation that will be necessary for an expanded economy.[18]

The Communist unionists mirrored this fact in their activities and became the most passionate and devoted advocates of undeviating prosecution of the war.

In 1945 the Soviet-Anglo-American coalition split wide open. Browder was expelled from the Communist party and his "revisionism" was officially denounced. The Communists once again "began to re-establish the independent vanguard role of our Party."[19] The "correct political orientation for the party" is to be found in a "key quotation" from the Resolution of the National Committee of the Communist party.

A sharp and sustained struggle must still be conducted to secure the complete destruction of fascism throughout the world and to guarantee that the possibilities which now exist for creating a durable peace shall be realized. This is so because the economic and social roots of fascism in Europe have not yet been fully destroyed. This is so because the extremely powerful reactionary forces in the United States and England, which are centered in the trusts and cartels, are striving to reconstruct liberated Europe on a reactionary basis. Moreover, this is so because the most aggressive circles of American imperialism are endeavoring to secure for themselves political and economic domination in the world.[20]

Here again the agitation of the party followers in the unions reflected this revised militancy. The foreign policies of Great Britain and the United States were violently attacked as imperialistic in union resolutions. The perspective of postwar collaboration cultivated during the war was abandoned and the doctrine of militant struggle came to the fore again. In August, 1946, editorial comment in the *Dispatcher,* organ of Harry Bridges's CIO Longshoremen, charged that there were "fifth column" elements in the CIO:

Recently, we had the spectacle of the leader of a major CIO union calling a joint conference with the bosses to discuss, not higher wages or better conditions, but increased production! In other words, he was willing to divert the power of his union to sweating more out of the workers to line the pockets of the employers.[21]

The leader of the "major CIO union" in question was Walter Reuther of the UAW.

In this brief historical survey of Communist unionism we have sought to develop the factual basis for the most significant generalization applicable to Communist unionism: that the various changes in attitude to broad domestic and international affairs in every instance were given their starting impetus by changes in the foreign policy of the U.S.S.R.

TACTICS—EXTRACURRICULAR

The most conspicuous tactic of Communist unionism is the systematic fashion in which its leaders identify themselves with the organizational vehicle and the tenets of the party line in force at any particular time.

There is always pressure on Communist unionists to display evidence of their ability to line up support for the party line. The time and energy consumed in agitating for the passage of resolutions favorable to the party line and warding off resolutions inimical to the line yield no useful results except as symbols of "mass influence" on the part of the Communist unionists. These symbols are very important to their standing in inner party circles, nationally and internationally.

Frequently, the drive to get resolutions passed generates opposition to the Communists which might not otherwise be provoked but so intense is the compulsion that the Communists persist in their efforts even after it is clear that their strength within the union is being weakened as a result. It is this kind of situation which an official national CIO investigation of Communist activities in the Chicago Industrial Union Council found:

> One of the contributing causes of bickering and friction within the Chicago Council has been a tendency on the part of certain delegates to bring controversial issues to the floor on which the CIO has not declared itself nationally, and which are remote from the interests of workers in the Chicago area.[22]

The pattern of Communist strategy can be traced through a series of organizations which reflected that strategy from shift to shift. The American League against War and Fascism, organized in 1932, was militantly antiwar. It "proposed a plan of action at specific points where the war machine can and must be stopped" and demanded "that neutrality legislation effectively cover all war supplies," according to a leaflet of the organization. In 1937 this organization was transformed into the American League for Peace and Democracy. It contended that "aggressor nations have, until now, used our isolationism and our so-called neutrality to go ahead with their plans of imperial conquest." "Moral pressure" and "economic measures" were advocated against the aggressor nations.[23] After the Nazi-Soviet Pact, the League for Peace and Democracy was dissolved. In 1940 the American Peace Mobilization was organized. The APM announced its opposition to the conscription law and lend-lease. When the APM died after Hitler invaded Soviet Russia, there were no further large attempts of comparable magnitude during the war to organize public opinion. The National Committee to Win the Peace was organized in 1946 to "promote understanding and agreement with our great ally, the Soviet Union." The committee stated: "We, the people of the United States, are not interested in Britannia's rule or even in defending Standard Oil's interests in Iran."[24] The committee was apparently not concerned with Soviet activity in Europe or Asia, since the Declaration of Principle does not refer to these situations.

The names of certain union leaders persist through most of these organizations. Donald Henderson of the Food and Tobacco Workers was successively associated with the American League against War and Fascism, American League for Peace and Democracy, American Peace Mobilization, and at the 1942 CIO convention viewed with alarm "the sabotaging of the war program." [25] In 1940 Michael Quill, president of the Transport Workers Union, became an officer of the American Peace Mobilization, and at the CIO convention of that year wanted "no part of any foreign war." [26] In 1941, after the Hitler invasion of Soviet Russia, Quill was for "all out aid for the forces fighting Hitlerism." [27] In 1946 Quill was again proclaiming against British and American imperialism as a speaker for the National Win the Peace Committee.

Joseph Curran of the Maritime Workers supported the American League for Peace and Democracy, the American Peace Mobilization, and at the CIO convention in 1941, and thereafter during the war, gave vigorous support to its prosecution. After V-J day, Curran led a demonstration strike protesting the delay in returning servicemen to home shores. Abram Flaxer of the State, County and Municipal Workers was a sponsor of the American League for Peace and Democracy, the American Peace Mobilization, and at the 1941 convention he declared his support of President Roosevelt's foreign policy "without equivocation" and his feeling that "this war was our war." [28] After the war Flaxer and his associates were instrumental in putting through the convention of the newly formed United Public Workers of America a resolution condemning American and British imperialism. A similar pattern is followed by Lewis Merrill of the CIO Office Workers, who at the 1941 CIO convention called for the production "of every implement necessary to exterminate Hitler." [29] Later Merrill became a member of the Win the Peace Committee Board.

Harry Bridges subscribed to the principles of the American League against War and Fascism, the American Peace Mobilization, and the National Win the Peace Committee. After the German invasion of Soviet Russia, no labor leader could outdo Bridges in his emphasis on relentless prosecution of the war. His sentiments at that time on the need for postwar co-operation have already been referred to. After V-J day Bridges became a member of the National Board of the Win the Peace Committee and again took up the cudgels of the class struggle. Ben Gold of the Furriers' Union and Louis Weinstock of the Painters are open and avowed members of the Communist party and/or the Communist Political Association.

The meaningful fact about the Communist line that should emerge from this recital is not the agenda of what it stands for at any particular time, but the *shifting* nature of the Communist party line. Thus, there are many people who are not Communists—who may, in fact, be anti-Communist—who will at a particular time believe many of the things the Communists profess to believe. But the Communist is distinguishable from the non-Communist by the faithfulness with which he holds to the line, no matter how it changes and no matter how the current line is at odds with the line that immediately preceded it.

Union Tactics

There is substantial evidence that the Communist party line in the unions, although it functions most publicly through what we have called extracurricular activities, functions as well through the trade union activities. When Communists become active in a union they can always be counted on to recruit faithful followers from the outside to perform the "Jimmy Higgins" work—distributing leaflets at plant gates in the early morning, picketing, and the infinite number of onerous tasks that constitute the heart of any movement. If the properly oriented recruits for these tasks cannot be got from within the union ranks, then the rosters of the Young Communist League (the Communist youth organization) or what is its equivalent at the moment are a fruitful source of supply. Minton and Stuart, favorably disposed toward the Communists, observe in respect to Bridges's conduct of the 1934 waterfront strike:

To Harry Bridges, it was obvious that the Communist Party would not only cooperate wholeheartedly and effectively with the maritime workers, but could also give invaluable advice on the conduct and development of the strike. In addition, the rank and file of the waterfront unions found that the Communist workers were the most militant, the most self-sacrificing, and the most consistent elements in their ranks.[30]

This zealousness of the Communist group in performing the "leg work" of day-to-day unionism provides much of the leverage by which a small Communist group in a union can command the support of a much larger but uncohesive non-Communist element.

The mechanism through which the Communists administer the

party line is known as the "party fraction." The fraction is a more or less secret group limited to members of the Communist party in a given organization. The function of the fraction is to apply Communist policy in the particular union. The fraction does not determine the policy. It follows the instructions of the fraction "leader," who in turn gets his instructions from the appropriate Communist party functionary. Foster defines a fraction as the "group of Communist members in the given union or other mass organization." [31]

The power of the fraction lies in its ironbound discipline and in its unity of purpose. Such concentrated force applied in expert fashion makes it possible for the fraction to put its loyal followers in the key committees and offices of the union, and exert vastly more authority than would be justified by the actual weight of numbers.

The most authoritative insight into Communist union tactics in a situation in which the party line followers dominate has been provided by Joseph Curran, who, as this is being written, is the president of the National Maritime Union (CIO).

Curran estimates that, although there are about 500 party members among the 70,000-80,000 members, "approximately 107 out of the 150 elected officials" of the NMU are Communists. Nor is there any question that the Communist party itself is determining union policy.

The Communist Party itself raised a fund of approximately $20,000 . . . among the people of the waterfront . . . to prevent the union from being destroyed.

This is a euphemism, Curran implies, for preventing his group from controlling the union.

One of the techniques of domination which the Communists use is, first of all, stuffing the union ballot boxes. In the elections during the spring and summer of 1946

the report of the Honest Ballot Association and the handwriting experts used by them prove beyond doubt that ballots were premarked and many forged. It was shown in membership meetings following elections that balloting committeemen had been handpicked in many cases and even sent from one port to another.

Another election technique was to put organizers on the payroll, nominally, to help in the campaign to organize the Isthmian Lines (in which the NMU was contending for representation rights with the Seafarers International Union [AFL] in an NLRB election) but actually to "insure the defeat of non-Communists" in the union election. This was not too difficult

because the Vice President in charge of the organizational Department of the union was also a member of the Communist Party—Frederick Myers, and at that time had full authority to appoint as many organizers as he needed to organize the Isthmian Line. Myers proceeded to appoint only those organizers who were members of the Communist Party . . . some of whom did not even have the qualifications of two years at sea.

In addition, the Communist party itself, with the proceeds of the waterfront collection to which Curran has referred, placed its members

on the waterfront on a full-time basis in the union halls in the various ports and their specific job was to coordinate the work of the Communists within the union in that port, in influencing the members, particularly the new members who knew very few of the officials, into voting for the right ones.

The party co-ordinators also distributed approved slates of candidates, helped those who did not know how to vote,

and in some cases, these Party members even voted the ballot for the new member. They were also responsible for seeing to it that the proper kind of smear and slander campaign was conducted in the port against those who were non-Communists running for office.

So much for Communist tactics in election campaigns. The tactics extend to the control of union membership meetings on shore as well. The Communists

come to the meetings well organized, having met before the meeting at outside meeting places. All of their members are fully instructed and have their resolutions in their pockets. Their speakers are chosen. They are trained and disciplined and above all are prepared to stay all night at a meeting in order to tire out the non-Communist members, make them disgusted, and leave the meeting, then they have full control of the meeting and are able to pass any resolutions and actions they want.

If the Communists cannot outlast the rest of the members at a meeting

they do everything possible to disrupt the meeting, raising points of order . . . and whenever votes are finally taken they make sure their people count the votes and if necessary make a short count on the vote if it is against them.

As for the internal government of the union,

> Communists make it their business to see to it that they are on every important committee and if you will notice in our union, the same faces, the same ones are on almost every committee. . . . They make it their business to stay on the beach as long as possible, obtain appointments to jobs and ship only enough to keep them in good standing as active seamen.

The party also controls the union paper, the *Pilot*. "Many issues have been deliberately suppressed from the *Pilot* by the Editor Chamberlain and the Secretary Ferdinand Smith, whenever they believed they were not in the interests of the Party members of the union." Curran cites a case in point, the resignation of the Houston port agent, news of which was kept out of the *Pilot* because party representatives "tried to run his job for him."

Party tactics carry over into the handling of grievances aboard ship. "Beefs are not being properly settled" by the Communist officials.

> Crews are told to tie up ships if they want beefs settled, in spite of the fact that the contract insures the membership of the settlement of beefs, without tying ships up. This is done purposely to disrupt and stampede our membership and to make it appear that they, the Communists, are the only ones who can settle beefs and they can do it by tying up ships.[32]

Insight into the functioning of the Communist unionists when they constitute only an element in a balance of power situation is gained from the experience of R. J. Thomas, former president of the UAW-CIO, who had occupied that position by virtue of the fact that neither Reuther nor Addes, the two "strong" men in the union, was powerful enough by himself to control the policies of the union.

"In his [Thomas's] search for troops," says the *Wage Earner*, a Detroit labor paper of anti-Communist persuasion but of consistent accuracy on these matters,

> Thomas accepted mercenaries of doubtful loyalty. Communists and Communist followers began to appear in key staff positions. The UAW's educational department became infiltrated. Soon Thomas himself began to talk the language of the Party line. The same man who, four years ago, angrily rejected Communist support at the Buffalo convention, now declared he couldn't help it if the Commies liked him.
>
> Strange things began to happen. Thomas caused a furore in a Senate Committee by an unexpected personal attack upon Senator Vandenberg.

Other auto union leaders charged that this statement was written by a pro-communist on the UAW staff and that the motive was to discredit Vandenberg's position on the United Nations Organization. It is doubtful if Thomas had any chance to analyze the statement before he made it.

Thus gradually, R. J. Thomas was knitted into the so-called "left-wing" of which Addes had been the leader.[33]

The party line is also translatable into strike policy. During the period September, 1939-June, 1941, when the party line was emphatically isolationist, at least two strikes were charged as having grown out of that line. One of these was the 1941 Allis-Chalmers strike in Milwaukee. The strike was led by Harold Christoffel, president of Local 238 of the UAW-CIO. Both Christoffel and the rest of the local leadership had, over a period of years, pursued faithfully the variations in the party line. The sworn testimony of a former Communist party member indicates that Christoffel had discussed with the state organizer of the Communist party the strategic value of organizing Allis-Chalmers, an important producer of defense materials, as a way of furthering the antiwar program. Louis Stark, the veteran labor reporter of the *New York Times*, concluded that the Communist party line was clearly evident in the Allis-Chalmers strike. The then attorney general of the United States, Robert H. Jackson, charged that the strike at Vultee aircraft plants during the same period also was of Communist origin.

During the war the Communists were the most devoted adherents of the "no-strike pledge" whatever the provocation. Samuel Wolchok, president of the CIO Department Store Employees, was subject to the most violent denunciation for calling a strike against Montgomery Ward after that firm had persistently refused to abide by an order of the National War Labor Board. The Communist-led group in the Chicago Industrial Union Council charged "that secretary Mann [leader of the anti-Communist group] was more concerned with expressions of support for the Montgomery-Ward workers than with the [reaffirmation] and defense of the no-strike pledge."[34] John Brophy of the national CIO headquarters, investigating the Chicago situation, found that

the Council and its Secretary were not only within their rights in declaring their support for the Montgomery-Ward employees, but might well have been regarded as remiss in their duty to organized labor had they failed to take a strong stand on that issue.[35]

After the war the demonstration strikes of the CIO Longshoremen and the Maritime Union have already been referred to. Only a direct

order from CIO President Philip Murray canceled another demonstration strike by the Communist-controlled New York City Industrial
Union Council.

In the bulk of day-to-day *union* activity—organizing, administration,
collective bargaining—the Communist-dominated unions have frequently
had to operate pretty much as other unions. This was not always so.
Foster characterized the Trade Union Educational League as a "mere
revolutionary propaganda organization." [36] The Trade Union Unity
League, again in Foster's words, tended to "develop its union programs
upon a too advanced revolutionary basis." [37]

Even when revolutionary attitudes are in vogue at a particular time
in the Communist party, there is no evidence that these attitudes are
consistently translated into action on the collective bargaining front.
The Electrical Workers (CIO) is perhaps the largest union under
Communist control. An examination of its collective bargaining demands does not distinguish it noticeably from the characteristic pattern
in mass production industries.

The minimum contract standards adopted by the UE 1946 convention
are:

1. Union security—at least maintenance of membership.
2. Hours—5-day week, premium overtime pay for hours in excess of 8
per day and 40 per week, Saturday, Sunday and night shifts.
3. Paid holidays.
4. Vacations—1 week for 1 year's service up to 2 weeks for 5 years' service.
5. Seniority if worker has ability to do the job.
6. Equal pay for women workers.
7. Protection of veteran's rights—incorporates protection already guaranteed by law.
8. Establishment of typical grievance procedure and arbitration of grievances which cannot be settled by union and management.
9. Leave of absence from plant for union activities.
10. Employer should provide to union information relating to seniority
roster, rates, job definitions and classifications.
11. Specific termination date for contracts with automatic renewal unless
notice of termination 30 days before expiration.
12. No discrimination by employer because of sex, national origin, color,
or creed.
13. Adequate provision for lost time for stewards.
14. If employee is called in at all he should receive a minimum guarantee irrespective of actual time worked.

15. Automatic top seniority for stewards and union officers.
16. Contracts should not include
    a. *company* security clauses.
    b. no-strike clause, if contract does not provide for arbitration.
    c. clause that union will not organize a specific group of workers.
    d. a broad management prerogative clause.[38]

Nor are other Communist-controlled unions exempt from many of the habitual union practices. Michael Quill's Transport Workers' Union opposed as vigorously as any so-called conservative unions such labor-saving devices as bimonthly instead of monthly billing of customers for electric utility services and the substitution of one-man operated buses for the current two-men buses in New York City. The work limitation rules of Harry Bridges's CIO Longshoremen are as widespread as any in the rival AFL union in the field. The National Maritime Union equivalent of "permit men"—the trip card seamen—will, as a matter of union policy, be required to give way to the superior rights of the unlimited union member. The union policies of James Petrillo have not visibly embarrassed the significant Communist element in the leadership of the New York Musicians local. Louis Weinstock, leader of the New York Painters and an open party member, espouses the need for curtailing the use of the spray gun as articulately as anyone else in the union.

Jurisdictional disputes are not foreign either to followers of the party line in the unions: the Farm Equipment Workers and the UAW, the CIO Longshoremen and the Department Store Employees, the Transport Workers and the UAW, the Conference of Studio Unions and the Moving Picture Machine Operators (the first named in every instance being the union in which Communist followers are in important positions).

If deemed necessary, Communist union leadership will send its members through picket lines. Julius Emspack, an officer in the United Electrical and Radio Workers and considered a follower of the party line, found it necessary to urge the members of the UE local at Westinghouse in Springfield to go back to work although the Westinghouse "salaried workers" were out on strike. In a letter to the local business agent, Emspack wrote:

As you know, the [UE Westinghouse] Conference Board authorized the issuance of an appeal to the salaried workers to abandon their strike and their phony leadership, to go back to work and join with UE. We will do everything in our power to expose the misleadership given to these people, and we will do everything in our power to see to it that our workers are not deprived of the right to work.

If the strike continues and it becomes necessary, we will engage in cross picketing, and in exposing in every possible way the connivings of the company union leadership with the Company to deprive the salaried workers of what was and what is justly due them. We will not worry about charges of strike-breaking from Bollens, because as a mouthpiece of the Company he has been busy for years in undercutting the standards of the white collar workers and working against the interests of the UE membership.[39]

<h2>APPRAISAL</h2>

Communist strength in the unions is much greater in the CIO unions than in the AFL unions. Because the CIO was a young organization it provided the kind of fluid situation that lends itself admirably to the process of infiltration at which the Communists are so skillful. From the time that John L. Lewis organized the CIO until the German invasion of Soviet Russia ran into conflict with his isolationism, the Communists in the CIO and Lewis were devoted allies. Lewis provided, therefore, a powerful base from which the Communists could assume positions of importance.

Yet it would be a mistake to assume from this that the Communists control the CIO. Only one union under Communist control now has a really large membership—the Electrical Workers, which claims 430,000 members: The Longshoremen, Maritime, Fur Workers, and Transport Workers, while important unions in their industry, are relatively small by American standards. The greatest strength of the Communists in the CIO is in unions which have still to establish themselves as permanent going concerns: Public Workers, Woodworkers, Office and Professional Workers, Food and Tobacco Workers, Communications Workers and Furniture Workers. While no AFL international union is controlled by a Communist administration, some local groups are: notably the Painters in New York and Cleveland, some of the studio unions in Hollywood, and a local of the Hotel and Restaurant Workers in New York.

Given the indisputable organizational adroitness and the large ambitions of the Communists in the unions, what explains their inability to build a really powerful labor movement? Although the Communist unionists are more conscious of the need to do a good union job in addition to agitating for the party line than has been true in the past, it yet remains true that a disproportionate amount of work and personnel is diverted to extracurricular activities. This means that union work suffers. Moreover, the tenacity with which the Communist unionists hold to their positions and seek to make converts generates countermovements within their unions. The resulting factional conflict siphons off energy and resources which might go into building the union.

The philosophy of communism, or of anything else, has nothing to do with the Communist party line in the unions. A philosophy implies a consistent viewpoint. The party line in the unions is more aptly characterized as a constantly shifting strategy in which accumulation of power in order to maximize the prestige of the Communist line is the expected end product.

The attitudes of Communist leadership to issues of social policy have had no demonstrable relationship to any thoughtful and rational adjustment to changing conditions but to the pronouncements of the U.S.S.R. As we have shown, the successive shifts from "boring from within" to "dual unionism," back again to "boring from within," and the shifts from an antiwar program to a prowar program, then to an antiwar program, back again to a war program and finally, as we write, to an antiwar program mirrored the zigzags in foreign policy of Soviet Russia, either for or against the rest of the world.

In the arsenal of union tactics which the Communists utilize, the record indicates ballot box stuffing, diversion of union funds for factional purposes, party domination of union personnel and their policies, systematic and planned disruption of union meetings and of the handling of grievances, and politically inspired strikes.

Nor is there evident any relationship between a philosophy and the policy of Communist unionism in the collective bargaining process. There have been instances in which collective bargaining by the Communist-controlled unions has followed the dictates of party line strategy but, by and large, Communist unionism has had to pursue the policies of nonparty unionism in order to survive.

CHAPTER XII

WHAT DO THE UNIONS WANT?

STEREOTYPES FIGURE PROMINENTLY IN THE ACCEPTED GENERALIZATIONS about the character of American unionism. Thus, it is widely held in academic and lay circles that unions are, in the last analysis, either "conservative" or "revolutionary." The conservative unions, according to the stereotype, base their policies and activities on an acceptance of the private enterprise, capitalistic system. The revolutionary unions act on the philosophy that the union is a vehicle to usher in a new social order of a Socialist or Communist kind. In short, those who seek to explain American unions in terms of these stereotypes are saying that ideology of one sort or another is the crucial vantage point from which union functioning is to be perceived.

How do these stereotypes as the pivotal factors in the shape of American unionism line up against the facts of union functioning as we have set them forth here?

First, it must be clear that unionism in general or in particular situations has reflected the impact of *many* influences of which ideology has been only *one* and invariably not the most crucial. The mainsprings of union functioning are to be found in the economic, technological, cultural, psychological, and intellectual currents of social living. As we have explored the diverse areas of union activities—organization, internal administration, collective bargaining, strikes, political action, education, welfare, community relations—the *complexity* of the underlying causes is consistently the impressive fact, which denies the potency of any single consideration like ideology as a controlling influence in the molding of unionism in the United States.

To see further the fundamental unreality of the stereotypes, it is only necessary to compare, say, the outcomes of collective bargaining of the unions in the building trades and the CIO electrical workers. By the conventional formulations, the building trades unions are the so-called conservative unions and the CIO electrical workers are reputed to be the left-wing type of union. But the building trades unions have much more to say about the conditions under which their members work than have the CIO electrical workers. Put another way, the conservative supporters of the private enterprise system—the building trades unions—have made far greater inroads into their employers' "prerogatives" than has yet even been demanded, much less granted, by the CIO electrical workers.

Pursue the validity of the stereotypes on another ground—militancy. Part of the conservative union stereotype is the notion that these unions are less prone to strike than are the revolutionary unions. Compare, therefore, the International Ladies' Garment Workers' Union, of acknowledged Socialist inspiration, and the unaffiliated Telephone Workers who, the union president conjectured, were probably predominantly Republican. The ILG has recently prided itself that in its most important market—New York—there has been no significant strike for twenty years. As this is being written, the "Republican" telephone workers have tied up the nation's vital telephone facilities with a country-wide strike.

If the unions are not *fundamentally* concerned with a conception of the brave new world as the decisive element in their functioning, what *do* they want? To answer this question with some discernment it is necessary to differentiate between what may be called the "core" functions and the extracurricular functions. For most unions, organizing new members, administering the affairs of the union, collective bargaining, and strikes are the core functions because the maintenance of the union as a going institution depends on the adequate discharge of these functions. In the category of extracurricular activities fall such functions as education, journalism, public relations, international relationships, union benefit and welfare programs. These are not crucial activities and the leverage for the extracurricular functions is provided by the effectiveness with which the union performs its core functions. In a

twilight zone is the group of activities related to influencing government policy. For unions intimately affected by government policy, this
group of activities falls into the core category. For other unions, these
activities are essentially extracurricular. It should be added that the influencing of government policy is increasingly becoming a core function.

The union's outlook toward its core functions is always colored by the
consciousness that normally there are more workers than jobs. Seniority
and work sharing, work rules and union security are important in the
union's scheme of things because they are union devices that seek to
minimize the effect of job scarcity. Job-scarcity consciousness is, therefore, an inextricable component of the fabric of unionism.

Against this backdrop of job scarcity the union is first of all concerned
with strengthening its standing (or, if on the defensive, at least maintaining it) as a union. At all costs the representation of the union as
anything but a powerful, effective, and successful enterprise is resisted.
The wave of recognition strikes that swept the country from 1933 to
1937 and the considerable expenditure of energy and finances in these
strikes are only more spectacular manifestations of the drive that per-
vades all the more pedestrian union activities.

In the process of holding the support of its constituents and maintaining its status, the union pursues the objective of "more"—more pay
and shorter hours, better working conditions—on the ground that, above
every other possible achievement, "more" is most readily recognizable
as an index of effectiveness. In the pursuit of more (or holding on to
what it has) the union attempts to put itself in a position where it can
influence what it regards as the *determinants* of more, wherever that
may lead.

The usurpation of management prerogatives in any wholesale sense
has little attraction for the union as an end in itself. Management
prerogatives are of concern only in a specific context and then not as
management prerogatives *per se* but as they appear to impinge on
wages, hours, and working conditions. Thus, unions do not indiscriminately seek to participate systematically in the formulation of job
evaluation and wage incentive programs even where managements
are quite receptive to joint participation. Now, the area over which
the union feels it necessary to exercise some control varies with each
situation.

The union's search for more is interlaced with other considerations inherent in the union as a political institution. Primary among these considerations for the union is the necessity for minimizing disruptions in the prevailing group relationships in the union or in the plant. In collective bargaining, it is perilous for the union to upset traditional relationships among various classes of jobs. In administering the internal affairs of the union appropriate recognition is given to all significant attachments—economic, political, national, racial, cultural, regional, and personal.

The whole setting in which union behavior functions is accommodated to the acceptable forms of doing things in a social *movement*— in this case the labor movement. In the process of a century and a half of growth, the labor movement has evolved a distinctive code of sentiments in which solidarity and democracy figure prominently. Much of the temper and coloration of unionism is derived from the belief in the intrinsic rightness of popular control and participation as a controlling principle in union affairs. Persisting, too, is the creed that "an injury to one is an injury to all," reflected, say, in the unionist's normal repugnance to crossing a picket line of another union. The measure to which unions *act* on these sentiments is something else again. Some unions are content with appropriate obeisances on public occasions; other unions are devout adherents; but *no* union flouts them indelicately. Broad social philosophy, then, whether it emphasizes the desirability of private enterprise or the need for profound economic change, is not reflected in the core activities of unionism.

In the extracurricular activities, ideology plays a more influential role. Here it is possible to see that the union's educational activities, or lack of them, its position on broad issues of public policy not too intimately related to union immediate interests, its support of causes bear a clearly discernible relationship to the leadership's economic and social philosophy. This is most distinctly apparent in the Communist-controlled unions, where the extracurricular activities are integrated with the demands of the party line. It is apparent, too, that non-Communist unions like the International Ladies' Garment Workers, the CIO Textile Workers, the Amalgamated Clothing Workers, the United Automobile Workers (CIO), the Pulp and Sulphite Workers (AFL), the Millinery Workers—with their roots struck deep in equalitarian thought —reflect their ideologies in their extracurricular activities. On the other end of the range the unions in the building trades and in the railroads are on the whole indifferent, if not opposed to, these types of activities since their attitudes are not sympathetic to wholesale social and economic reform programs.

It may be that this analysis of union purposes has some implication for the future course of organized labor. Let me hazard some forecasts which flow from this analysis.

Unionism has its seamier side, but this is in major part a reflection of the seaminess of the total society. Legislative enactments which seek merely to modify the technicalities but leave untouched the profound insecurities of all social living will not legislate out of existence the "abuses" of unionism. Rather, punitive legislation will only make things worse when the reaction to it sets in, as it must. Then the forces of social darkness will have so much more bitterness and tension to flourish on.

It is extremely unlikely that the organized labor movement as a movement, or any substantial segment of it, will lend itself seriously to any revolutionary political upheaval in the United States. Its basic mechanisms are so profoundly tied up with the existing general social and economic pattern that any substantial involvement in a conscious revolutionary movement with its inevitable disruptive consequences is unthinkable. This is not to say that organized labor has not itself substantially reordered economic group relationships or that it will not continue to do so, but if it does it will be within the framework of a gradually changing private enterprise system. Here and there, it is likely, unions will pass resolutions and even give financial assistance to causes in support of a new order. The main sectors of union functioning, however, will not be much affected by this incidental support.

But even within a private enterprise system, the status of the unions will be beset by many difficulties. Sometime, soon perhaps, the kind of unionism called forth by the exigencies of functioning in an economy increasingly dominated by *massive* aggregates of industrial and financial managements, and therefore taking on a massiveness of its own, will have to reflect on the administrative dilemma inherent in conserving power and conserving democracy at the same time.

The responsiveness of unionism to the preservation of human values has been its major source of strength with respect to both its own constituents and the progressive groups in American life from whom it has received much support. The American labor movement will need to devise ways of solving the power-democracy dilemma in a manner to sustain that strength.

CHAPTER I. THE UNIONS AND THE AMERICAN ENVIRONMENT

1. Charles A. Beard, *The Rise of American Civilization* (New York: Macmillan, 1930 ed.), II, p. 176.
2. Vernon L. Parrington, *Main Currents in American Thought* (New York: Harcourt, Brace and Co., 1930), III, p. 17.
3. Louis Adamic, *Dynamite* (New York: Viking Press, rev. ed., 1935), p. 62.
4. Terence V. Powderly, *Thirty Years of Labor*, p. 494, as quoted in Commons and Associates, *History of Labour in the United States* (New York: Macmillan, 1926), p. 371.
5. Terence V. Powderly, *The Path I Trod* (New York: Columbia University Press, 1940), pp. 268-270.
6. Samuel Gompers, *Seventy Years of Life and Labor* (New York: E. P. Dutton & Co., Inc., 1-vol. ed., 1943), p. 284.
7. U.S. Commission on Industrial Relations, "Report on the Colorado Strike," as quoted in Samuel Yellen, *American Labor Struggles* (New York: Harcourt, Brace, 1936), p. 106.
8. Interchurch World Movement, "Report on the Steel Strike of 1919," as quoted in *ibid.*, p. 230.
9. *New York Times*, April 7, 1914, as quoted in *ibid.*, p. 222.
10. Dudley Kennedy, "Industrial Management," as quoted in Harry A. Millis and Royal E. Montgomery, *Organized Labor* (New York: McGraw-Hill, 1945), p. 872.

The History of Labour in the United States by John R. Commons and Associates, and Vol. 4 by Selig Perlman and Philip Taft (New York: Macmillan, 1935) are indispensable to any general appraisal of union development in the United States. Equally indispensable is Selig Perlman's *A Theory of the Labor Movement* (New York: Macmillan, 1928).

The cultural background is admirably treated in *Main Currents in American Thought*, by Vernon Louis Parrington, particularly the first two volumes, Charles A. and Mary R. Beard's *The Rise of American Civilization*, and *The American Spirit* (New York: Macmillan, 1942).

More specific examinations of the attitudes of American institutions on labor questions can be found in Merle Curti's *The Social Ideas of American Educators* (New York: Scribner's, 1935), James Dombrowski's *The Early Days of Christian Socialism in America* (New York: Columbia University Press, 1936), and *The Autobiography of Lincoln Steffens* (New York: Harcourt, Brace, 1931).

Valuable insight into the nature of labor's efforts to build a movement can be gained first of all from the autobiographies of two of the chief protagonists: *Seventy Years of Life and Labor,* by Samuel Gompers, and *The Path I Trod—* Terence V. Powderly's edited autobiography.

The best single account of violence in American strikes is Samuel Yellen's *American Labor Struggles. Dynamite,* by Louis Adamic, is more flashy but also more opinionated. Nobody has grasped the "feel" of the Knights of Labor as well as Norman J. Ware in *The Labor Movement in the United States 1860-1895* (New York: D. Appleton, 1929).

Radical unionism finds its best chronicles in *Left-Wing Unionism,* by David J. Saposs (New York: International Publishers, 1926), *The I.W.W., A Study of American Syndicalism,* by Paul F. Brissenden (New York: Columbia University Press, 2nd ed., 1920), *The Decline of the I.W.W.,* by John Gambs (New York: Columbia University Press, 1932), and *Bill Haywood's Book,* William D. Haywood's autobiography (New York: International Publishers, 1929).

Company unionism and its variations are given useful treatment in U.S. Bureau of Labor Statistics Bulletin 638, *Characteristics of Company Unions* (Washington: 1938) and the Twentieth Century Fund study *Labor and the Government* (New York: 1935), particularly Chaps. IV and V.

The most exhaustive analysis of employer antiunion tactics is in the monumental La Follette Committee Hearings, more formally titled as *Violations of Free Speech and the Rights of Labor,* Subcommittee of the Committee on Education and Labor, Pursuant to S. Res. 266, 74th, 75th, and 76th Congresses (Washington: Government Printing Office).

Chapter II. HOW AND WHY UNIONS ARE ORGANIZED

1. Clinton S. Golden and Harold J. Ruttenberg, *The Dynamics of Industrial Democracy* (New York: Harper & Bros., 1942), p. 170.
2. J. R. Robertson, *Organize Now,* International Longshoremen's and Warehousemen's Union, p. 9.
3. National Women's Trade Union League, *How to Organize; A Problem,* 1929, p. 13.
4. Golden and Ruttenberg, *op. cit.,* pp. 128-129.
5. Pacific Coast Marine Firemen, Oilers, Watertenders and Wipers Asso-

ciation, *The Story of the Marine Firemen's Union* (San Francisco, June 1, 1943—rev. Feb. 10, 1945), pp. 26-27.

6. Steel Workers Organizing Committee, *Proceedings of the Second International Wage and Policy Convention* (Pittsburgh, Pa.: 1940), p. 157.

7. Powderly, *The Path I Trod, op. cit.*, p. 24.

8. Frank Fenton, "A Chat on Organization," *American Federationist*, July, 1940, p. 8.

9. Amalgamated Clothing Workers of America, *Documentary History, 1936-8* (New York), p. 169.

10. Textile Workers Union of America, *Manual of Instruction for TWUA Shop Stewards* in the Plants of the American Viscose Corporation (New York), p. 6.

11. Women's Trade Union League, *op. cit.*, p. 16.

12. A. Philip Randolph, as quoted in B. R. Brazeal, *The Brotherhood of Sleeping Car Porters* (New York: Harper & Bros., 1946), pp. 40-41.

13. Louis Stark, "AFL Warns South of CIO Radicals," *New York Times*, May 11, 1946.

14. Fenton, *op. cit.*, p. 8.

15. Joseph Buckley, in the *Seafarers Log*, March 29, 1946 (Seafarers International Union of North America, AFL), p. 14.

16. International Ladies' Garment Workers' Union, *Handbook of Trade Union Methods* (New York: 1937), p. 10.

17. California CIO Council, *Proceedings of the 6th Annual Convention* (Fresno, Calif., 1943), p. 117.

18. Based on a personal interview with Alan Strachan. The real names of the town and the company have not been used in this account.

Much of the material for this chapter is based on my own observations and discussions with direct participants in union organizing activities and others who were in a position to see at first hand the incidents described. Unless otherwise noted, the situations which come in this class are the organizing activities in the automobile industry, Bethlehem Steel, Montgomery Ward, the Ohio public utility incident, the garment industries, and the southern organizing drive. The following named people should not be held responsible for my interpretations, but my debt to them should be acknowledged: Clinton S. Golden, Frank Fenton, Myrna Siegendorf, Ted Silvey, Brendan Sexton, Agnes and Kenneth Douty, Greg Bardacke, Edward Levinson, William H. Munger, Anna Kula, Philip Clowes, R. J. Thomas, and E. J. Lever. I am particularly grateful to Alan Strachan, who took the trouble, at my request, to put his Hanan experience in memorandum form.

Published material in this aspect of union functioning is relatively scarce. I found the following interesting for background and orientation even when the material may not have been used directly: Robert R. R. Brooks, *When Labor Organizes* (New Haven: Yale University Press, 1937), particularly Chap. I; Rose Pesotta with John Nicholas Beffel, *Bread Upon the Waters* (New York: Dodd, Mead, 1944), the best account in book form of the trials and tribulations of an organizer; Edward Levinson, *Labor on the March* (New York: Harper & Bros., 1938).

The Harlan County situation is treated at length in the La Follette investigation hearings (*op. cit.*), Parts 9-13 inclusive and summarized in an unpublished master's thesis, Jack Barbash, *Employer Attitudes and Tactics in Industrial Disputes* (New York University, 1937), Chap. VIII. The estimate of District 50's expenditures is based on James A. Wechsler, *Labor Baron* (New York: Morrow, 1944), p. 191. The reference to Henry Miller, the first president of the Electrical Workers (AFL) is based on International Brotherhood of Electrical Workers, *Biography of a Labor Union*—A Chronicle of the International Brotherhood of Electrical Workers, Washington, D.C., undated. The organizing strategy of the Teamsters is discussed in Samuel Hill, *Teamsters and Transportation* (Washington, D.C.: American Council on Public Affairs, 1942), pp. 96 ff.

William Z. Foster, *From Bryan to Stalin* (New York: International Publishers, 1937), Chap. XIV, is the authority for the reference to Communist organizing. The Kaiser story is based on the speech of his counsel, Harry F. Morton, in *Proceedings of the 35th Annual Convention of the Metal Trades Department of the American Federation of Labor*, 1943, pp. 130 ff. The incident relating to the raffles as a method of getting names is from the *Handbook of Trade Union Methods* (*op. cit*). The temper of the AFL in the southern organizing drive is effectively conveyed in the addresses comprising "Southern Campaign, American Federation of Labor," *Report and Policy*—3rd Biennial Southern Labor Conference, Asheville, N.C., May 11-12, 1946 (Atlanta, Ga.). The public releases of the CIO Southern Organizing Committee and the *CIO News* during 1946 serve a similar purpose for the CIO. The reference to the Detroit Teamsters is based on the accounts in the *New York Times*, Dec. 18, 1946.

CHAPTER III. UNION STRUCTURE AND JURISDICTION

1. Currently outside of the AFL and CIO, among the substantial unions, as this is written, are the National Federation of Telephone Workers; the Engineers, Firemen, Trainmen, and Conductors constituting the so called "operating" union among the railroad brotherhoods; the Brewery Workers; and the Machinists.
2. International unions are so called because many have membership in Canada and a few in Mexico.

3. As of the 1944 conventions of both AFL and CIO.
4. National Labor Relations Board, *Report of the NLRB to the Senate Committee on Education and Labor,* upon S 1000, S 1264, S 1392, S 1550, and S 1580 (April, 1939), p. 162.
5. There is a movement on foot to merge the maritime unions, including the Longshoremen, the Maritime Union, and the American Communications Association, into a subfederation within the CIO.
6. Seafarers' International Union, *West Coast Sailors,* Oct. 19, 1945, p. 4.
7. UAW-CIO International Education Department, *Apprenticeship and the UAW-CIO,* May 1, 1941, p. 20.
8. Harry A. Millis and Others, *How Collective Bargaining Works,* (New York: McGraw-Hill, 1942), p. 139.
9. *Ibid.,* p. 140.
10. Philip Taft, "The Problem of Structure in American Labor," *American Economic Review,* March, 1937.
11. *Proceedings of the 25th General Convention of the United Brotherhood of Carpenters and Joiners of America,* April 25, 1946, p. 14.
12. Frank Duffy, in American Federation of Labor, *Report of the Proceedings of the American Federation of Labor,* 1938, p. 509.
13. U.S. Department of Labor, *Report of the Commission on Industrial Relations in Great Britain* (Washington, 1938), p. 8.
14. Quoted in *Fortune,* "Boss Carpenter," April, 1946, p. 121.
15. *AFL Proceedings, 1938, op. cit.,* p. 444.
16. Report of the secretary treasurer, *Forty-Second Annual Convention of the Kentucky State Federation of Labor,* Louisville, Ky., 1946, p. 8.
17. Selig Perlman, *Theory of the Labor Movement* (New York: Macmillan, 1928), p. 232.
18. Congress of Industrial Organizations, *Daily Proceedings of the Third Constitutional Convention* (Atlantic City, 1940), p. 161.

The facts in the problems of structure and jurisdiction are adequately set forth in Florence Peterson, *American Labor Unions* (New York: Harper & Bros., 1945), Chaps. III, IV, V, VI; Millis and Montgomery, *Organized Labor (op. cit.),* Chap. VI; David J. Saposs, *Readings in Trade Unionism* (New York: Macmillan, 1927), Chaps. VIII, IX, X, for the period prior to 1925; Philip Taft, *Economics and Problems of Labor* (Harrisburg, Pa.: Stackpole, 1942), Chap. XV. A convenient summary of the facts relevant to the jurisdiction of particular international unions can be found in Florence Peterson, *Handbook of Labor Unions* (Washington, D.C.: American Council on Public Affairs, 1944). Philip Taft's two articles in the *American Economic Review* are among the most thoughtful analyses of the problem: "The Problem of Structure in American Labor," March, 1937, and "New Unionism in the United States," June, 1939.

The references to the structure and jurisdiction in the Teamsters, ladies' and men's garment workers, Automobile Workers, Boilermakers, Machinists, Steel Workers, Electrical Workers (CIO), are based on personal observation.

The exact citation for the NLRB case in the telegraph industry is: In the matter of the Western Union Telegraph Company and the American Federation of Labor, Case 17-R-742, decided Oct. 23, 1944, 58 NLRB 1283.

The first report of the CIO Jurisdiction Committee can be found in a mimeographed release issued Jan. 28, 1946.

The recapitulation of AFL jurisdictional disputes between 1938 and 1944 is taken from the respective AFL convention proceedings. I know about the Amalgamated-ILGWU and the UAW-CIO-Farm Equipment jurisdictional disputes from firsthand observation. The details of the UAW-CIO-Transport Workers dispute can be found in the *New York Times,* Oct. 14, 1945. The instance from the Bakery Workers came from Taft, *Economics and Problems of Labor, op. cit.,* p. 551.

CHAPTER IV.   UNION GOVERNMENT AND ADMINISTRATION

1. The AFL has no education department as such. AFL educational responsibilities are carried on by the Workers Education Bureau.
2. "President's Biennial Report," *Proceedings of the Seventeenth Session of the Cigarmakers International Union of America* (Buffalo, N.Y.: 1887), p. 6.
3. Transport Workers Union of America, *Fifth Biennial Convention Report of Proceedings* (New York, 1946), p. 192.
4. Quoted in James A. Wechsler, *Labor Baron, op. cit.,* p. 79.
5. Daniel J. Tobin, "Chicago Independents Belong in IBT," *International Teamster,* International Brotherhood of Teamsters, September, 1945, p. 11.
6. "N.Y. Newspaper Strike Useless," *ibid.,* p. 16.
7. International Brotherhood of Paper Makers, *Labor Unrest and Dissatisfaction* (Albany, N.Y., June 15, 1944), p. 23.
8. Textile Workers Union of America (CIO), *Executive Council Report,* (New York, 1943), p. 68.
9. *Labor Unrest and Dissatisfaction, op. cit.,* p. 56.
10. "Judicial Procedure in Labor Unions," *Quarterly Journal of Economics,* May, 1945, p. 377.
11. *Ibid.,* p. 385.
12. "Expelled Boston Men Reinstated," *International Teamster,* September, 1945, *op. cit.,* pp. 22 ff.

13. United Automobile and Agricultural Implement Workers of America, *Proceedings of the Eighth Convention*, 1943, pp. 426 ff.
14. American Civil Liberties Union, *Democracy in Trade Unions* (New York, 1943), p. 37.
15. *Ibid.*, p. 34.
16. Herbert R. Northrup, *Organized Labor and the Negro* (New York: Harper & Bros., 1944).
17. Philip Murray and M. L. Cooke, *Organized Labor and Production* (Harper & Bros., 1940), p. 43.
18. *Proceedings*, Carpenters and Joiners, *op. cit.*, April 30, 1946, p. 7.
19. Ross Blood, "Blood Urges Prudent Expenditures of Funds, Expansion of Union Service," *Shipyard Worker*, Industrial Union of Marine and Shipbuilding Workers of America, Sept. 17, 1945, p. 2.
20. P. J. King, "Grand Lodge Gets Too Much," *Machinists Monthly Journal*, International Association of Machinists, July, 1945.
21. *Typographical Journal*, International Typographical Union, July, 1945, p. 334.
22. Carpenters' 1946 Convention, *op. cit.*, April 30, 1946, p. 8.
23. *Guild Reporter*, American Newspaper Guild, Sept. 14, 1945, p. 11.
24. "Why Trade-Union Group Insurance Rather Than a Benefit Plan," *American Photo-Engraver*, April, 1930; quoted in *Monthly Labor Review*, February, 1947, p. 202.
25. W. J. Buckley, "Discussion of Methods To Be Used in Organizing Campaigns," *Chicago Conference*, International Brotherhood of Boilermakers, Iron Shipbuilders, and Helpers of America (Chicago, Ill., Sept. 20-24, 1944), p. 36.
26. Millis and Montgomery, *Organized Labor, op. cit.*, Vol. III, p. 264.
27. "Democracy in Labor Unions," *Antioch Review*, Fall, 1943, p. 408.
28. *Labor Unrest and Dissatisfaction, op. cit.*, pp. 39-40.

General discussions of this phase of union functioning are, on the whole, rare. Most of the material is, therefore, based on personal knowledge. Philip Taft has made several useful contributions, some of which have been referred to in the text. In addition, his "Understanding Union Administration (Cambridge: *Harvard Business Review*, Winter, 1946) and "Opposition to Union Officers in Elections" (*Quarterly Journal of Economics*, February, 1944) and "Dues and Initiation Fees in Labor Unions" (*Quarterly Journal of Economics*, February, 1946) should be cited. The report and supplement on *Democracy in Trade Unions* (*op. cit.*) is another worth-while study. The details of union government are conveniently summarized in Miss Peterson's *American Labor Unions* (*op. cit.*), Part II, and with somewhat greater insight by Millis and Montgomery in *Organized Labor* (*op. cit*), Chapter

VI. Of an even more analytical and philosophical turn are Joel Seidman's *Union Rights and Union Duties* (New York: Harcourt, Brace, 1943), Chap. II particularly, and Will Herberg's "Democracy in Labor Unions" (*Antioch Review*), which is one of the most thoughtful and provocative pieces available on contemporary unionism. The operation of union conventions has been subjected to interesting treatment by Joseph Kovner in "Union Conventions," *Labor and Nation* (New York, June-July, 1946). The entrance requirements of contemporary unions is summarized in Clyde W. Summers, "Admission Policies of Labor Unions" (*Quarterly Journal of Economics*, November, 1946).

Chapter V. COLLECTIVE BARGAINING

1. Jacob Loft, *The Printing Trades* (New York: Rinehart & Co., 1944), p. 141.
2. United Automobile, Aircraft and Agricultural Implement Workers of America, *Proceedings of the Eighth Convention* (Buffalo, N.Y., 1943), pp. 169 ff.
3. United Electrical, Radio and Machine Workers of America, *UE Guide to Wage Payment Plans, Time Study and Job Evaluation*, 1943.
4. *Ibid.*, p. 91.
5. Ken Eckert, "About Piecework," *Union*, International Union of Mine, Mill and Smelter Workers, CIO, May 1, 1946, p. 4.
6. International Brotherhood of Electrical Workers, *Wage Trends and Related Subjects* (Washington, 1945), p. 22.
7. *Ibid.*, p. 27.
8. William Gomberg, "Union Interest in Engineering Techniques," *Harvard Business Review*, Spring, 1946, pp. 363-364.
9. *Ibid.*, pp. 362-363.
10. Draft ms. of the Summary of a Conference of Union Technicians held in Chicago, December, 1946.
11. International Union, United Automobile and Agricultural Implement Workers of America, *Proceedings Second Education Conference*, 1945, p. 211.
12. Office Employees International Union. AFL, *Are You Confronted With Job Evaluation?* (Washington, D.C.), p. 25.
13. Harvey W. Brown, *Human Relations vs. Human Engineering*, International Association of Machinists (Washington, D.C., 1947), pp. 6-7 (mimeographed).
14. American Federation of Labor Proceedings, 1921, *Executive Council Report*, pp. 68-69, quoted in David J. Saposs, *Readings in Trade Unionism, op. cit.*, p. 272.

15. *Wage Trends, op. cit.,* p. 25.
16. *Dynamics of Industrial Democracy, op. cit.,* p. 163.
17. "Hosiery," *How Collective Bargaining Works, op. cit.,* p. 484.
18. "On the Beam," *Dispatcher,* International Longshoremen's and Warehousemen's Union, San Francisco, Calif., Sept. 7, 1945, p. 2.
19. "A Program for Economic Equality," *Report of the UAW-CIO Buffalo Conference,* July, 1945, p. 5.
20. Solomon Barkin, *Provisions for Vacations with Pay* in Agreements with the Textile Workers Union of America, Textile Workers Union of America (CIO) (New York, 1941), p. 1 (mimeographed).
21. *Justice,* March 1, 1947, p. 9.
22. *Boilermakers Chicago Conference, op. cit.,* p. 92.
23. "Knoxville Local 90," *Glass Workers Edition, CIO News,* Oct. 1, 1945, p. 9.
24. United Electrical, Radio and Machine Workers of America, *UE News,* May 18, 1946, p. 6.
25. *Labor Unrest and Dissatisfaction, op. cit.,* p. 48.
26. Quoted in U.S. Dept. of Labor, Bureau of Labor Statistics, *Labor News,* December, 1944, p. 2 (mimeographed).
27. *New York Times,* Nov. 10. 1945.
28. Eric Peterson, "Apprenticeship Standards," *Machinists Monthly Journal,* November, 1945, p. 346.
29. Robert F. Handley, "Apprenticeship . . . What It Means to Organized Labor," *Machinists Monthly Journal,* September, 1945, pp. 261 ff.
30. Upholsterers International Union of North America, *Construction and Administration of a U.I.U. Local Union,* p. 20.
31. United Electrical, Radio and Machine Workers of America, *UE Guide to Group Insurance* (New York, 1944), p. 15.
32. Quoted in Helen Baker and Dorothy Dahl, *Group Health Insurance and Sickness Benefit Plans in Collective Bargaining,* Industrial Relations Section (Princeton, N.J.: Princeton University, 1945).
33. Quoted in Inter-Union Institute for Labor and Democracy, "Royalties, Taxes and Assessments," *Labor and Nation,* August, 1945, Part II.
34. Quoted in Baker and Dahl, *op. cit.,* p. 19.
35. *United Mine Workers Journal,* "Text of President Lewis' Speech to Joint Conference in Support of UMWA Demands," March 15, 1946, p. 10.
36. United Retail, Wholesale and Department Store Employees of America (CIO), *Report of Samuel Wolchok* to the 1946 Convention, New York, 1946.
37. ILGWU, "In Defense of Labor's Basic Rights," *Justice,* March 1, 1947, p. 9.
38. James C. Petrillo, *International Musician,* April, 1946. p. 1.

39. Brotherhood of Painters, Decorators and Paperhangers of America, *Proceedings of the Seventeenth General Convention*, September, 1946 (San Francisco, Calif.), pp. 326 ff.

40. Testimony of Mr. Goodman, quoted in National War Labor Board, *Report and Findings of a Panel of the National War Labor Board in Certain Disputes Involving Supervisors*, Jan. 19, 1945, p. 63.

41. *Ibid.*, p. 22.

42. Economic and Business Foundation, *Relationship Between Supervisory Management and Shop Stewards* (New Wilmington, Pa., 1946), pp. 244-245.

43. Testimony of H. Parker Sharp, *Labor Relations Programs*, Hearings before the Committee on Labor and Public Welfare, U.S. Senate, 80th Congress, 1st Session, on S. 55 and S.J. Res. 22, Part I, p. 338 (Washington, D.C.: U.S. Government Printing Office).

44. Quoted in "The Foreman Abdicates," *Fortune*, September, 1945.

45. U.S. House of Representatives, 80th Congress, 1st Session, *Labor-Management Relations Act, 1947*, Report No. 245, p. 15.

46. Robert F. Hoxie, *Trade Unionism in the United States* (New York: D. Appleton, 1923), p. 262.

How Collective Bargaining Works (op. cit.) and Sumner Slichter's *Union Policies and Industrial Management* (Washington, D.C.: Brookings Institution, 1941) I found extraordinarily useful as storehouses of facts.

Van Dusen Kennedy's *Union Policy and Incentive Wage Methods* (New York: Columbia University, 1945) is the most exhaustive treatment of its subject. My conversations with William Gomberg, as well as his publications in the field, were the sources of much of my background in the general problem of technical methods of wage determination. Gomberg's (as this is written) unpublished Ph.D. dissertation, *Limitations of Time and Motion Study*, and "The Relationship between the Unions and the Engineers" (*Mechanical Engineering*, June, 1943), as well as the article cited in the text, I found particularly instructive. See, too, Solomon Barkin's "Wage Determination: Trick or Technique" (*Labor and Nation*, June-July, 1946) for a devastating attack on job evaluation, and the same author's series of articles in *Textile Labor*, March-August, 1941, and October, 1941. The Research Department of the Textile Workers Union of America, which Barkin heads, prepared a good critical bibliography on this general subject.

The definitive labor point of view on the relationship of wages to the cost of living with particular reference to the inadequacy of the BLS index is *Cost of Living* by George Meany and R. J. Thomas (Washington D.C., 1944), which is the report of the labor members of the National War Labor Board Cost of Living Committee appointed by President Roosevelt.

The piece of folklore about the AFL and CIO men on the opposite sides of the wall was thrust at me practically everywhere in Detroit during the 1945 reconversion period. The illustration from the steel industry with respect to wage inequities comes from Golden and Ruttenberg, *op. cit.*, pp. 173-174.

The railroad wage reduction movement is based on the section on "Railroads" in *How Collective Bargaining Works, op. cit.*

McAllister Coleman tells a vivid story of Lewis's attempts to maintain union conditions in the coal fields in his *Men and Coal* (New York: Rinehart & Co., 1943). The building trades' tacit acceptance of wage reductions is noted in Millis and Montgomery, *op. cit.*, p. 409 n.

On the importance of the "Hours" movements in American labor history see Yellen's account of the Haymarket strike in 1886 in *American Labor Struggles, op. cit.*, also Commons's *History of Labour in the United States, op. cit.* The major portion of the seniority section is based on personal observation. The references to seniority on the railroads and in the printing trades are taken from the appropriate sections in *How Collective Bargaining Works, op. cit.*

See *Organized Labor, op. cit.*, pp. 260 ff., for its treatment of the "closed" union. The incident relating to the Ford negotiations was told to me by one of the participants. Henry Kaiser's support of the closed shop was explained by his general counsel, Harry F. Morton, in a speech before the 1943 convention of the AFL Metal Trades Department.

I found the following the most useful for the discussion of industry-wide bargaining: U.S. Bureau of Labor Statistics, *Collective Bargaining with Associations and Groups of Employers* (Bulletin 897, 1947), as an exhaustive repository of facts; Richard A. Lester, *Wages Under National and Regional Collective Bargaining* (Princeton, N.J.: Princeton University, Industrial Relations Section, 1947), for its authoritative insights into the problem; and Senator Wayne Morse's address in the U.S. *Congressional Record* (March 10, 1947, pp. 1900 ff.). The reference to the Air Line Pilots is based on the *New York Times* coverage during May, 1946.

The best analysis of the economic functions of apprenticeship is in Slichter's *Union Policies and Industrial Management, op. cit.* Northrup's *Organized Labor and the Negro, op. cit.*, pp. 25-26, is the authority for the references to the barring of Negroes from acquiring apprenticeship status. The kinship requirement for apprenticeship I found in an investigation I made in New York City, *Apprenticeship Admittance Requirements in New York City Trade Unions* (New York: New York University, Division of General Education, 1935). Millis and Montgomery, *op. cit.*, carry an excellent discussion of the permit system. A forceful statement on the relationship of union policy to technological change can be found in *Technological Unemployment*, by Philip Murray (Pittsburgh: Steel Workers Organizing Committee, 1940).

The reference to the printing trades' vacation policy is from *How Collective Bargaining Works* (op. cit.), pp. 84-85. See also U. S. Bureau of Labor Statistics, *Paid Vacations in American Industry, 1943 and 1944,* Bulletin 811, 1945.

The sources for the instances relating to restrictive union practices when not indicated below are based on personal knowledge: 1A, Slichter, *op cit.,* pp. 196-197; 1C, *Report to the President* by the Emergency Board appointed March 8, 1946 (Chicago, Ill., April 18, 1946), p. 35; "Court Sets Aside 2-Deck Bus Ruling," *New York Times,* Aug. 9, 1946; 2A, *Utility News,* Transport Workers Union, September, 1945, p. 1; *Labor Bulletin,* Belleville Central Labor Union, Belleville, Ill., Oct. 20, 1945, p. 4; Jacob Loft, *The Printing Trades,* op. cit., p. 124; Jack Barbash, "The Strike Wave," *New Leader,* Supplement, March 30, 1946, p. 7; 4, *Allen Bradley Company, et al., Petitioners* v. *Local Union No. 3, International Brotherhood of Electrical Workers, et al.,* Supreme Court of the United States, 702—October Term, 1944; Joel Seidman, *The Needle Trades* (New York: Rinehart & Co., 1942), p. 204; Richard L. Neuberger, *Our Promised Land* (New York: Macmillan, 1938).

On the modification of restrictive practices see Joseph B. Eastman, "Featherbed Rules," *Railroad Manpower and the T. P. and W.,* Office of Defense Transportation, Washington, D. C., 1943; *Proceedings of the Thirty-Fourth Annual Convention* of the Metal Trades Department of the American Federation of Labor, Washington, D.C., 1942, p. 29.

A competent summary of union participation in health and welfare programs is in "Royalties, Taxes and Assessments," *Labor and the Nation,* August, 1945, Part 2. For more on Walter Reuther see the extended treatment of the Reuther philosophy in the chapter on Union Leadership.

Additional background material on the foreman issue is presented in Research Institute of America, *Supervisory Employees,* (New York, undated); U.S. Department of Labor, Bureau of Labor Statistics. *Union Membership* and Collective Bargaining by Foremen (April, 1943). The best analytical material on the foreman issue is in the various National Labor Relations Board decisions, specifically: the Maryland Drydock case, 49 NLRB 733; the Packard case, 61 NLRB No. 4 and 64 NLRB No. 204; and the Jones and Laughlin case, 66 NLRB No. 177.

CHAPTER VI. COLLECTIVE BARGAINING (Cont.)

1. *New York Times,* Dec. 17, 1946.
2. *Ibid.*
3. *Wage Earner,* Dec. 7. 1945, p. 2.

4. *Ibid.*, Feb. 15, 1946, p. 2.

5. George Soule, *Sidney Hillman* (New York: Macmillan, 1939), p. 213

6. Benjamin Stolberg, *Tailor's Progress* (New York: Doubleday, Doran, 1944), p. 220.

7. Quoted in the *New York Times*, Dec. 15, 1945, p. 1.

8. Quoted in National Labor Relations Board, *In the Matter of Times Publishing Company*, etc., Case No. 10-C-1860 (Washington, D.C., 1947), p. 3.

9. *Ibid.*

10. Steel Workers Organizing Committee, *Handling Grievances* (Pittsburgh, Pa., 1938), pp. 16-18.

11. United Automobile Workers-CIO, Proceedings, *First Annual Education Conference*, 1943, p. 133.

12. Upholsterers International Union, *Duties of Shop Delegates, Shop Committees* (Philadelphia), No. 8, p. 8.

13. *Manual of Instruction for TWUA Shop Stewards*, *op. cit.*, p. 11.

14. Janice Rogin, "Sally in Our Alley Has Her Price," *Hat Worker*, Aug. 15, 1946, p. 8.

15. *Organized Labor and Production* (New York: Harper & Bros., 1940), p. 260.

16. Quoted by Frederick H. Harbison, *op. cit.*, pp. 246-247.

17. Andrew H. Whiteford and others, "From Conflict to Cooperation," *Applied Anthropology*, Fall, 1946, p. 12.

18. *UAW-CIO Education Conference*, *op. cit.*, p. 132.

19. "U.S.A.," *Fortune*, November, 1946, p. 254.

20. "Union Interest in Engineering Techniques," *op. cit.*, p. 364.

21. International Brotherhood of Electrical Workers, *Your Trade Union— The IBEW*, pp. 15 ff.

22. This account is taken from a report of Fay's testimony in the Federal Court in Newark, N.J., in the *New York Times*, Jan. 14, 1947.

23. *New York Times*, June 8, 1946.

24. Martin Gerber, "A Program for Economic Equality," *op cit.*, p. 6.

25. Woodruff Randolph, *Typographical Journal*, July, 1945, Supplement, p. 7.

26. "Arbitrator's Fees," *Pact News*, Northwestern Union of Telephone Workers, September, 1945, p. 12.

27. *Thirty-fifth Annual Convention of the Metal Trades Department*, *op. cit.*, p. 131.

28. *Report and Record, Twenty-Third Convention*, International Ladies Garment Workers Union, Atlantic City, 1937, pp. 70 ff; *Executive Board Report*, pp. 167 ff.

29. Hearings before the Select Committee to Investigate Seizure of Mont-

gomery Ward and Co., House of Representatives, 78th Congress, 2nd Session, Pursuant to H. Res. 521, p. 298.

30. *Ibid.*, p. 325.

31. *Ibid.*, p. 353.

32. Education Department, United Mail Order, Warehouse and Retail Employees Union, Local 20, *The Avery Formula*, p. 12.

33. *Investigation of Montgomery Ward Seizure, op. cit.*, pp. 482-487.

34. *Employer Attitudes and Methods, op. cit.*, p. 32.

The published material relating to the central concern of this chapter is mostly in the nature of advice to management and, in a few instances, to labor. Little has been done by way of analysis and insight. Consequently, I have had to rely to a considerable degree on my own observations. In addition to Slichter and Millis (*How Collective Bargaining Works*), Frank C. Pierson's *Collective Bargaining System* (Washington, D.C.: American Council on Public Affairs, 1942) is useful for background.

The variations in the mechanics of negotiation have been explored by Neil W. Chamberlain in *Collective Bargaining Procedures* (Washington, D.C.: American Council on Public Affairs, 1944). Wechsler in his biography of Lewis, *Labor Baron* (p. 68), recounts the negotiations with Taylor. See my *Strike Wave (op. cit.)* and the discussion on Reuther in the chapter on Union Leadership for more detailed discussion of the UAW-GM negotiations.

An infinite number of stewards' manuals have been prepared by unions. The Division of Labor Standards of the U.S. Department of Labor has the best collection. Benjamin Selekman is one of the few who have grasped some of the emotional complexities of the union representative's job in administering the collective agreement. His articles have appeared in the *Harvard Business Review* throughout 1945 and 1946.

The business agent as an institution in American trade unionism is treated sympathetically by Millis and Montgomery (*op. cit.*) and unsympathetically by Winifred Raushenbush in the brief chapter on business agents in *American Labor Dynamics*, edited by J. B. S. Hardman (New York: Harcourt, Brace, 1928).

The most penetrating analysis of arbitration I have ever read is William M. Leiserson's "The Impartial Machinery" in the *Amalgamated Illustrated Almanac* (1924, Amalgamated Clothing Workers of America, New York).

The Naumkeag and B. & O. plans are treated in Slichter's *Union Policies and Industrial Management (op. cit.).*

The most recent systematic account of collective bargaining in the construction trades is William Haber's section in *How Collective Bargaining Works*. Joel Seidman's *The Needle Trades (op. cit.)* is the most reliable and current examination of labor problems in the garment industries.

Chapter VII. THE STRIKE

1. Stan Smith, *Liberal Press* (Chester, Pa., Nov. 2, 1945), p. 1.
2. Quoted in *Labor Relations Reporter* (Washington, D.C.. Oct. 4, 1943), p. 162.
3. "Strikes and Lockouts in 1944," *Monthly Labor Review*, U.S. Department of Labor, May, 1944, p. 957.
4. Delegate Busbey of the Alabama Federation of Labor in *Report of the Proceedings of the 63rd Annual Convention of the American Federation of Labor*, Boston, 1943, pp. 507 ff.
5. *New York Times*, Dec. 21 and 28, 1945.
6. *American Photo Engraver*, September, 1945, pp. 812 ff., 833 ff.
7. "Papers Confused in Chicago Strike," *International Teamster*, August, 1945, p. 7.
8. "The United Front," *International Teamster*, Sept. 21, 1945, p. 1.
9. *Seafarers Log*, Oct. 19, 1945, p. 3.
10. *New York Times*, Jan. 3. 1946.
11. Quoted in *New York Times*, Nov. 22, 1945.
12. *Retail, Wholesale and Department Store Employee*, January, 1946, p. 3.
13. Joseph Curran quoted in *New York Times*, Nov. 29, 1945.
14. Wilfrid H. Crook, *The General Strike* (University of North Carolina Press, 1931), p. vii.
15. Charles Rumford Walker, *American City* (New York: Rinehart & Co., 1937), pp. 94-95.
16. "From Conflict to Cooperation," *op. cit.*, p. 9.
17. St. Louis *Post-Dispatch*, June 16, 1937, quoted in the New York *Herald Tribune*, June 18, 1937.
18. "The Chicago Memorial Day Incident," *Violations of Free Speech*, p. 32.
19. This description is taken from A. H. Raskin's report in the *New York Times*, Jan. 5, 1946, p. 1. The quotations are all from this account.
20. *New York Times*, Nov. 14, 1945, p. 13.
21. Final Report, *Committee on Industrial Relations*, under Act of Congress of Aug. 23, 1912 (Washington, 1915), p. 142.
22. Quoted in National Association of Manufacturers, *Labor Relations Bulletin*, No. 18, March 21, 1937.
23. *Labor on the March*, *op. cit.*, p. 152.
24. *Bread Upon the Waters*, *op. cit.*, pp. 238-239.
25. Charles Rumford Walker, *op. cit.*, p. 99.
26. From Walter Reuther's testimony at the *General Motors Fact-Finding Panel*, as quoted in the *New York Times*, Dec. 29, 1945.

The strike is one of the few aspects of union functioning that have stimulated good writing. Outstanding are Yellen's *American Labor Struggles* (*op. cit.*) and Charles Rumford Walker's *American City.* (*op. cit.*). The authoritative data on strike magnitudes, causes and results are produced by the U.S. Department of Labor, Bureau of Labor Statistics.

Edward Levinson's *Labor on the March* (*op. cit.*) is the best account of the "recognition" strike wave. For a description of the "first round" of strikes following World War II see *Strike Wave,* (*op. cit.*).

The garment workers' stoppages are discussed in *The Needle Trades* (*op. cit.*), pp. 242-243. The wartime quickies I saw at first hand as an employee of the War Production Board. *Organized Labor and the Negro* (*op. cit.*) contains several instances of strikes against the employment of Negroes.

The account of the strike of several AFL maritime unions against the action of the Wage Stabilization Board is based on the reports appearing in the *New York Times* during September, 1946. The account of the building trades' sympathetic strike is from the *New York Times,* Dec. 21 and 28, 1945. The telephone and railroad situations I know about from personal observation.

I have relied on Yellen's chapter on the San Francisco Longshoremen's strike in *American Labor Struggles* (*op. cit.*) and Walker's *American City* for the Minneapolis Teamsters' strike. On racketeering, Harold Seidman's *Labor Czars* (New York: Liveright, 1938) is the most thorough and the best balanced study. I learned about the Donnelly Printing Co. strike from some of the participants. The Engineers and Trainmen's strikes on the railroads were given ample coverage in the *New York Times* during May, 1946. Mr. A. F. Whitney has provided a clinical account of the events immediately before and after the Engineers and Trainmen's strike in *Causes of Labor Unrest* (Cleveland: Brotherhood of Railroad Trainmen, 1946), which is a reprint of his testimony, July 9, 1946, before the special subcommittee of the House of Representatives Committee on Labor.

CHAPTER VIII. UNIONS, GOVERNMENT, AND POLITICS

1. Painters Convention Proceedings, *op. cit.,* p. 330.
2. Amalgamated Clothing Workers of America, *Advance,* April 1, 1946, p. 16.
3. *Proceedings of the Sixteenth Convention* of the International Brotherhood of Boilermakers, Iron Shop Builders and Helpers of America, 1937, p. 271.
4. Congress of Industrial Organizations, *Proceedings,* 1944 Convention, p. 204.

5. *Ibid.*, p. 207.

6. *Proceedings*, Grand Division, Order of Railway Conductors, 42nd Session, 1941, p. 38.

7. *CIO News*, Oct. 1, 1945, p. 5.

8. Report of President Philip Murray to 1943 CIO Convention, quoted in Joseph Gaer, *The First Round* (New York: Duell, Sloan and Pearce, 1944), p. 61.

9. CIO-PAC, *What Every Canvasser Should Know*, p. 138.

10. Ohio CIO-PAC, *Should Labor Take Political Action?*, Columbus, Ohio.

11. Keating, *op. cit.*, p. 38.

Most of the material in this chapter, unless otherwise credited, is based on personal observation as an economist in government agencies concerned with labor matters and discussions with union people engaged in political and governmental activities.

The varying ways in which organized labor has viewed its attitudes to government are painstakingly documented in George G. Higgins, *Voluntarism in Organized Labor in the United States, 1930-1940* (Washington, D.C.: Catholic University of America Press, 1944).

The CIO Department of Research and Education and the CIO Political Action Committee have been prolific sources of published materials on almost every phase of national and economic policy. The AFL is much less articulate in a literary way about these matters and its annual convention proceedings are the best original source for AFL attitudes. Among CIO international unions, the United Automobile Workers, the United Electrical Workers, the Textile Workers Union, the National Maritime Union, and the International Ladies Garment Workers and the American Federation of Teachers among the AFL internationals, have been the most active in passing judgment on broad public issues.

The Taft-Hartley law is so new that there is no extensive, thoughtful literature on the subject. For the best digest of the text and legislative history see the Bureau of National Affairs, *The New Labor Law*, Washington, D.C., 1947.

Chapter IX. EXTRACURRICULAR UNION ACTIVITIES

1. Fannia M. Cohn, *Workers Education in War and Peace* (New York: Workers Education Bureau, 1943), p. 6.

2. U.S. Department of Labor, Division of Labor Standards, *The Educational Program of the Textile Workers Union of America, CIO* (May, 1946), p. 1.

3. Frank Marquart, *First Annual Education Conference, op. cit.*, p. 123.

4. Smith Steel Workers Federal Labor Union No. 19806, AFL, *Manual and Guide to Good Stewardship* (Milwaukee, Wis.), p. 13.

5. United Paperworkers of America, CIO, *For UPA-CIO Stewards and Committeemen* (Cleveland, Ohio), pp. 12-23.

6. St. Louis Joint Council, United Retail, Wholesale and Department Store Employees of America-CIO, *The Joint Council Steward at Work* (St. Louis, 1945), pp. 23-27.

7. Larry Rogin and Joseph Glazer, "Training for Union Service," *Labor and Nation*, March-April, 1947, pp. 17 ff.

8. International Brotherhood of Pulp, Sulphite, and Paper Mill Workers, *Report of Jacksonville, Florida Zone Conference* (Washington, 1945).

9. U.S. Department of Labor, Industrial Relations Division, *Labor News*, February, 1945.

10. American Federation of Labor, *Report of the Executive Council* to the 65th Convention, Chicago, 1946, p. 69.

11. *International Teamster*, September, 1945.

12. *American Photo-Engraver*, September, 1945, pp. 823-829.

13. *Fur and Leather Worker*, October, 1945, p. 20.

14. *International Molders and Foundry Workers Journal*, July, 1944, p. 386.

15. Quoted in Congress of Industrial Organizations, *Report of the CIO Delegates to the World Trade Union Conference*.

16. Samuel Gompers, *Seventy Years of Life and Labor* (New York: E. P. Dutton, 1943 ed.), II, p. 509.

17. Cigarmakers Proceedings, *op. cit.*, p. 6.

18. *Your Trade Union—The IBEW*, *op. cit.*, p. 27.

19. U.S. Department of Labor, "Brotherhood of Railroad Trainmen," *Labor Information Bulletin*, February, 1940, p. 8.

The section on workers' education is based substantially on my personal involvement in these activities over a period of fifteen years. The two best general treatments of workers' education are Mark Starr's pamphlet *Workers' Education Today* (New York: League for Industrial Democracy, 1941) and the series of essays edited by Theodore Brameld, *Workers' Education in the United States* (New York: Harper & Bros, 1941).

The three major sources of information on workers' education in the United States are the Workers Education Bureau, which is the educational arm of the AFL, the American Labor Education Service, and the Labor Education Services Branch, Division of Labor Standards, U.S. Department of Labor.

Some personal familiarity with union research has been my major resource in the preparation of this section. I have not run across any really analytical account of union research activities. The one which has the most facts is by Nelson Bortz, in the *Monthly Labor Review* of February 1943, titled "Research Work of Trade Unions."

The public relations section is another case of piecing together bits of personal observation and experience.

J. B. S. Hardman's 3-page essay on the labor press, which was written almost twenty years ago, is still the most discerning analysis that I know of: "A View of the Trade Union Press and its Function" in *American Labor Dynamics* (*op. cit.*).

The standard work on labor interests in international affairs before 1929 is Lewis Lorwin's *Labor and Internationalism* (Washington: Brookings Institution, 1929). *The International Labor Movement,* by John Price (New York: Oxford University Press, 1945), brings the flow of events just short of the formation of the World Federation. A thoughtful analysis of the current situation can be found in *Labor and Nation* supplement on the World Federation of Trade Unions, December, 1945. See also the AFL and CIO convention proceedings for 1944 and 1946.

The opening pages of the AFL convention proceedings normally carry every year a detailed itemization of benefit payments, by purpose and by affiliated union. The U.S. Bureau of Labor Statistics Bulletin 465 which is *The Beneficial Activities of Trade Unions* (Washington, 1928) is probably the most comprehensive description, but it is now sadly out of date.

There is a well-written description of Amalgamated Clothing Workers activities in banking and housing in its publication *The Amalgamated Today and Tomorrow* (New York, 1939). See also Millis and Montgomery's (*op. cit.*) treatment, pp. 343 ff. On *Union Counselling* see the pamphlet of the same name published by the CIO War Relief Committee (New York, 1945). The role of union counseling in Chicago during the 1946 steel strike I learned about from Myrna Siegendorf, who acted as liaison between the CIO and the Chicago Council of Social Agencies.

Chapter X. UNION LEADERSHIP

1. *Pilot,* Sept. 28, 1945, p. 11.
2. "Labor Unrest and Dissatisfaction," *op. cit.,* p. 22.
3. "The Trade Union Leader: A Collective Portrait," *Public Opinion Quarterly,* Summer, 1945, p. 174
4. "Labor Unrest and Dissatisfaction," *op. cit.,* p. 36.
5. Local 9, *Coopers International Journal* (Philadelphia), January, 1945, p. 5.
6. National Federation of Telephone Workers, *Wisconsin Stewards Training Program* (unpublished report), 1946.

7. Quoted in the *New York Times,* Dec. 26, 1945.

8. Quoted in Milton Mayer, "Mussolini of Music," *Esquire,* July, 1937.

9. Quoted in Neuberger, *op. cit.,* p. 184.

10. Cecil Carnes, *John L. Lewis, Leader of Labor* (New York: Robert Speller, 1936), p. 303.

11. *Labor Baron,* op. cit., p. 3.

12. *Ibid.,* p. 233.

13. "Changing Status of Bituminous Coal Miners, 1937-1946," *Monthly Labor Review,* August. 1946.

14. *Sidney Hillman, op. cit.,* p. 67.

15. *New York Times,* July 14, 1946.

16. Quoted in Herbert Harris, *American Labor* (New Haven: Yale University Press, 1939), p. 335.

17. International Ladies' Garment Workers' Union, *Report of the General Executive Board* (New York, 1937), p. 197.

18. Quoted in Benjamin Stolberg, *op. cit.,* p. 276.

19. *Wage Earner,* March 29, 1946, p. 3.

20. *New York Times,* Dec. 29, 1946.

21. *United Automobile Worker,* August, 1946, p. 4.

22. *Ibid.,* p. 4.

Union leadership is another of the aspects of union functioning which have been largely ignored by the professional writers. Norman Ware's chapter on "The Working Class and Its Leaders" in his *Labor and Modern Industrial Society* (Boston: D. C. Heath, 1935) is one of the few I know about in a labor textbook. The analysis, with occasional flashes of insight, is uneven in quality. The November, 1946, issue of *Fortune,* which is devoted to labor issues, contains some attractively written pieces on labor leaders who normally do not get into the news.

Several labor leaders have been autobiographically inclined: Powderly, Gompers, Haywood, Foster, have already been referred to in these notes. In addition, there have been a number of biographies. Walter McCaleb has written what amounts to an official biography of A. F. Whitney in *Brotherhood of Railroad Trainmen* (New York: Boni, 1936). Elsie Gluck has done a much more creditable job with the life of John Mitchell of the United Mine Workers in *John Mitchell—Miner* (New York: John Day, 1929). There are penetrating judgments of A. Philip Randolph of the Sleeping Car Porters in Brailsford R. Brazeal's *The Brotherhood of Sleeping Car Porters* (New York: Harper & Bros., 1946). *The Autobiography of Lincoln Steffens* (*op. cit.*) has some interesting appraisals of an earlier generation of labor leadership.

The section on imperatives of union leadership is based on personal observation. Milton Mayer's article on Petrillo is the best I have seen. The same for Richard Neuberger on Dave Beck in *Our Promised Land.*

There is a voluminous literature on John L. Lewis. I think the best accounts are those of McAllister Coleman in *Men and Coal (op. cit.)* and James Wechsler in *Labor Baron (op. cit.).*

John Chamberlain's article on Philip Murray in *Life* magazine of Feb. 11, 1946, is better than anything else I have seen on the CIO leader. Wechsler's treatment of Murray is unflattering, and unjustly so.

George Soule's biography of Hillman is the most current but is largely in the nature of an "authorized" work. It lacks a critical perspective. Stolberg's *Tailor's Progress (op cit.)* has much about Dubinsky in it but the author's interest in the turn of a phrase frequently conflicts with a balanced appraisal. I do not know of any really good appraisal of Walter Reuther.

I have had the opportunity to make some personal appraisals of Dubinsky, Hillman, and Reuther, as a sometime casual employee of their organizations, supplemented by discussions with people who knew these men reasonably well. My judgments of Murray, Petrillo, Lewis, and Beck are based on some observations of them in action as well as on talks with individuals who have had a much closer contact than I have had.

CHAPTER XI. COMMUNIST UNIONISM

1. Foster, *From Bryan to Stalin, op. cit.,* p. 134.
2. Lorwin, *Labor and Internationalism, op. cit.,* pp. 228-229.
3. *From Bryan to Stalin, op. cit.,* p. 139
4. *Ibid.,* p. 139.
5. *Ibid.,* p. 163.
6. *Ibid.,* p. 165.
7. *Ibid.,* p. 195.
8. Quoted in Eric Achorn, *European Civilization and Politics since 1815* (New York: Harcourt, Brace, 1934), p. 535.
9. *From Bryan to Stalin, op. cit.,* pp. 213-214.
10. Quoted in *ibid.,* p. 218.
11. *Ibid.,* p. 278.
12. Georgi Dimitroff, *Working Class Unity—Bulwark Against Fascism* (New York: Workers Library Publishers, 1935), p. 64.
13. *From Bryan to Stalin, op. cit.,* p. 274.
14. *Ibid.,* p. 271.
15. Earl Browder, *Second Imperialist War* (New York: International Publishers, 1940), p. 289.
16. *Ibid.,* p. 143.

17. Quoted in Irwin Ross, "It's Tough to be a Communist," *Harper's Magazine*, June, 1946, p. 532.
18. International Longshoremen's and Warehousemen's Union, CIO, *A Postwar Perspective for Jobs* (leaflet).
19. William Z. Foster, "One Year of Struggle Against Browderism," *Political Affairs*, September, 1946, p. 772.
20. *Ibid.*, p. 772.
21. "The Fifth Column in Labor," *Dispatcher*, Aug. 23, 1946.
22. John Brophy, *Instructions to the Chicago Industrial Union Council*, Congress of Industrial Organizations (1945, mimeographed), p. 9.
23. *New Masses*, March 15, 1938, p. 19.
24. National Committee to Win the Peace, *A Call to the Washington Conference to Win the Peace* (leaflet).
25. Congress of Industrial Organizations, *Daily Proceedings of the Fifth Constitutional Convention* (Boston, 1942), p. 267.
26. *Proceedings* (Atlantic City, 1940), p. 229.
27. *Proceedings* (Detroit, 1941), p. 140.
28. *Ibid.*, p. 157.
29. *Ibid.*, p. 153.
30. Bruce Minton and John Stuart, *Men Who Lead Labor* (New York: Modern Age, 1937), p. 185.
31. *From Bryan to Stalin, op. cit.*, p. 275 n.
32. National Maritime Union, "Report to the Membership," *Pilot*, July 5, 1946, p. 23.
33. "Defeat of R. J. Thomas, May End UAW 'Balance of Power,'" *Wage Earner*, Association of Catholic Trade Unionists, March 29, 1946, p. 5.
34. John Brophy, Director Industrial Union Councils, CIO, *Instructions to the Chicago Industrial Union Council, CIO*, April 26, 1945.
35. *Ibid.*
36. *From Bryan to Stalin, op. cit.*, p. 195.
37. *Ibid.*, p. 278.
38. *UE News*, Sept. 21, 1946, p. 4.
39. Westinghouse Industrial Union, *United Front* (Official News Organ, Local 202, UER&MW), Sept. 21, 1945.

The two best books on the subject are now unfortunately out of date: David J. Saposs, *Left-Wing Unionism* (*op. cit.*), and Lewis Lorwin, *Labor and Internationalism* (*op. cit.*): Communist unionism in particular situations is given informed treatment with varying degrees of sympathy in the following autobiographies: *Bill Haywood* (*op. cit.*), Foster's autobiography referred to in the footnotes, Morris Hillquit's *Loose Leaves from a Busy Life* (New York: Macmillan, 1934), Fred E. Beal, *Proletarian Journey*

(New York: Hillman-Curl, 1937), and Benjamin Gitlow's *I Confess* (New York: E. P. Dutton, 1940).

Communist unionism in specific unions is discussed in Seidman's *The Needle Trades* (*op. cit.*), Vernon Jensen's *Lumber and Labor* (New York: Rinehart & Co., 1945), and James Wechsler's *Labor Baron* (*op. cit.*).

The most current analysis is that of the Research Institute of America, *Communists in Labor Unions* (New York, April 4, 1946). Of course, the official publications of the Communist party are indispensable sources of information: notably the *Daily Worker,* the *Communist* (monthly) succeeded by *Political Affairs* (monthly).

The organizational affiliations of Donald Henderson, Michael Quill, Joseph Curran, Abram Flaxer, Lewis Merrill, Harry Bridges, were compiled from the publications of these organizations reproduced in Special Committee on Un-American Activities, House of Representatives, 78th Congress, 2nd Session, on H. Res. 282, *Investigation of Un-American Propaganda Activities in the United States,* 1944 (Washington, D.C.). The statements of purposes of the organizations are from the same source. The references to the National Win the Peace Committee are from the publication of that organization cited in the footnotes.

The account of the Allis-Chalmers strike is based on an unpublished master's thesis by Donald A. Schwartz, *The 1941 Strike at Allis-Chalmers* (University of Wisconsin, 1943). The reference to the Vultee strike is from *Business Week,* Jan. 4, 1941, p. 28. The New York City general strike details can be found in the *New York Times,* Feb. 7, 1946. The Transport Workers Union item is based on an account in the *Utility News,* Transport Workers organ, September, 1945.

The references to jurisdictional disputes is based on personal knowledge. On Communists in the CIO see Joseph Loftus's reports on the CIO convention in the *New York Times,* Nov. 15-23, 1946, inclusive.

Throughout the chapter there are characterizations which are not documented of certain unions as Communist-controlled. To cite the proof on which the characterization is based would be a laborious process. I have firsthand knowledge of all the unions cited and accept full responsibility for the accuracy of the judgment.

Chapter XII. WHAT DO THE UNIONS WANT?

Within the past year or so, the man who, to my mind, has done the most fruitful thinking about the labor movement in its broad character is E. Wight Bakke. See particularly his *Goals of Mutual Survival* (Labor-Management Center, Yale University, 1946) and his contribution to the symposium on *Wage Determination and the Economics of Liberalism* (Chamber of Commerce of the United States, Washington, 1947).

Selig Perlman's *Theory of the Labor Movement* is still the most probing of the philosophical treatments. Some years ago I formulated an earlier version of the approach in this chapter in *"Ideology and the Unions," American Economic Review*, December, 1943.

176; jurisdictional disputes, 35; organizing of, 20; quoted, 227; re-
moval of racketeers, 55; research,
165; as semi-industrial union, 30;
trade department in, 52; types of
locals, 32; as unaffiliated union, 29.
See also S. Hillman, Men's clothing
industry

Clowes, Philip, 227

Coal industry, antiunionism, 134; Harlan County, 12; industry-wide bargaining, 87; union foremen in, 98;
union strength in, 4. *See also* Mine
Workers, John L. Lewis

Cohn, Fannia M., 159, 241

Coleman, McAllister, 235, 245

Collective Bargaining, Chapter V,
Chapter VI

Collective bargaining, process in Taft-
Hartley law, 157; terms in Taft-
Hartley law, 156; training, 163. *See
also* Industry-wide collective bargaining

Color requirement, for apprenticeship,
89

Colorado Federation of Labor, 163

Colorado Fuel and Iron Corporation,
and Ludlow "massacre," 4, 5

Columbia University, 179

Commission on Industrial Relations in
Great Britain, 229

Committee for Industrial Organization,
and Dubinsky, 195; formation of,
40; and the ILGWU, 13

Common Laborers' Union, International Hod Carriers' Building and,
of America, 114

Commons, John R. and Associates, 225,
235

Communications Association, American,
cited, 229; communist control in,
217; organizing techniques, 24; in
the telegraph industry, 33

Communist Unionism, Chapter XI

Communist, AFL charges CIO is, 20;
issue at conventions, 51; line, 60;
fraction in unions, 211; tactics,
207-10

Communist International, 1935 meeting, 205

Communist party, and Bridges, 210;

members in unions, 209; and Philip
Murray, 49; reasons for organizing
unions, 16; and rival unionism, 39

Communist Political Association, 209

Communist unionism, 222

Communist unions, against discrimination, 62; on union security, 86; on
wage incentives, 120

Communists, 147, 187-8, 219; in
American Labor Party, 150; fought
by Beck, 184; cited, 247; in the
CIO, 48, 180, 189; and Dubinsky,
195; and Hillman, 193; and Lewis,
185; in Machinists, 54; and Murray,
190; in Taft-Hartley law, 157; in
Electrical Workers-CIO, 180; and
World Federation of Trade Unions,
172

Community chests, 175, 196

Company security, in UE contracts,
216

Company unions, 5, 6, 54; as training for union leaders, 11

Conference of Studio Unions, and
Communists, 29; jurisdictional disputes, 125, 216

CIO News, 148, 170

Congress of Industrial Organizations,
Anti-Discrimination Department, 62;
attitude on BLS cost of living index,
75; communist strength in, 217; and
Democratic Party, 149; Department
of Education and Research, 161;
electoral activity, 150; Industrial
Union Council, Michigan, 152; and
issue of structure, 40-43; Jurisdiction
Committee, 25,230; jurisdictional disputes, 49; legislative organization,
148; on national policy, 146; as organizing mechanism, 47; Political
Action Committee, 147, 189, 193;
reasons for organizing, 16; relationship to international unions, 100;
southern drive, 9, 13, 19, 48, 228;
strikes, 145; structure of, 28. *See also*
Philip Murray, Committee for Industrial Organization, Political Action

Conservative unionism, 219

Construction industry, grievances, 108;
piecework systems, 71; seniority, 119;

International Union of United Brewery, Flour, Cereal and Soft Drink Workers of America. *See* Brewery Workers
International Union of Wood, Wire and Metal Lathers. *See* Lathers
International unions, 228; importance of, 29; number of in AFL and CIO, 28
International Woodworkers of America. *See* Lumber Workers, CIO
Inter-Union Institute for Labor and Democracy, 233
Italian groupings in unions, 20, 180, 196

Jackson, Robert H., 214
Jensen, Vernon, 247
Jewish workers, 13
Job classification, 70, 94
Job dilution programs, 95
Job evaluation, attitude of Electrical Workers, AFL, 72; attitude of Steelworkers, 72; effect of, on foremen, 97; grievances, 111; union attitudes, 74; union participation in, 221; plans and union technicians, 57
Job scarcity, 221
Jones and Laughlin Steel Corp., 98, 107
Journeyman Stonecutters' Association of North America. *See* Stonecutters
Journeymen tailors, 52
Judicial process, 58
Jurisdiction, allocation, 45; and business agent, 114
Jurisdictional disputes, 34-9, 125; and D. Beck, 184; of communist unions, 216; in Taft-Hartley law, 156-7
Jurisdictions, and work rules, 94

Kaiser, Henry, attitude toward unions, 19; cited, 235; on collective bargaining, 121; on union security, 86
Kaiser-Frazer Corp., 133
Kaplan, David, 56
Kaplan, Sam, 60
Keating, Edward, quoted, 241; quoted on legislative activity, 148; quoted on political action, 152; quoted on

railroad unions' legislative activities, 146
Kennedy, Dudley, 225
Kennedy, Van Dusen, 234
Kenosha Labor, 170
Kentucky Federation of Labor, 163, 229
Keyes, Robert, 97
King, P. J., 231
Knights of Labor, 2-3, 13
Kovner, Joseph, 232
Kula, Anna, 227

Labor, 170
Labor and Nation, 236
Labor banking, 192
Labor Health Institute, 91
Labor-management cooperation, 117-18
Labor Management Relations Act of 1947, 155
Labor movement, 194, 222
Labor party, 204
Labor press, 168-171, 220
Labor supply control, 118
Labor's Nonpartisan League, 150
Ladies' Garment Workers' Union, International. *See* Garment Workers
LaFollette Committee investigation, 134, 226, 228
LaFollette, Robert M., Jr., 4
Language local unions, 32
Large-scale industry, 6, 38. *See also* Mass production industry
Lathers, International Union of Wood, Wire and Metal, apprenticeship requirements, 89
Latin-American labor, 173
Laundry industry, craft locals in, 33
Laundry workers' unions, 15
Law department, in AFL and CIO, 44
Lawyers, in collective bargaining, 166; in unions, 156
Layoff provisions, 82
Leadership, Chapter X, 11
League of Nations, 171
Leave of absence, 215
"Left-wingers," in CIO, 189. *See also* Communists
Legislation, as AFL and CIO function, 44
Legislative department, 56